SHAKESPEARE IN A CHANGING WORLD

SHAKESPEARE IN A CHANGING WORLD

essays edited by

Arnold Kettle

INTERNATIONAL PUBLISHERS
NEW YORK

© INTERNATIONAL PUBLISHERS CO., INC., 1964

Library of Congress Catalog Card Number: 64-17899

Printed in the United States of America

The Contributors

ROBERT WEIMANN
Professor of English, Pädagogische Hochschule, Potsdam

V. G. KIERNAN
Senior Lecturer in History, University of Edinburgh

KENNETH MUIR
*King Alfred Professor of English Literature,
University of Liverpool*

ZDENEK STRIBRNY
*Head of the Department of English,
Charles University, Prague*

J. K. WALTON
Lecturer in English Literature, Trinity College, Dublin

G. M. MATTHEWS
Lecturer in English Literature, University of Leeds

ARNOLD KETTLE
Senior Lecturer in English Literature, University of Leeds

DIPAK NANDY
Assistant Lecturer in English, University of Leicester

DAVID CRAIG
*Organising Tutor, Workers' Educational Association,
North Yorkshire*

RAYMOND SOUTHALL
*Assistant Lecturer in English Literature,
University of Sheffield*

CHARLES BARBER
*Senior Lecturer in English Literature,
University of Leeds*

ALICK WEST
Author and critic

CONTENTS

EDITORIAL NOTE

The text used for all quotations from Shakespeare is the one-volume Tudor edition of the Complete Works edited by Peter Alexander (London, 1951).

I should like to thank Mr. Dipak Nandy for his help in standardising quotations and reading proofs.

A.C.K.

INTRODUCTION

The title is intentionally ambiguous, for the ambiguity expresses a truth. We cannot read or watch a Shakespeare play spontaneously, as we respond to the writers of our own time, unless we bring to the plays some deeply absorbed sense of the historical context in which he wrote. To try to read a Shakespeare play as though he were our contemporary is to ask for trouble: we shall see what is not there and miss too much of what is. Yet to read the plays as though they belonged utterly to the past, like fine fossils, is fatal too: the living core, what we read Shakespeare *for*, is lost. We cannot, however soaked in history, pretend that we are members of the audience of the old Globe theatre.

A solution of the problem must – we might as well face the word as well as the fact – accept its dialectical nature. It is no use hunting for a pure essence of Shakespeare, outside time and space, nor can we ever become pure readers, unaffected by *our* experience. We are all, Shakespeare and ourselves, characters in history. The better we succeed in seeing ourselves as such, the better we shall understand him. And *vice versa*; for no other literature can help us more than Shakespeare's plays to see ourselves as we are. Paradoxically, yet obviously, by reading him we learn how to read him. And the more we read him the better we understand those words of Juliet's:

> My bounty is as boundless as the sea,
> . . . the more I give to thee
> The more I have . . .

We should not slur over the word bounty. Any approach to literature that does not start from the recognition of the pleasure we get from it must always be suspect.

The changing world, then, is neither Shakespeare's nor ours, yet it is both Shakespeare's and ours. And it is not to claim any superiority of sensibility to recognize that his sixteenth-century world and our twentieth-century one have at least one characteristic deeply in common: the rate and the density of change is, as these things go, exceptionally powerful, so that, whatever conclusions they may draw from the changes, men are unusually conscious of change and its necessities.

Already, two generations before Shakespeare, Thomas Wyatt in a fine image had penetrated to the heart of the matter:

> Processe of tyme worketh suche wunder,
>   That water which is of kynd so soft
> Doeth perse the marbell stone a sonder,
>   By litle droppes faling from aloft.

There can be no doubt, as every essay in this book in its own way demonstrates, that Shakespeare had absorbed in his very being the insight Wyatt here expressed. No one tells us as much as he of the processes of time and all that they involve in pain and wonder. It is upon the tensions of the changing world that he builds his poem-plays. From his apprehension of these tensions come his discovery of what is drama, his revelation of human beings in all the complexity of their living relationships, his evocation of the outside world of nature, his inexhaustible sense of the resources and potentiality of language.

No one, in this book, has written specifically about Shakespeare's language, though from every essay comes, through quotation, a glimpse of its marvellous power and variety. Perhaps this is, in the long run, the best way of discussing the subject. Any linguistic approach which tends, even for the temporary purposes of exposition, to abstract a word from its context or to consider it apart from its unique significance of meaning within that context, must run the risk of doing violence to the words it is examining. But this does not mean that the contributors to this book undervalue the importance of linguistic approaches to Shakespeare or want to underwrite a facile separation of 'literature' from 'language'. Shakespeare is the greatest figure in our literature because he is the greatest master of our language.

Our starting-point, then, is a common conviction that the best way to emphasize the value of Shakespeare in *our* changing world is to see him in *his*, recognizing that the two worlds, though very different, are at the same time a unity. And there is, closely bound up with this conception, a further unifying factor in this book of separate essays. If change is one of the recurring words in these pages, man is another. It is a humanist Shakespeare that is being discussed.

The word humanist, in this context, has a wide but essential significance. The humanist tradition cannot be described as though it were a set of unchanging ideas, much less a revealed philosophy. It implies, rather, an evolving outlook which has developed with man's increasing knowledge and control of the world he lives in and hence of his own destinies. One would not expect a twentieth-century humanist to hold all the same opinions or even share all the same attitudes as a humanist of the sixteenth or seventeenth century. What distinguishes both, and brings them into the same tradition, is a fundamental tough confidence in the capacity of men (though not necessarily the individual man) to master – with whatever difficulty, error and tragedy – the particular problems and challenges with which, at the particular stage their world has reached, they are faced. I do not want to suggest that the humanist is – as his opponent always makes him – an easy optimist committed to some comfortable belief in inevitable progress. Certainly most humanists of Shakespeare's time thought the world was getting worse rather than better (to put it mildly); certainly almost all accepted some kind of religious explanation of the world and man's fate; while even among those most concerned with the new science there was as yet little of what a modern scientist would call scientific theory or method. Many of the humanists of this time were in fact rather nervous intellectuals whose comparative isolation made optimism difficult. Yet there shines out from their work (one recalls the famous 'upward turn' at the close of Shakespeare's most heartrending and blackest tragedies) a refusal to accept despair, a firm determination to see the social being man and the world he lives in as clearly, truly, objectively as possible, and a deep conviction – which, whatever its particular philosophic form or colouring, is the essence of the humanist spirit – that this can be done. Humanism in the very nature of things can only be seen and understood in terms of actual human experience and history.

Shakespeare lived during the period of the great flowering of modern humanism which we still tend to call, for want of a better agreed name, the Renaissance. That flowering was a direct consequence, as well as a hastener, of the break-up of medieval feudal society and the release of human energy and aspiration which the needs of a new society called forth. Behind the essays in this book is the contention that the nature and value of Shakespeare's work is inseparable from the myriad human developments – social, artistic, political, religious, scientific – of this time, and that it was they that made Shakespeare possible. Such a view does not, of course, seek in some mechanical way to 'explain' Shakespeare, even less to reduce him. The humanist advances of the sixteenth century made his work possible: his work itself, in ways that nobody could well have foreseen, tremendously strengthened and deepened humanist advance.

Marxists call the immense social change which in England reached its climactic point with the Civil War of the seventeenth century the bourgeois-democratic revolution. The term is worth pausing over because its significance is not always understood, even by those who tend to accept it. It was the bourgeoisie – the class of town-merchants and profit-making landlords, whose power, position and way of life was based on the accumulation of capital through the employment of wage-labourers – who led the anti-feudal revolution and became the backbone of the new ruling class. But from the earliest stages of the revolution forces were involved and deployed on the anti-feudal side which were by no means, in any precise sense of the word, bourgeois. This applies to literature as much as to actual life. No one in his senses would describe *Don Quixote*, the great literary manifesto of a new realism dedicated to the undermining of feudal chivalric romance, as a *bourgeois* book. The arguments put forward in Thomas More's *Utopia* in the early sixteenth century or by the radicals of the New Model army in the Putney debates on the *Agreement of the People* in 1647 are not *bourgeois* arguments; on the contrary they are fundamentally anti-bourgeois. For the bourgeoisie the main thing about the great change was that it led to the acquisition of power for themselves and freedom to satisfy their needs. But many who rejoiced in the ending of the old order and fought, sometimes to the death, for new conceptions of freedom and equity had quite other aims and ideas. To them the new individualist go-getters who, like Volpone, treated gold as a goddess and men and women as commodities, were no more sympathetic than the lords of the old feudal hierarchy, often a good deal less so. The humanist ideas of the Renaissance have, it can be seen, a very complex social basis and we should not be surprised to find that a figure like Shakespeare refuses to be placed tidily in some convenient pigeon-hole marked 'Representative of Bourgeois Ideology' or 'Feudal Reactionary'. It is only to the extent that the rich complexity of the term 'bourgeois-democratic revolution' is appreciated that its helpfulness in clarifying the historical position of a Shakespeare can be claimed. One would make, in this connection, only one emphasis. We should never underestimate the democratic aspects and content of the bourgeois-democratic revolution in its early stages. To do so is to make ourselves immune to much of the bite and vital tang of Shakespearian drama with its often staggering irreverence and down-to-earth homeliness.

For while all the contributors to this book would strongly resist any suggestion that Shakespeare was, consciously or unconsciously, some sort of modern democrat or socialist born before his time, there is an important sense in which the *popular* nature of his achievement can scarcely be exaggerated – and not only in relation to his own time.

The nineteenth-century Chartists drew inspiration from him and in Leicester in 1841 one of their leaders, Thomas Cooper, started 'The Shakespearian Association of Leicester Chartists'. Nor is it by chance that the great socialists of the pioneering days valued Shakespeare so much. Karl Marx's son-in-law Paul Lafargue described 'a veritable Shakespeare cult in the Marx family' and Marx's unbounded admiration for the poet, much of whose work he knew by heart. 'Every friend of Tom Mann' wrote Dona Torr[1] 'recalls his passion for Shakespeare and has probably drunk Shakespeare's health and celebrated Shakespeare's birthday with him. For his family, in Manchester, he instituted "joyous evenings" when everyone had to sing, recite or at least read something of Shakespeare.' Tom Mann, we recall, was no professional intellectual but a working lad sent down the pit at the age of ten.

Many difficulties stand in the way of twentieth-century working-class people of his own country enjoying Shakespeare's plays. The changes of language are of course a real difficulty,

---

[1] *Tom Mann and his Times.* Vol. I (1956) 67.

though – bearing in mind the extraordinary popularity of Shakespeare's plays in translation, not least in the new socialist societies – one should not regard this as an insoluble problem. More important is the lack of a living popular dramatic tradition in modern British society – the fact that in the industrial towns, where most of us live, relatively few people go to the theatre and that state financial aid and encouragement of the drama is, even by Western European standards, pitifully inadequate. In a society in which culture is dominated by commercialism and the money-makers set the tone, it is not at all easy for the people as a whole to get to know and love Shakespeare. Yet, nevertheless, Shakespeare *does* mean a great deal to the British people. To no other dramatist do thoughtful and aspiring people, young and old, turn so readily or return with such delight. And we have all had the experience, some-time or other, of witnessing the impact of a Shakespeare play on someone who has not expected (and whom perhaps we have not expected) to like it. We easily underestimate our own people and culture, and the number of excellent school and college productions of Shakespeare plays in Britain is something we ought to be more proud of. Sometimes these get nearer to the heart of the plays than expensive professional productions and it is one of the evidences of the extraordinary toughness and many-sided richness of the plays that they respond as they do to non-professional and youthful approaches. It would be absurd to pretend that in 1964 Shakespeare is a great immediate conscious factor in the lives of the British people as a whole. This is in itself a criticism of our society, yet it is the bare truth that no great writer has *more* impact on our people than Shakes-peare and that in circles which are not normally thought of when cultural matters are discussed – I mean in particular the most active and deep-thinking members of the working-class movement – his language is cherished and his plays known and loved above all others.

This is perhaps the place to make a further point. Experience suggests that this book is not unlikely to be described somewhere or other, and with whatever overtones of sympathy or the reverse, as 'the Marxist interpretation of Shakespeare'. About this one would wish only to make two observations. First, not all the contributors to this volume would describe themselves –

at any rate without qualification – as Marxists; though none would wish to deny the relevance of Marxist thinking to his approach. Secondly, those of us who are Marxists would wish emphatically to repudiate any suggestion either that we regard our particular contribution as definitive or that there can properly be any narrow or dogmatic orthodoxy in the sort of enterprise we are engaged in. We do not believe that Marxism is that kind of philosophy or Shakespeare that kind of writer.

Some of the contributors to this volume discuss the more directly political and ideological connections between Shakespeare and his time. Most, however, are concerned with particular plays and the nature of their value.[1] Between the two sorts of essay there is not, I think, at all a hard-and-fast distinction. For all the authors would agree that 'critical' and 'historical' are not really – as they are so often considered in twentieth-century literary criticism – alternative or mutually exclusive approaches. On the contrary, the literary historian who eschews criticism can have no guide as to what to include in his history, while the critic who ignores history cannot well expect to find (whatever the justice of his particular insights) any satisfactory theoretical basis for his value-judgments. Once again, humanism is the unifying word. For history is human history and value – literary as much as any other kind – means what is valuable to human beings. And human beings, unless they are to be treated as more or less meaningless abstractions, are always individual creatures of flesh and blood, living in a particular place and time, faced with particular problems and choices – in a word, people in history.

None of us would wish, of course, to assert that the relations between literary judgments and other factors are simple and obvious. Shakespeare is not a great writer because he supported the Elizabethan monarchy. He is not even a great writer because he was an exceptionally wise and intelligent man, though he could not have been the former without being in some sense or other the latter. But in what sense? To such a question, however fascinating, this is not the place to attempt a general theoretical answer. In so far as we have the answer it is in

---

[1] The actual choice of subject-matter within the volume is largely arbitrary, depending on space and the personal inclinations of the contributors. There is no reason of policy behind the omission of full discussion of particular plays.

the pages that follow. If, out of this volume, any suggestive hints about such general critical principles were to emerge, that would seem to all of us as much as we could hope.

Each of the essays that follow is an independent contribution and, quite clearly, no contributor will feel responsible for the opinions expressed in any pages but his own. Nor has any attempt been made to eliminate or resolve differences of judgment or approach which the reader will notice in comparing different essays. Yet the *raison d'être* of this volume as a contribution to the quatercentenary commemoration of Shakespeare's birth would not be obvious if the contributions had no connecting links of common interest and assumption.

Such links might be summed up, negatively, as a rejection of – on the one hand – mystical, purely impressionist, anti-rational, anti-historical approaches, and – on the other – of the kind of pedantic academicism which, losing sight of the whole in its concern for the parts and (to borrow an image from Blake) creeping into literary criticism like a caterpillar to destroy, ignores the living and not infrequently disturbing content of great literature. More positively, what unites the contributors, as far as method goes, is a desire to approach Shakespeare's work as objectively and – if the word can be given its right weight in a literary context – as scientifically as possible, while at the same time recognizing that the impact of literature is both personal and complex and that literary judgments are as difficult – though also as unavoidable – as the judgments we make in actual life. For literature is a part of living and it is from its relationship with the whole of life that it draws its energy and delight and value; and a great piece of literature like one of Shakespeare's major plays is great not only because it makes us apprehend on our pulses the area of life it presents for our inspection, but because in doing so it has the power to affect the way we ourselves live. The Shakespeare honoured here is, above all, a writer who, in the complex ways of art, better than any other helps men and women to understand what it means to be a man or woman and hence affect and change their world.

A. C. K.

THE SOUL OF THE AGE:
TOWARDS A HISTORICAL APPROACH
TO SHAKESPEARE

Robert Weimann

In Britain and America today any historical approach to Shakespeare runs the risk of falling between the two stools on which sit the subtle critic and the painstaking scholar. Most of the recent trends in critical practice owe their momentum not to an awareness of, but an indifference to, the facts of economic and social history. The critics, especially the second or third generation of what is still called the 'new' criticism, have turned a somewhat contemptuous back not only on the study of sources, influences and characters, but also, of course, on 'historicism'; their charge being that the pedantry of the scholar has obscured the nature of the poetry and each work's unique wholeness and specific organization through language. The scholars, in their turn, have been annoyed rather than influenced by all the detailed studies of the verbal structure and texture, the patterns of imagery and symbolism, irony, paradox and ambiguity; *their* irritation amounting to the charge that the critics' concern for words, while obscuring both literary background and context, has outrun verifiable knowledge and sense of proportion.

This picture is of course too neat a simplification, but perhaps it will serve to suggest that in recent years important critical tenets have failed to come to terms with the background study of history (and *vice versa*), and that against either of the two it will be useful to distinguish the present approach – a Marxist one – which attempts to be both historical and critical.

It will be useful, at the outset, to state briefly certain underlying assumptions and to raise the question of the relevance of our present study of past literature. This question must indeed be faced: in its bluntest terms it involves the consideration of how a historical insight can be made to deepen our under-standing of Shakespeare and, consequently, enrich our own lives and human and social potentialities. To put it like this may appear provocatively superficial, but it is nevertheless a useful, if humbling, reminder of both our own historical point of view and our critical purpose. It reminds us of what we, historically, cannot do and, on this basis, helps us to proceed to what is, critically, within our reach. For we cannot, however hard and however conscientiously we try to do so, assume the point of view of the Elizabethan spectator watching, say, a performance of *Hamlet*. Of course we can (and we must) reconstruct the economic conditions, the social status, the moral assumptions, and the literary tastes of the typical representatives of Shakespeare's audience. We may, as historians, even try to define their attitudes and explain their reactions to specific plays, but we cannot, if we are honest, pretend to recreate and share their experience of Shakespeare. We cannot critically approach Shakespeare from the same point of view as that of the Elizabethans – nor should we attempt to do so. The experience of works of art is so essential and so organic a part of a man's human needs and social nature, that we cannot and ought not to attempt to become a different being when watching Shakespeare's dramas or reading Cer-vantes' fiction.

However, one of the objections raised against the historical approach seems to assume that an investigation into the historical origins of past art is bound to preclude an illumina-tion of its living value. This may perhaps be true of a certain critically inert type of sociological or even Marxist writing, but as a generalization it must be rejected as profoundly mis-leading. As long as literature is regarded as literature (and not as a medium of sociological reference and exemplification), the contradiction between the historical origins and the enduring values of art cannot honestly be ignored or belittled. On the contrary, it involves the necessary tension between the work of art as a historical phenomenon and as a living force in our present-day culture. This relationship is a dialectical one and, in aesthetics, finds its correspondence in the mimetic and the moral aspects of great literature, which, although reflecting one given moment in history, yet does not cease to be significant or influential outside that particular historical period.

A historical approach to Shakespeare, then, does not identify the poetic value of his plays with their ideological or biographical significance, and to elucidate the latter is not in itself identical with an awareness of the former. And yet the historical approach remains a *sine qua non*; for although it does not necessarily involve critical standards, it makes the application of these standards meaningful.

No one can hope adequately to explore the moral and artistic values of literature (its *aut prodesse ... aut delectare* aspects), unless he has previously considered its *mimesis* (the way it holds 'the mirror up to nature'). The poetics of Renaissance humanism never dissociated these two basic aspects, and modern critics do so at their peril. There is no antinomy between a critical concern for living values and the scholarly study of their historical background: present values are themselves a product of history, and to realize their historical character is to be more deeply conscious of the nature of one's critical awareness.

The application of all this to the study of Shakespeare is obvious. A good deal of background research seems so irrelevant (and so dull) and a good deal of otherwise very subtle criticism is so lacking in meaningful precision, simply because this relationship has been overlooked, whereas it ought to concern the background scholar as well as the literary critic.[1] Ultimately this relationship is expressed in the contradiction, so often noticed, between Shakespeare's drama as the perfect expression of his time and the dramatist's 'timelessness'. It was Ben Jonson who first said that Shakespeare 'was not of an age, but for all time'. This early assertion of Shakespeare's greatness has been characteristically misread by latter-day eulogists, who ignore the context in which it occurs and in which the present problem first emerged; for Jonson, a few lines before he abstracts Shakespeare from his time, declares that he was the 'Soule of the Age'.

---

[1] Cf. the present writer's critique of recent trends in Shakespearean criticism: *New Criticism und die Entwicklung bürgerlicher Literaturwissenschaft* (Halle 1962), 142-277.

I

The age into which Shakespeare was born was, to an extent
that only the twentieth century can surpass, an epoch of
transition. Sixteenth-century English society, in its economic
relations and political structure, its morals and manners, was
in many significant aspects unlike those forms and organiza-
tions that we normally associate with either the heyday of the
feudal classes or the rise to power of the bourgeoisie. It was an
age of social compromise and economic confusion which yet
achieved, politically, a temporary stability and a cultural
balance distinctly its own. In the sphere of economics, traditional forms of trade and agriculture existed side by side with
the newly emerging modes of capitalist enterprise, and an
unprecedented and often conflicting number of heterogeneous
developments and activities resulted. The growth of the market,
first for commodities, then for land and labour and finally for
money, the development of an extensive cloth industry serving
overseas export markets (which accelerated enclosures), the
extraordinary influx of gold and silver, and the remarkable
rise in prices – these and their concomitant factors had proved
powerful dissolvents of the traditional economy. At the same
time, they had weakened the position of those landowners
whose very existence was based on the system of feudal tenure
and service, the manor and the self-sufficient community of the
village with its open fields. The rule of the barons was past, and
their bankruptcy was military and political as well as economic.
After the Wars of the Roses their ranks were thinned, their
castles and strongholds had become too vulnerable, their
housekeeping too expensive, and their retainers unlawful; after
the last feudal rising, the Northern Rebellion of 1569, their
decline was an irrevocable trend.

But while the feudal aristocracy was no longer in a position
to rule the country at large, those sections that a hundred
years later succeeded in winning the civil war were as yet too
immature to achieve political supremacy. The bourgeoisie,
together with the 'improving' gentry and the lower middle
classes that ultimately shared (or aspired to share) their modes
of living, were politically not yet emancipated. They were
more concerned about the settlement of the succession, the

threat of foreign invasion, the maintenance of civil order, and their more immediate economic interests, than with the challenging of state power by advancing their own (as distinct from the national) policies and ideologies. Like the merchants, the moneyed landlords who owned most of the abbey lands, enclosed the commons and introduced capitalist practices into agriculture, did not for a moment think of challenging the prerogative of the Tudor monarchs under whose peaceful rule they had obtained vast estates and had thrived so unprecedentedly. Policy-making was as yet the undisputed privilege of the crown.

It was the crown and the court, then, which became the focal point of the nation's political, religious and cultural life. The immense prestige of the monarchy, the homage paid to it by men such as Ascham, Spenser, Hooker and Bacon, cannot be dismissed as empty eulogium; for the Tudors – as Shakespeare viewed them in *Richard III* – had overthrown the warring factions of the nobility and thus made possible that 'smooth-fac'd peace, with smiling plenty and fair prosperous days', of which the Elizabethans were so gratefully conscious. Although themselves of the nobility, the Tudors were prepared (and indeed they had no other choice) to compromise with those forces which had opposed the disastrous rule of the barons and which still were suspicious of the rebelliousness of the over-mighty subject. By providing favourable conditions for trade and shipping the Tudor monarchs developed their customs revenues; by promoting a stable and more centralized administration, they reorganized their fiscal system and controlled their own landed revenues much more effectively; at the same time, they advanced the economic development of the country by welding together hitherto local communities of exchange into a larger national whole. In doing all this, the Tudors, without breaking with the more conservative aristocracy, promoted the interests of the newer gentry and the middle classes which, especially in the economically advanced south and east, were moving closer together. In Tudor England those who upheld the independence of the nation supported the sovereignty of the crown; its authority was accepted not only as against the claims of the Roman church but also in the face of domestic unrest and foreign invasion.

The new monarchy, even before the secession from Rome, found active supporters in the newly promoted aristocracy from which, in Elizabeth's time, the great courtiers and administrators were to be recruited. These were the Dudleys, Russells, Seymours, Sidneys, Herberts, Cecils and, of course, Ralegh and Walsingham; in contrast to the more conservative Norfolk, Sussex, Oxford, the remnants of the older nobility and the unenterprising country gentry, such men were firmly committed to the expansion of commerce and industry. They stood behind the maritime expeditions of the 'sea dogs' and often advocated a more aggressively protestant foreign policy. At home they – particularly Leicester, the Sidneys, Herberts and Russells – patronized, or shared in, the pursuit of humanist knowledge and letters.[1]

Even before their patronage became most effective, many of the earlier humanists, who were mostly descended from burgess families, had been preferred by the monarchy. Despite his barbarous treatment of More and Fisher, it might be said of Henry VIII that 'throughout his reign he regarded the relation between humanism and affairs of state as indispensible'.[2] But as the monarchy, aided by the new aristocracy, encouraged a learned vindication of its new policies and the use of a more polished Latin in diplomatic intercourse, the humanists themselves were commissioned with practical tasks. With men such as Thomas Elyot, Edward Fox, Thomas Starkey and Richard Morison, humanism and patriotism became fused; to them learning was no longer a private form of virtuosity but a means of public service. Of burgess descent, supported by the monarchy, in close contact with the new aristocracy, the new pedagogues were permitted to introduce their political and educational ideas into the many new or reorganized schools. The humanists, here as elsewhere, endeavoured to implement a policy which, while it served the absolutism of the Tudors, helped to consolidate the autonomy of the nation. And it was Elyot and his

[1] See J. Buxton, *Sir Philip Sidney and the English Renaissance* (London 1954); E. Rosenberg, *Leicester: Patron of Letters* (New York 1955); E. H. Miller, *The Professional Writer in Elizabethan England* (Cambridge, Mass., 1959), chap. 4. The position of the new aristocracy is well brought out by P. Siegel,*Shakespearian Tragedy and the Elizabethan Compromise* (New York 1957), 12 ff.

[2] W. G. Zeeveld, *Foundations of Tudor Policy* (Cambridge, Mass., 1948), 6. See also F. Caspari, *Humanism and the Social Order in Tudor England* (Chicago 1954), 132 ff.

followers who had sown the seeds that came to fruition in many of the grammar schools throughout the country in which the young generation, among them Shakespeare of Stratford, received their introduction to the classics and to a view of human nature that was, in essential points, no longer medieval.

Marx, considering western Europe as a whole, summed up the general significance of the trends we have been considering when he wrote that 'absolute monarchy presents itself as a civilizing centre, as the initiator of social unity. There it was the laboratory, in which the various elements of society were so mixed and worked, as to allow the towns to change the local independence and sovereignty of the Middle Ages for the general rule of the middle classes, and the common sway of civil society.'[1] Obviously a full historical description of the ways of transition in England would have to assess – as we cannot do here – the precise balance of class forces at each particular stage as well as the general economic and social processes by which capitalist modes of production became the dominant ones. What it is important to emphasize here is that in the period we are concerned with the middle classes (although steadily advancing) were as yet in no position to repudiate the Tudor compromise, and that the monarchy, whose rise to power was based on a transitional balance of socio-economic forces, endeavoured to maintain the equilibrium politically. It was this endeavour (and it accounts for both the success and the ultimate contradictions of the Tudor position) which determined most of their legislation, ecclesiastical as well as economic. The Elizabethan church settlement was in itself the epitome of that 'laboratory' in which 'the various elements were so mixed and worked' as to contain all the parties within the platform of national alliance. Elizabeth's one distinctive doctrine was the doctrine of royal supremacy; once this was accepted – and there was no reluctance to do so, since 'royal' was as yet synonymous with 'national' – the queen did not bother to press for ideological definitions or really strict conformity. On a different plane, economic legislation such as the Statute of Artificers (1563) or the Usury Act (1571) was Janus-faced, designed to serve both trade and stability: the monarchy was willing to consider the bourgeoisie as a junior

[1] K. Marx and F. Engels, *Revolution in Spain* (New York 1939), 25.

partner, but determined to prevent any rapid growth of those new men who, like Peter Wentworth, had – as the queen was sure to perceive – a way of becoming too independent too quickly.[1]

And yet, as the balance of power gradually changed, it became more and more difficult to contain the puritans and to conceal the cracks in the Tudor alliance. Elizabeth, as late as 1601, still could fall back on compromise measures and the crown's long-standing prestige which neither her subtle evasiveness nor her many studied ambiguities were quite able to undermine. As James Harrington sarcastically remarked, she succeeded in 'converting her reign through the perpetuall Love-tricks that passed between her and her people into a kind of Romanze'.[2] Part of this 'Romanze' may – in the words of a later historian – have consisted in 'bribing her people with prosperity'. But when the old queen died, prosperity – now that it was taken for granted – was no longer good enough at its traditional level; and (what proved more important) there were indications that its growth was to be less secure than before. At the same time, the compromise in religion and the platform for an all-inclusive national church had become increasingly tenuous, until James I discovered (in 1604, at the Hampton Court conference) that 'Presbytery agreeth as well with monarchy as God and the devil'. Now Hooker (in the seventh book of his great *Laws*) might well deplore 'those extreme conflicts of the one part with the other, which continuing and increasing' (were reminiscent of) 'those words of the Prophet Jeremiah, "thy breach is great like the sea, who can heal thee?" ' English absolutism ceased to be an absolutism by consent, and out of the national alliance emerged the gradual (although by no means straightforward) formation of two increasingly antagonistic class positions.

Facing these far-reaching divisions (there were significant, if almost imperceptible, changes from at least 1588) – how was the humanist scholar or poet to react? Was he still, like Gabriel Harvey, to consider the court as 'the only mart of praeferment and honour'? Or could he honestly, as Stephen Gosson did,

[1] For a more detailed discussion of the Tudor compromise in legislation, religion, etc., see my *Drama und Wirklichkeit in der Shakespearezeit* (Halle 1958), 34-139.

[2] *James Harrington's Oceana*, ed. S. B. Liljegren (Heidelberg 1924), 49.

throw in his lot with the puritans? As early as 1586 the death of Sidney, followed by that of Leicester, was a blow to poets and all those who might have continued to reconcile humanism with the principles of militant protestantism; in affecting the national position of both movements it was an event scarcely less significant than the execution of Essex (1601) to whom, in the 1590's, the leadership of Leicester's court party and the popular support of the citizenry had passed. But while the new aristocracy was losing valuable territory at Whitehall, the court – at least since the appointment of Archbishop Whitgift to the Privy Council – was drawing nearer to an episcopalian church increasingly determined to oppose and suppress puritan innovations. As, under James, the court grew to be part of a corrupt administration (in which anyway preferment and a public career had for long become rare to unprivileged scholars), the more advanced sections of the bourgeoisie showed an increasing hostility to the arts and a growing impatience with the philological traditions of Christian humanism.

Thus the foundations of the national compromise – so essential to Gascoigne, Sidney or Spenser – were crumbling away, and neither side proved really acceptable to the humanist imagination. Now classically trained poets, even before the end of the century, turned to satire, and their writing reflected an attitude to experience more sardonic, sombre and savage than that of the earlier decade. The melancholy malcontent became a symbol of the disillusioned academic, and the Italianate courtier, his affected imitator, the fashionable 'gull', was held up to ridicule, while the covetous puritan was attacked with equal scorn.

With Chapman and Donne, the modes and values of Renaissance poetry underwent remarkable changes in the course of which Elizabethan standards were replaced by a more private and less secure outlook, symptomatic of a new awareness of unresolved tensions, a 'kind of doublenesse of heart' (Richard Sibbes' term) unknown to the earlier humanist integration of values. But in introducing new accents, as in the development of satire, poets and pamphleteers preceded the popular dramatists. For the latter, under increasingly precarious conditions, there continued to exist a national institution. Amidst the growing divisions of early Jacobean society the theatre remained unique for its popularity, unshaken – or so it seemed – in its social foundations until, even before its greatest representative left London, attendance at the public playhouses began to fall.[1]

II

To view Shakespeare historically is to approach his plays through the theatre for which they were written. If the greatest of the Elizabethans appeared as the 'Soule of the Age' – an age which Ben Jonson to some extent already viewed in retrospect – it was because his medium, and the theatrical organism on which it was based, reproduced the workings of that larger 'laboratory' which – as our rapid and necessarily incomplete survey has tried to suggest – was at the very centre of Tudor society. The Elizabethan theatre flourished in conditions no less rapidly transitional than the society to which it was so deeply related. To illuminate the nature of this relationship in terms of historical criticism is one way of defining the quality of its cultural values in the plays that embody them.

In a bird's-eye view of the Elizabethan theatre, its most distinctive qualities may be seen to result from the survival of traditional popular attitudes to art at a time when these attitudes could be newly vitalized and enriched under conditions superior to those of traditional medieval society. For one short season in English history the springs of folk-drama and the people's enthusiasm for the arts of acting were not yet smothered by puritanism and the rise of capitalism; while broad sections of the population were still capable of enjoying first-rate drama, they were – as never before in modern history – already in a position, economic and social, to support a large-scale theatrical organization. The very conditions which made possible the modern theatre, with its professional and financial apparatus, had not yet transformed the minds of its audience. Capitalism, not having as yet gained a decisive hold over the consciousness of the majority of the people, provided – in the centre of the country – the necessary material conditions much superior to those of the seasonal and amateur stage of the Middle Ages. A time-honoured tradition and a deep-seated demand of the popular imagination could now be developed

[1] A. Harbage, *Shakespeare's Audience* (New York 1941), 38.

in an entirely new direction; it could be met by a theatre which, while not essentially dependent on aristocratic patronage, was – despite formidable pressure – free from the immediate control of the leading London bourgeoisie.

These are, of course, the barest of generalizations (and as such can only be helpful if we are aware of their limitations). They do not suggest the nature, let alone the values, of the popular tradition. The relevance of that tradition to the Elizabethan theatre is perhaps still best approached through its early manifestations in morris and maying, sword-dance and mummings. Historians of the early drama have shown that although these folk ceremonies and disguisings never achieved mature dramatic forms, they became an important sustenance of the medieval drama once this had left the church and its yard. They constituted a communal element in art, best studied in the great craft cycles and their huge amateur performances, based on multiple individual contributions of a corporate community in which spectators and actors had assumed only imperfectly separate identities. But when the great cycles declined or were – as 'popish impostures' – suppressed, the communal interest in mimetic activities continued; its sources were more central to the people's living needs than the Christian ritual, and its strength derived from its not being administered from above. Its essential virtues, the realism, honesty and healthiness of folk culture, its lack of escapist attitudes and its readiness to face and accept natural limitations, were intimately associated with a vital experience in living at first hand, a living itself so honest and so concrete because its processes and tools were the very objects of individual and communal experience alike. There is a continuity from the great passages of the Wakefield cycle (the *Killing of Abel*, the *Lazarus*, the *Secunda Pastorum* scenes) right up to Shakespeare and Jonson. It is a tradition which enriched standards of perception as well as, ultimately, the poetic realism of expression and allowed both 'a huge zest for life and the moral strength to see through its glitter, its hypocrisies, its shame, and its rewards'.[1]

There is no space here to indicate the various ways in which

---

[1] A. P. Rossiter, *English Drama From Early Times to the Elizabethans*, (London 1950), 75. See also L. C. Knights, *Drama and Society in the Age of Jonson* (London 1937), esp. chap. 6.

this popular tradition sustained the Elizabethan theatre; but a glance at the homely though crude English of the miracle plays suggests that its channels were not primarily verbal – as some modern critics seem to assume. Apart from the language (otherwise a tremendously important vehicle of tradition) and apart from the Morality habit of allegory and direct literary 'influences' (the survival or transformation of certain stock elements, figures such as Herod, Vice, and so on), its vitality asserted itself in complex ways and on various levels. Its continuity revealed itself not only in certain basic conventions of the Elizabethan stage, such as the spaciousness of the scene, freedom in the handling of time processes, the mixture of comic and tragic elements, or the emphasis on 'matter' and 'shewes' (on which, as Puttenham remarked, 'the common people' have their eyes and their ears 'so attentive'[1]), but in the general pervasive attitude to art as a positive communal activity. Something of this attitude was, at any rate up to the 'war of the theatres', alive in the anonymous and still rather impersonal and self-effacing process of play-making, in which the playwright's self was submerged in the activity of the group. He did not see his task as that of expressing his purely personal vagaries. Something similar could be said of the supreme responsiveness of the Elizabethan audience to imaginative 'matter' and poetic language, their more than physical closeness to a Tarlton, Alleyn or Burbage.

In this context, it is illuminating to glance at the social background of the Elizabethan actor, those common players whose numerousness is in itself a remarkable phenomenon. It will not do simply to say – as historians of the stage have so often done – that at a certain point minstrels turned actors and thus filled the ranks of the companies (more than 150 of them were traced by G. W. Wallace and J. T. Murray). Rather, I suggest that all those 'freshe starteupp comedanties'[2] – as a contemporary observer calls them – had by and large the same origin as those innumerable 'ruffyns, vagabonds, Masterless men, Comon players' as well as those 'Fencers Bearewaredes . . . Juglers Pedlers Tynkers Pety Chapmen'[3] that Tudor legis-

[1] *Elizabethan Critical Essays*, ed. G. G. Smith (O.U.P. 1904), II, 86.
[2] Cf. E. K. Chambers, *The Elizabethan Stage* (O.U.P. 1923), II, 5.
[3] *The English Drama and Stage under the Tudor and Stuart Princes*, ed. W. C. Hazlitt (London 1869), 6f./22.

lators listed (and maltreated) so indiscriminately. Of course
there was no clear demarcation between minstrel and player,
and the language of contemporary records is often ambiguous.
But when traditional minstrels, far from joining the acting
profession, are on record to complain about unlawful competition by 'rude rustics and craftsmen' (*rudes Agricolae et Artifices*[1]),
this should give us pause to think. Nowhere else in Europe –
with the partial exception of Italy – were there large sections
of the rural population uprooted at a time when popular
attitudes to art were as yet largely unaffected by puritan or
bourgeois standards. The significance of this must strike us
when we learn that at York, for instance, amateurs *had to be
fined* 40s. for taking more than two parts in communal playing.
But then England as well as Italy became famous in Europe
for its agricultural revolution and (subsequent) export of
both, commodities and 'comedanties'. If this is more than
fortuitous we may perhaps gather that the origin of the Elizabethan actor is no disreputable one and that, as he was of the
people, he helped to keep a popular tradition intact, at any
rate up to the time that the *Theatre* and the *Curtain* gave the
best of his descendants a more solid footing and a new basis
for a superior practice of their art. Thus, in England, the vitally
important transition from amateur actors to professional
players may be said to have involved no essential break in the
popular background of the mimetic arts.

Yet, in assessing the popular contribution to the Elizabethan
drama, we should not allow ourselves to be tempted to over-
emphasis. Although it is in one way difficult to exaggerate its
importance, the repeated reference to the communal element
tends to produce an unfortunate note of vagueness if we conceive it unhistorically as against the background of what a
well-known English critic has called the 'organic community'.
The reason why this – historically, and hence as criticism –
appears so unsatisfactory is not merely the somewhat abstract
or symbolic use of the organic community concept which, one
understands, is more than a modern synonym for Merrie
England. But even stripped of its mythical or nostalgic under-

---

[1] Cf. E. K. Chambers, *The Mediaeval Stage* (O.U.P. 1903), II, 260. See also
W. L. Woodfill, *Musicians in English Society from Elizabeth to Charles I* (Princeton
1953), 127.

tones and accepted simply as a convenient shorthand formula –
is it at all helpful in describing social relations at the time of,
say, the first public playhouse (1576)? For a pamphleteer
like Robert Crowley, writing in the middle of the century, it was
possible to say of London: '. . . this is a Citye in name, but,
in dede, / It is a packe of people that seke after meede; . . . /
But for the wealth of the commons not one taketh pain. / An
hell with out order, / I maye it well call, / Where every man
is for him selfe, / And no manne for all.'[1] Again, William
Harrison in the second edition of his *Description* goes out of his
way to insert the warning 'that everie function and severall
vocation striveth with other, which of them should have all
the water of commoditie run into hir owne cesterne'.[2] Such
contemporary reactions (and they could be multiplied) are
scarcely reconcilable with the conception of the 'organic
community', even though it must be granted that statements
by Elizabethan pamphleteers cannot always be taken at their
face value. The point that has to be made is not, of course, that
acquisitive and competitive attitudes had already displaced
the communal outlook but that the latter – existing side by
side with new ways – became increasingly vulnerable to the
pressure of the former. As there are no statistics it may be
safest to stress the resulting contradictions and to suggest
that the preponderance of traditional standards was being slowly
but gradually undermined; that, furthermore, this process was
lagging behind the development, in the economic sphere, of
new modes of production and living until, sometime in the
first decade of the seventeenth century, their combined effects
were acutely felt in the declining attendance at the public
theatres. It was at this time that those forces first began to
triumph who held that theatre-going was a 'great wasting both
of the time and thrift of many poore people'.[3]

But if the Elizabethan communal attitudes to art had positively ceased to rest on the corporate foundation of an organic
community, this does not mean that they were no longer potent.
On the contrary, the conditions of their survival, the very fact
that they were partly uprooted and no longer unchallenged,

1 *The Select Works of Robert Crowley*, ed. J. M. Cowper (E.E.T.S. 1872), 11.
2 *Harrison's Description of England*, ed. F. J. Furnivall (London 1877), Pt. I, 132.
3 Cf. Chambers, *The Elizabethan Stage*, IV, 291.

allowed for a new kind of potency on the basis of a much greater adaptability. On the continent, in the French *confrères de la passion* and the German *Gilden*, the social background remained traditional; but one more reason why we should not be unduly nostalgic about the decline of the medieval organic community is that where it remained intact it did not produce great drama, but the *Fastnachtspiel*, while in Paris (through the theatrical monopoly, since 1548, of the French *confrères*) it stubbornly resisted the inspiration of humanist letters. In England this was not so and the popular tradition in the drama, once it was no longer controlled by conservative guilds, became free – before it seriously decayed – to enter into fruitful combination with whatever elements of a more broadly national culture offered themselves. Among these humanism was foremost: it had developed in closest touch with the growth of a national (as distinct from a provincial or corporate) outlook, whether in political theory, education, translation or drama.

The contribution of the humanist drama, its models in Seneca, Terence and Plautus, the French imitations by Garnier and Jodelle, its classical examples as seen in *Gorboduc* and the later tragedies by Fulke Greville and Sir William Alexander, need not detain us here. What is less of a commonplace is the changing moral nature and the deeper dramatic significance of the humanist contribution, as it reached, and was transformed by, the popular stage. The familiar interpretation (it reached the textbooks long ago) stresses the ways in which – beginning with Kyd – Senecan elements, such as the revenge theme, the declamatory uses of rhetoric, the stricter adherence to the unities, the prominence of the monologue and so on, in comedy, the *Miles gloriosus*, the parasite and servant types, parallelism in construction, etc., constitute the humanist contribution to the Elizabethan drama. However, these elements (whose importance is not in question) do not adequately define the moral vision and the dramatic potency of what humanism – as an approach to life and art rather than as doctrine or philology – gave to the theatre. If we approach it at its greatest level, as seen in *Doctor Faustus* or *Hamlet*, the inadequacy of the customary approach becomes evident: the humanist element in either of the plays (in so far as it is possible to abstract it) can no longer be reduced to its Senecan sources or understood in terms of the older synthesis of Christian faith and classical reason. Once humanism had entered the popular theatre and modified its rigid poetic dogmas, it achieved a new social dimension and a new freedom of imagination, through which its artistic potentialities were tremendously enriched. Although it remained deeply indebted to the study of the classics and to traditional concepts, such as the hierarchical analogies and 'the great chain of being', it was now able to question their meaning and validity through imaginative conflicts with more practical and revolutionary principles. In *Tamburlaine* and *Doctor Faustus* these involved a new confidence in man's capacity for self-determining action, a new awareness of 'Nature's treasure' and the freedom of man to be 'on earth as Jove is in the sky, / Lord and commander of these elements'. It is out of the new consciousness 'to have aspiring minds' that the 'fearful pride' of Tamburlaine results,

> . . . whose faculties can comprehend
> The wondrous architecture of the world,
> And measure every wandering planet's course.
> Still climbing after knowledge infinite,
> And always moving . . .

This spirit (if it can be summed up in a quotation) achieves so great an importance in the drama precisely because it is *not* a doctrinal statement but part of an imaginative perspective from which a great poet illuminates human experience. It produces the grand rhetoric of Marlowe's 'mighty line' and – through this – the towering stature of his heroes; less directly it informs the enhanced capacities for tragic action in Shakespeare and Webster, where human destiny is no longer subject to some inscrutable fate – determined by arbitrary gods or the wheel of fortune – but ultimately conditioned by the deeds, though not the will, of men. The grandeur of man is unlimited: 'in action, how like an angel! in apprehension, how like a god!'; but the will of the individual is not, for his deeds clash with what is greater than fate and no longer subject to his will: something that can best be described as order and the laws of its existence.

Once the humanist contribution to the drama is seen in its

wider moral and imaginative implications, it can more significantly be related to the popular tradition. The interplay of
popular taste and humanist endeavour has indeed often been
observed; it has been pointed out that classical models, Senecan
or Terencean, enriched the popular drama while the popular
tradition, in its turn, saved the drama from academic stiffness.
Hence resulted 'the union of classical artistry and refinement
with Romantic life and vigour, of the classic sense of form and
simplicity with the Romantic love of colour and luxuriance, of
the classic care for words and style with the Romantic insistence
on action . . .'.[1] This is all very well as far as it goes, but
scarcely suggests the strength and meaning of the ties between
the popular and the humanist traditions. In exploring their
relations, one might be tempted to ask why and how in the
1580's a number of young university-trained poets first were prepared to popularize their rhetoric in public places of entertainment traditionally associated with fencing, bear-baiting,
'clownage' and 'the jigging veins of rhyming mother wits'.
From this, many further questions arise which do not admit of a
simple answer. Is the young poets' readiness to be attributed
merely to the desperate position of penniless intellectuals in
want of either preferment or patronage? Or did they willingly
assume the roles of public moralist and dramatic commentator?
And if so, were they flattered by popular fame or attracted by
the remarkable freedom of expression which the theatre allowed
them? To ask these questions is to realize that the poetic achievement of the university wits cannot be explained in terms of their
private intentions. Biographical evidence, even if it were
exhaustively sifted, will hardly illuminate the distinctive quality
of their work, which involves the seeming paradox that, as
leaven to art, humanism in the drama was greatest when
closest to the people.

In order to illuminate the problem we may refer to Marlowe's
greatest play which is so profoundly indebted to a popular
source *par excellence* – the *Volksbuch*. Or we may ask: why is
Nashe's satire and prose most effective when most intimately
in contact with popular speech and jest book traditions? Again,
why is Shakespeare's greatest single representative of humanism
so created as to be not only in favour with the multitude, but

[1] F. L. Lucas, *Seneca and Elizabethan Tragedy* (Cambridge 1922), 103.

in intimate touch with popular speech – as appears in the very imagery of *Hamlet*? (It would be possible to ask similar questions about the work of Boccaccio, Rabelais and Cervantes.) Since the Renaissance allowed for an astonishing proximity of popular tradition and humanist innovation, some kind of common ground might be expected to exist between them.

Although we cannot here hope to offer a definitive answer to these problems, it may at least be noted that the two traditions involved have more in common than might at first sight appear. To give only one illustration, humanist criticism of society – never more scathing than in More's *Utopia* – finds a good many parallels in popular literature from *Piers Plowman* to the mystery plays, where a similar tradition of critical attitudes to landlords and 'thyse gentlery men'[1] can be traced. But if some ultimate concord between the humanist and popular points of view seemed at all possible, this must have been particularly so in the 1590's when patriotic sentiment and national unity still served as unifying factors among humanist-trained playwrights and popular audiences. When, at the turn of the century and shortly after, divisions among the ruling classes gradually upset the much-praised harmony of City, Court and Country, important sections of the theatre-going population were likely to remain unimpressed by either the case for puritanism or that for the prerogative of an increasingly conservative (not to say corrupt) court. For a few precious years, the 'public' (as distinct from the increasingly important 'private') playhouses not only defied the emerging social divisions but actually seemed to thrive on the richness of their contradictions. Consequently the popular dramatist continued to find in the theatre the support that allowed him a measure of independence of the rival ideologies. Outside the theatre his position as author was, by and large, one between the declining patronage of the aristocracy and the as yet immature opportunities of a money-market for books. This, too, involved contradictions which fostered a relative blurring of class alignments and a certain kind of double-edged social criticism which a popular audience might be expected to encourage rather than resent.

As an illustration, the Janus-faced point of view in Nashe's

[1] *The Towneley Plays*, ed. A. W. Pollard (E.E.T.S. 1897), 117.

picaresque *Jack Wilton* and the blurred commitments of his pamphlets are perhaps most characteristic. For Nashe, like most of the humanist-trained popular writers, was fearless in his attacks on puritans and newly-rich landlords: 'There is none hath any wealth which he getteth not from another', he could write – without, however, making concessions to 'the ruinous wals of Venus court' and corresponding standards of aristocratic literature and ideology (as in *Jack Wilton* the ironic rejection of chivalry in the description of the Florence tournament reveals). Nashe could *in one sentence* attack the hypocrisy of the trading puritan and the dishonesty of the warring knight. Thus he defines 'our common calamitie, that the cloake of zeale shoulde be unto an hypocrite in steed of a coate of Maile' – an extraordinary statement which, summing up the twofold angle of popular humanist criticism, indicates the way its emphasis was gradually shifting.[1] Eventually, this kind of attitude (it was to be elevated into the moral vision of *Volpone*, *King Lear* and *Timon of Athens*) developed along lines identical with neither of the leading sections of the dividing classes. Instead, it was written from a position which, while it ultimately reflected the interests of the people, was not congruent with that of one class alone.

In suggesting some of the common ground between the humanist and the popular points of view, we must not overlook their combined relations to the new monarchy. As early as Bale's *King Johan* it is 'Imperial Majestie' that overthrows the enemy 'Sedycyon' so as to make room for the triumph of 'Cyvyle Order': this is the major *motif* taken up and varied from the humanist *Gorboduc* to the popular chronicles and history plays. Under the transitional conditions of Elizabeth's reign the crown would assume the role of arbiter pretending to what Hooker regarded as 'the soundest . . . and most indifferent rule'. It kept in check not only the feudal reaction of the Northern earls but also (in Crowley's words) those new 'men that would be alone on the earth, . . . that would eate up menne, women and chyldren'.[2] It protected the stage against the

---

[1] This is based on my more detailed discussion of "Thomas Nashe and Elizabethan Humanism", in: *Filológiai Közlöny* (Budapest 1962), VII, 285-99, with English summary in *Supplément*, 40-44. The above Nashe quotations are taken from *Works*, ed. R. B. McKerrow (London 1904-10), II, 64; I, 37; I, 22.

[2] Crowley, op. cit., 132.

chronic indignation of the city authorities and helped both the playwrights and their audiences in preventing the puritans from 'preaching awey theyr pastime'.[1] Most important of all, the crown stood for and upheld the conditions to which the theatre owed so much. By deliberately promoting mercantile capital and blurring the lines of gentry and aristocracy, old and new, the Tudors helped to bring about that 'mingle-mangle' which the theatre in its organization and audience, the drama in its genres, structures and speech conventions, reflected. Most clearly this was seen when, in the 1580's, the 'gallimaufry' was about to be complete, by a humanist who (like Lyly) was in close contact with the court:

> At our exercises, Souldiers call for Tragedies, their object is bloud: Courtiers for Commedies, their subject is love: Countriemen for Pastoralles, Shepheards are their Saintes. Trafficke and travell hath woven the nature of all Nations into ours, and made this land like Arras, full of devise . . . Time hath confounded our mindes, our mindes the matter; but all commeth to this passe, that what heretofore has been served in several dishes for a feaste, is now minced in a charger for a Gallimaufrey. If wee present a mingle-mangle, our fault is to be excused, because the whole worlde is become an Hodge-podge.[2]

Unlike Sidney's assault on 'mungrell Tragy-comedie', this statement is already confidently apologetic, but its classically-trained author is still too bewildered to realize that the contradictions (which he points out) are about to yield a new and superior kind of unity. It was a synthesis achieved by the great Elizabethan laboratory – so remarkably effective both in society and in the theatre. Against the 'hodge-podge' of a transitional age, the medieval estates of the realm were no less mixed and transformed than the various dramatic genres: the craft cycle tradition, the drama of the schools, the interlude of the hall, the masque and courtly revels were now no longer 'served in several dishes'. Instead they were so 'minced' that in the country's metropolis the result was a drama neither

---

[1] From Laneham's letter: see its recent discussion by M. C. Bradbrook, *The Rise of the Common Player* (London 1962), 141-61.

[2] *The Complete Works of John Lyly*, ed. R. W. Bond (Oxford 1902), III, 115.

farcical nor learned nor courtly. It was a drama unlike any of the continental burgess or classical or pastoral genres, but one whose bewildering medley of kinds could indeed be defined as 'tragedy, comedy, history, pastoral, pastoral-comical, historical-pastoral, tragical-historical, tragical-comical-historical-pastoral, scene individable, or poem unlimited'. It was in truth a theatre 'individable' with a poetry 'unlimited' in its social and aesthetic appeal; for it embraced many of the popular, humanist and some of the courtly elements, together with their theatrical equivalents such as rhetoric, allegory, singing, dancing, clowning, dumb-shows, disguisings, and corresponding modes of speech, presentation and acting. But by fusing these elements in the light of a unifying and exalting experience of nationhood, the Elizabethan theatre brought forth something new which *nevertheless* appealed to all sections of its audience ('from potboy to prince', as a great authority on the subject writes). 'This three years', says Hamlet (v. i.), 'I have took note of it: the age is grown so picked that the toe of the peasant comes so near the heel of the courtier, he galls his kibe'. It is an observation that might have been made by a spectator in Shakespeare's theatre. Its audience was made up of every rank and class of society; its greatest literature so written that (as a contemporary observed) 'it should please all, like Prince *Hamlet*'.[1] Through underlying tensions and in the face of imminent divisions Shakespeare's theatre achieved a 'unity of taste'.[2] It was a multiple unity based on contradictions, and as such allowed the dramatist a flexible frame of reference which was more complex and more vital to the experience of living and feeling within the social organism than the achievement of any other theatre before or since.

III

The integration, in the theatre, of heterogeneous elements is a historical process, and as such it affects the history of the stage as a social institution; but it also – and more deeply –

[1] Scoloker's remark (1604), cit. E. K. Chambers, *William Shakespeare* (O.U.P 1930), II, 215.

[2] Harbage, op. cit., 114; similarly C. J. Sisson, H. S. Bennett, and recent writers on Shakespeare's audience. But Marxist critics have done well to point to the contradictions involved in this unity: cp. A. Schlösser (on the populace in Shakespeare) in: Z.A.A. (Berlin 1956), IV, 148-71; L. Goldstein (on Elizabethan acting) in: *Bull. New York Publ. Libr.*, vol. 62 (1958), 330-49; A. Anikst

affects the quality of *the plays themselves*, their themes, forms and structures. If it is a truism to say that Shakespeare's subject-matter is as rich in potentialities of experience as the world in which he lived, it perfectly corresponds to his own ideas of how the art of the theatre was related to the contemporary world. Hamlet's words about 'the purpose of playing' (III. 2.) illuminate a relationship which, in an earlier scene (II. 2.), is summed up by a reference to the players as 'the abstracts and brief chronicles of the time'. The point here that is worth making is of course not that Shakespeare's drama – in line with the Aristotelian concept of *mimesis* – reflected the issues of his time (in this he was not at all unique); but that he, more than any of his con-temporaries, succeeded in the discovery of how the issues of his time, its 'form and pressure', could most significantly be turned into material for great art. It was a discovery that involved the capacity for so absorbing and moulding the varied themes and modes of drama that its latent tensions might be released into dramatic poetry.

As an illustration (although space permits only the barest of hints), we might not unreasonably be expected to select one of those plays in which Shakespeare most freely transforms reality into poetry. In *A Midsummer Night's Dream* the 'form and pres-sure' of his age – far from being at all consistently reflected in plot or character – is transmuted into that larger imaginative vision which comprehends, and is expressed by, the sum total of the characters' dramatic interrelations and statements about the world. Its basic levels are well-known: the courtly world of Theseus and Hippolyta is brought into contact with the amorous intrigues of 'Athenian' upper-class society, which contact, in turn, is related to the playmaking activities of the craftsmen, as well as the fairy creatures who, like Oberon, Titania and Puck, are a fantastic 'mingle-mangle' blending classical and Germanic mythology with native folklore. It is through the intimate interplay of delicately woven threads (one silken, one homespun, one sheer gossamer, as the Victorians might have said) that the varied attitudes and moods are made to merge in one com-plex perspective which defines the unique quality of the play. When the muddy boots of the mechanicals thump through the

(on Shakespeare as playwright of the people) in: *Shakespearovski Sbornik* (Moscow 1958), 7-44.

airy wood of the fairies the result is much more than a series of colourful contrasts: their imaginative interrelation is such that the varied attitudes and statements illuminate one another, and the play as a whole achieves a poetic substance infinitely larger than the sum of its parts. Thus the craftsmen's robust sense of reality at once heightens and limits the airy phantasia of the fairies, while in turn their graceful intrigues form a dramatic commentary on the thick-witted earthiness of late medieval amateur acting and guild life.

It is the dramatic integration of varied social values and cultural elements that, as Shakespeare progresses from his early work, makes the structure of the plays so balanced and the poetic perspective of experience so satisfying. In *Twelfth Night*, although it does not blend courtly romance with popular custom and the fairy world, the exquisite poise of the play's vision is, despite the romantic exuberance, maintained through the comic interplay of material non-existent in Shakespeare's Italian source: Malvolio's 'yellow-legged' stalking (with its puritan undertones) and Sir Toby Belch's merry banquets (somewhat in the old style of feudal hospitality) flank the central plot of romantic love and comic disguise, but are so closely integrated that they can no longer be described as a mere subplot. By illuminating one another, these varied attitudes again heighten and help to define the play's comic vision as expressing a complex poetic impression of life. At its centre, in the country house of Olivia, it is Feste the fool rather than Olivia or even Viola who is closest to it. As in other plays of this period, the fool's part becomes so important because his attitude (and, for that matter, the cultural traditions behind this figure) epitomize the theatrical 'gallimaufry' on which Shakespeare, in contrast to Beaumont, Fletcher and their followers, could still draw so successfully. (It is of course an oversimplification to say that the fool as a dramatic figure was equally indebted to the tradition of the courtly jester, the Vice in popular drama and the literary impulse of the humanist *moriae encomium*, but vestiges of all these elements may be traced in several of the great Shakespearian fools. It is perhaps not fortuitous that the fool, whose position is so central to the social 'hodge-podge' of the Elizabethan compromise, is also the figure closest to some of the unformulated assumptions of the people.)

It is the pregnant interplay of varied social and theatrical elements that is so characteristic of Shakespeare's plays. The richness and complexity of its dramatic effects, however, must not be dismissed as a happy exploitation of colourful subject-matter or a skilful arrangement of contrast and relief. Nor is the customary (and somewhat impressionistic) reference to Shakespeare's 'breadth' or 'width of outlook', his 'objectivity' or 'impartiality' likely to be much more helpful. These, indeed, have for a long time been his proverbial epithets, but they can hardly claim to focus the essential qualities of the plays themselves. To say, at this stage, that the richness of their dramatic content draws on the contradictions and tensions in the larger social 'laboratory', may be yet another hint at their historical background but, as criticism, is likewise unsatisfying. None of these gives us a meaningful suggestion of what constitutes the living quality and the moral nature of Shakespeare's art.

It is perhaps an oversimplification to say that in the Elizabethan drama the astonishing range of values and attitudes is dramatically usable because it achieves an imaginative dimension as large and as lively as the social organism itself. To make this dimension an imaginative possibility, it is clearly not sufficient to have, say, various social concepts of 'honour', 'merit' or 'virtue' existing side by side (as by and large was the case in many European countries at the time). For in Shakespeare's England the varied moral attitudes towards experience did not merely coexist: their relative strengths were so balanced and hence so 'minced' that popular dramatists were capable of evaluating experience from a singularly fortunate position. As we see from *Henry IV*, the concept of 'honour' could still be dramatically defined in terms of Hotspur's attitudes, but it was no longer possible to view it solely as 'bright honour', exclusively from the angle of feudal chivalry. Falstaff's complementary commentary on the same subject reveals an alternative of considerable vitality. But while important standards of the older class-morality could already be questioned, the social attitudes of the new era of capitalism (among them, individualism, acquisitiveness, etc.) were not yet their *necessary* alternative; in neither social morality nor dramatic conventions were they yet accepted as a matter of course.

It was from this singularly fortunate position that the dramatist proceeded to realize the dramatic and imaginative possibilities which the conflicting standards of his age allowed. As in *Twelfth Night*, Shakespeare could now express moral evaluations in terms of structural organisation: for the dramatist, through Malvolio and Sir Toby, comically rejects both the puritan disapproval of, as well as the cavalier indulgence in, sensuous pleasure. Instead, something healthier than either asceticism or hedonism is envisioned from a position whose strength and moral poise are altogether admirable. Here, as in the great tragedies, this involved a relative independence of either social alternative as long as it was possible to fall back on a living tradition of popular attitudes to experience. These were in many ways related, but not subservient, to ruling-class concepts of morality. Consequently, there was a margin of imaginative evaluation which embraced, but was not quite identical with, the ruling social standards. Thus, the playwright could dramatically juxtapose *and evaluate* the ideals or attitudes of *both* service and individualism, honour and property, family pride and family feeling, lasciviousness and chastity, sophistication and simplicity, cynicism and naïvety. These attitudes were usable in dramatic composition precisely because the resulting tensions were not slurred over but transformed into tragic conflict or comic incongruity. (On a different plane, they informed important conventions of speech and disguising: Falstaff imitating the king, Orlando a shepherd, Edgar a Bedlam beggar, King Henry a soldier – these and similar extensions of character were part of a dramatic convention, but the effectiveness of the convention was due to the proximity of the actual attitudes, not to the loss of their social identities.)

The vast range of conflicting values and standards within the Elizabethan situation retained its imaginative pregnancy just as long as the dramatist was in a position honestly to face and incorporate their tensions within his poetic vision of society. He could do this only as long as he possessed, as a touchstone to test any experience or concept, a standpoint more valid and profound than the particular social attitude or moral concept in question. Shakespeare's superiority over his material was of course based on his incomparably deep feeling for reality and humanity; but it was so secure and remained essentially unshaken because a living tradition of popular culture sustained it, giving his vision – amidst the temporary 'mingle-mangle' of social values – the strength to achieve so often a more valid and enduring position. It was a position which only partly was one of genial detachment, amused tolerance and dispassionate irony. For apart from the negative virtue of avoiding a facile identification with any of the emerging class concepts, this vision possessed the positive capacity for bringing to bear varied perspectives on the actions and morals of men, thus creating the experience rather than the ideologies of heroism, love and tyranny. The universalizing pattern in Shakespeare and the 'myriad-mindedness' of his art were never outside history, but they live beyond the historical conditions that made them possible. The basis of Shakespeare's 'negative capability' is itself socio-historical. It was because Shakespeare and his theatre were so much the 'Soule of the Age' that his work continues to live, as it were, 'for all time'.[1]

[1] I wish to express my thanks to the editor and Dr. Leonard Goldstein for reading and commenting on this essay in manuscript.

HUMAN RELATIONSHIPS
IN SHAKESPEARE

V. G. Kiernan

Elizabethan drama grew in a no-man's-land between the two
historical epochs that we call the feudal and the capitalist.
All around it old habits and ways were crumbling, new ones
beginning to take shape, in a medley of fragmentary relics and
experiments. In the medieval society that was falling to pieces
the individual had been enclosed, snugly though crampingly,
inside a narrow framework of institutions and beliefs, like an
apprentice safe and warm in his airless cupboard-bed in one of
the old houses of the Hansa merchants still to be seen in Bergen.
Now the snug crib which was also a prison was releasing or
ejecting him into a strange environment where he must learn
to find his way about, among others groping likewise.

Life was thus both exhilarating and frightening. The epoch of
free competition was coming in, the world was an oyster waiting
for anyone's sword to open it. Competition was at its most
venomous among the jarring factions at court, where the
shortest cuts to fortune lay – and where the theatre had close
links: Lear's

> packs and sects of great ones
> That ebb and flow by th' moon.   (v. 3. 18-19.)

Many risks had to be run, not only at court. Lieutenant
Bardolph came to the gallows while still struggling to get
his oyster open. Men had been haunted ever since the Renaissance by the thought of 'blind Fortune' and her wheel, emblem
of the instability of all earthly affairs; it was fed by the separation
of man from man as the old social order faded, the dissolution of
accustomed ties and mutual duties. Success might come to
some, the most unblushingly egotistic, but it was likely to be
paid for by the isolation which makes one of Shakespeare's

43

most successful men, Henry IV, feel in the weariness of disillu-
sion and insecurity that no-one who could foresee his future
would ever want to live through it.

To see how disturbing and unnerving this climate was, to
the same Englishmen who in more sanguine moods could
identify themselves in fantasy with Marlowe's world-conqueror

> And ride in triumph through Persepolis,
>
> (1 *Tamburlaine*, II. 5. 758.)

one has only to read Burton's *Anatomy of Melancholy*. This
indispensable though unintended commentary on Shakespeare
depicts a whole generation grown morbid, anxiety-ridden; at
bottom because, then as now, an old society and its morality
were dying and a new one coming to birth. When men feel so
unfathomably uneasy it is always because they have lost touch
with one another.

> O, what's become
> Of the true hearty love was wont to be
> 'Mongst neighbours in old time,   (II. 2. 222-4.)

laments a pessimist in Middleton's *Women Beware Women*.
Needless to say, there was the usual quota of illusion here: the
times, like *Punch*, have never been quite as good as they used to
be.

Dramatic art had a sudden flowering in many parts of
Europe, where the change from medieval to modern was in
progress, all the way from the Globe to Hungary. Between the
theatre in England and in Spain the resemblances are astonishing. Men's heightened consciousness of themselves and of one
another found a natural outlet in drama, the social art of all
arts. They went to the theatre first of all no doubt in search of
entertainment, and a casual remark of Burton's indicates how
popular it was in London: in all lands people have hit on some
favourite way of shaking off their troubles – Italians sleep them
off, Danes drink, 'our countrymen go to Plays'.[1] But it is not
fanciful to suppose that in this hectic, disoriented society,
especially in dizzily growing London where newcomers poured
in from every province, men went to the theatre also as a

---

[1] *Anatomy of Melancholy* (Bohn edition), vol. II, 213.

place where they might learn something about life and their fellow-creatures.

In a season of change one artist will fasten chiefly on what is bad in the situation, decline and decay, another on what is good, birth and growth. Shakespeare belongs emphatically to the second sort. It is hard to resist the temptation to read a symbolic meaning into the words of a speaker in one of the late Romances, which sound so full of prophecy and vision – 'Thou met'st with things dying, I with things new-born' (*Winter's Tale*, III. 3. 108). Most of his rivals in the theatre belong as unmistakably to the first sort. These literary men were descendants of the humanist scholars of the Renaissance, brilliant talents whose fate it was to float unattached, except precariously to rich patrons, in a Europe whose ordinary people they had no contact with. Humanism meant belief in man; but this was harder to hold on to than disbelief in God, when it was not strengthened by faith in men's ability to live and work together, to co-operate fruitfully with one another. As a result the humanism we associate with Erasmus and the educationalists had been a vulnerable and short-lived growth. Elizabethan playwrights were similarly unattached, though writing for a popular audience was itself an attempt to escape from this situation. Struggling to make a living by their pens, they were forerunners of all artists in modern society, and peculiarly exposed to the uprooting influences of the age. Not seldom they had to fall back on private patronage, if they could find any. They have an air of being chronically on bad terms with an audience that seemed to them tasteless and ungrateful; Ben Jonson cannot help falling foul of it even in the preface to a Masque.[1] An artist is always inclined to judge the human race by the calibre of his own public. Shakespeare was more tolerant than Jonson of both. Part of the reason may be that he had roots in Stratford, one of the little towns where something of an older neighbourliness lingered on, as well as in feverish London. Another part of it must be that he was actor and theatre-man as well as writer, professionally involved like Molière with a company, a group of men dependent for success on one another's efforts and on their team spirit.

Over a great part of Elizabethan and especially Jacobean

[1] *Masque at Lord Haddington's Marriage* (1608).

drama hangs a cloud of gloom and embitterment. Its pre-
occupations are with death and with madness, the two things
that separate the human being most totally from the rest of
humanity. Its characters tend to be hard, distinct, unmingling
entities, repelling like billiard-balls, imparting to one another
only a mechanical kind of movement. Most typical among the
bad ones are the 'Machiavels', self-proclaimed villains emancipated from all bonds of conventional virtue. Machiavelli's
conception of human beings as unfused particles, each completely self-contained and self-centred, had a creepy fascination
for the men of this century, and it did become, in less melo-
dramatic forms than on the stage, the philosophy of life of many
of them. Shakespeare himself has his Richard III and Iago,
and, rather less inhuman, his Edmund. Marlowe brings on the
ghost of Machiavelli as Prologue to one of his plays (*Jew of
Malta*). At the opposite pole the same acceptance of isolation
as the bedrock of the human condition found expression in a
cult of stoicism, the lofty individual rising above society, rejecting its laws as meaningless and making higher laws for his
own unfettered self. Chapman especially always seems to be
trying to strip his Hero down to an inmost core, to find out
what he is made of, like a philosopher stripping away from
matter its form, colour, taste, in search of ultimate reality, and
in the end finding that matter has disappeared.

Contemporaries appear to have thought of Shakespeare and
his poetry as 'sweet'; an epithet which may not at first sound
very appropriate, but which ceases to surprise as soon as we
compare him with almost any of the other playwrights. The
difference between one of his plays and one of theirs – between
a *Twelfth Night* and a *Chaste Maid in Cheapside*, to take two at
random – is the difference between a living earth, a landscape
with a warm sunshine of human feeling playing over it, and a
frozen moon. Among his characters the self-enclosed natures,
moving about among their fellow-men without any emotional
need of them, stand out the more remarkably by their fewness.
Iago alone is completely alienated from humanity; Falstaff,
Hotspur, Henry IV and Prince Hal, however self-sufficient,
crave at least for the applause of those about them. Collectively
Shakespeare's men and women may be described, as Iago with
a possible touch of envy describes Othello, as 'of a free and open

nature'. They move freely and unhesitantly in a world not foreign to them because they have an assured knowledge of its inhabitants and an assured place among them; whereas the other denizens of the Elizabethan stage seem often to live by the rule of Dickens's lawyer 'Foxy': 'Always suspect everybody'. Shakespeare is making fun of this over-worldly wisdom when he puts it into Pistol's mouth:

> Trust none;
> For oaths are straws, men's faiths are wafer-cakes.
> (*Henry V*, II. 3. 50-1.)

A kind of diffused kinship among all human beings, or the suggestion at least that there ought to be such a kinship, pervades a play of his in a way difficult to define but impossible to miss. We might venture to call it, in Dr. Johnson's language, *clubbability*. One sign of it is the rich flow of humour, compared with the narrow trickle in most of the other plays. Another is that conversation among these people is really conversation, not declamation. They continue to interest us because they are willing to be interested in one another. Instead of being turned in on themselves they have an out-going quality, an ability to feel with and associate themselves with something outside them: another person, a cause, an ideal, a nation. In the Comedies, where women reign, the enchanting heroines overflow with a golden readiness of fellow-feeling for the world and everything in it, a readiness to be amused by it, to help it, to scold or reform it. In the Tragedies the great figures come to find themselves isolated, Timon last and most absolutely, and that is indeed their tragic destiny; but they are not at all solitary by disposition. They have a gift of spinning threads out of themselves in many directions, of linking themselves with other men and women and with the ideas of their time. Only Julius Caesar tries to play the part of a self-conscious Superman, to be like 'the northern star' with 'no fellow in the firmament'; and Caesar is a sick old man, his rhetoric pathetic as well as magnificent. Cato the arch-Stoic, much admired by both Chapman (in *Caesar and Pompey*) and Ben Jonson (in *Catiline*), only comes in for a mention from Shakespeare as the father of Portia – which Cato himself might have thought was damning him with very faint praise.

Shakespeare-criticism, growing up in days of fully-fledged individualism, was apt to fix its attention on characters as separate units, 'portraits', each a work of art in itself. Some of Shakespeare's own words show him thinking rather of the individual as the sum of his relationsips, actual or possible, with his fellows. Brutus has to see himself in the mirror of Cassius's mind before his duty becomes clear to him. Achilles has to look at himself in that of Ulysses, who goes on to argue at some length:

> That no man is the lord of anything . . .
> Till he communicate his parts to others;
> Nor doth he of himself know them for aught . . .
>
> (*Troilus and Cressida*, III. 3. 115-19.)

Shakespeare was concerned with men in combination, interacting, entering into one another's lives, becoming part of one another. Macbeth would have been a very different man, and Lady Macbeth a very different woman – or things slumbering under the surface of their minds would never have woken into life – with any other wife or husband. We think often of Shakespeare's characters, seldom those of the other playwrights, in pairs; and Beatrice and Benedick, Brutus and Cassius, Goneril and Regan, signify when brought into contact much more than a simple arithmetical addition.

His finest speeches are likely to grow directly out of men's feelings for one another; those of the other dramatists are likelier to be inspired by men's feelings about themselves, or by sensations or speculations concerned with impersonal things, fate or death or heaven. These others knew how to emulate 'Marlowe's mighty line' and write 'the style of gods' (or to borrow from Scott about his own work, 'the big Bow-wow stuff'); what lay more out of their reach was the kind of brief and unadorned but extraordinarily poignant phrase that multiplies towards the climax of any Shakespearian tragedy. When Antony learns that his follies have at last driven one of his oldest followers over into the enemy camp:

> Call for Enobarbus,
> He shall not hear thee,
>
> (*Antony and Cleopatra*, IV. 5. 7-8.)

the words have a crushing impact, a blank finality as of a door closed for ever. They fall so on our ears because they fall so on Antony's. There is an opposite effect, of something imperishable, in Brutus's promise to mourn his dead friend:

> I shall find time, Cassius, I shall find time.
>
> (*Julius Caesar*, v. 3. 103.)

This intense simplicity, in which the plainest words are transfigured like a group of plain notes in a symphonic development when it is a Beethoven who is writing, is made possible only by the intense strength of the human relations that generate it.

Shakespeare's paramount interest in what human beings mean to each other was not at all the same thing as that 'slavery to the confined interlocking of personal relationships, intricate as clockwork',[1] that a critic has complained of in present-day English drama. He was not concerned to count the yawns of a husband and wife coexisting in a corner of suburbia, or to chronicle the mannerisms of acquaintances who after getting on each other's nerves for twenty years remain at the end just what they were to begin with. Real contact, a real meeting of selves, depends on mutual knowledge, which comes only out of activity, out of joint doing and striving by individuals working with – or against – one another. Shakespeare's folk acquire such knowledge because they live venturously together on a planet where many things are as untried as the daffodils 'that come before the swallow dares'.

It is on public life that this proclivity of theirs and his has its most practical bearing. Historical progress is regulated not alone by the pace of objective development but also by the capacity of those who desire progress to form coherent leagues, to pool their energies in furthering it. Modern history is the history of the political party. But this political faculty is conditioned in any society by its members' ability to form stable relationships in private life. It is a cardinal error to suppose that the requisite aptitudes are natural rights of man, and come to him by instinct. They are the fruits of long, painful evolution, and they have matured variously under diverse social conditions, as anyone transplanted to a fresh environment, trying to join in activity with people of a different inheritance,

[1] L. Kitchin, *Twentieth Century*, February 1961, p. 172.

quickly learns. And if such aptitudes are lost, as they may easily be in a period of rapid change, much else will be lost with them. History like Nature produces nothing out of nothing, and a new society struggling to grow can only draw upon the moral, or psychological, as well as the economic resources bequeathed to it by its past.

We can see Shakespeare as one of the men of that age who were trying to salvage the consciousness of a social whole made up of its human parts; to preserve and adapt, that is, the talents humanity had acquired for combining and co-operating otherwise than by blind compulsion. In other quarters more artificial frameworks were being offered, to take the place of the old one. Patriotism and religion provided the two most obvious means of lessening men's distance from one another. In an age of religious wars, and of wars needed for the promotion of capitalism, the two often went together, and a great deal of humbug and worse went with both. Shakespeare did his share of patriotic tub-thumping when he wrote *Henry V*, where his idealizing of the English army as a 'band of brothers' is illuminating: it was a lost brotherhood (part reality, part myth) that Englishmen were trying to regain. Where Shakespeare was more truly himself he was looking for more vital relations between men, and men and women, to infuse a new spirit into the commonweal. For the same reason his profoundly humanistic outlook made him profoundly unreligious; he was not interested, as some of the dramatists were, in ropes to link human beings together that had to be slung over the pulley of a remote heaven.

The society fading away had for its metaphysical counterpart the 'Chain of Being' that united everything in the universe, angel and man and dust, in one ordered hierarchy. This was too static a notion, and too blatantly feudal, to retain much force, though it went on and on being repeated. Shakespeare was in search of fresh and living, instead of fossilized, connections. His quest was part of the all-round emancipation of the individual that was unfolding; but if he wanted a community enlivened by free choice and opportunity, he did not want one in which the individual would be 'set free' by being turned loose in a moral wilderness, abandoned to mere egotism and the survival of the most rapacious. Like poets in many epochs he put the contrast of old and new sometimes into the form of two contrasting generations. In *Hamlet* all the older people are warped and dehumanized by habits of mind that have grown petrified; nearly all the younger people share at least an impulsive, spontaneous quickness to feel, and to feel for others more than for themselves. Art, and drama in particular, is an active agent in the formation of new states of mind and of society. Shakespeare can be thought of in all his work as a preserver, modernizer, transmitter of the values of an older time for the benefit of a later one. All cultural values are delicate, and do not easily survive the transmutations they must undergo; those that arise directly out of men's relationships are the most fragile of all, most in need of a Shakespeare's genius for *psychochemistry*.

To try to reduce any part of Shakespeare to statistics invites his own question:

> Will you with counters sum
> The past-proportion of his infinite?
> (*Troilus and Cressida*, II. 2. 28-9.)

Reduction to cold figures of his world of life and movement can scarcely avoid travestying it; no tabulation can catch unique qualities, and nothing is more remarkable in Shakespeare than his way of making each chief relationship among his characters something unique. What there is between Hamlet and Horatio can be classified as 'friendship', but it is quite unlike anything that might grow between either of them and anyone else, or between any other pair. Any attempt at cataloguing must, besides, be biased by personal feeling as to what is more or less significant. In spite of these difficulties (and many more) there may be something to be gained from an experiment in putting Shakespeare's treatment of relationships into figures and columns, as a basis for comparing one part of his work with another in this respect, and his work with that of other Elizabethans.

His plays abound, needless to say, in fathers and sons, husbands and wives, friends, confederates, neighbours, and so on. Among each of these sorts of relationship there are some that stand out and impress us by a special vitality or colouring; something that makes them, as well as the individuals concerned in them, memorable. They may be referred to for

convenience as 'positive relationships'; they are connections
that engender some active, working force, able to alter the
human beings who take part in them, and through them to
alter the lives of others also. A play rich in this kind of ingredient is *Julius Caesar*. Here we may distinguish a 'positive
relationship' between, first and foremost, Brutus and Cassius;
another uniting these men and the whole band of conspirators;
a third between Brutus and Portia. Then there is the binding-
force between Caesar and Antony. There is besides some genuine
feeling between Caesar and Brutus; between Caesar and his
wife Calpurnia; between Brutus and his attendants and sub-
ordinate followers; and between Cassius and the friend after
whose supposed death he commits suicide, Titinius.

All these possess the electric spark; but clearly they are not
all on the same level of emotional or dramatic importance. The
first three among them may be singled out as of the highest
significance. In a second class may be placed the next tie,
that between Caesar and Antony. All the remaining four,
striking or touching as each of them is at certain moments,
seem to fall into a third class, of inferior weight, because
they do not affect leading figures in the plot, or do not affect
them vitally. Collectively 'positive relationships' such as these
last do much to add depth and tone to the Shakespearian
background; but for purposes of discussion it is the first and
second classes that matter most. The same three-fold classifi-
cation may be applied to family or other relationships, whether
of a 'positive' character or not. Thus, to take a mixed set of
married couples, none of which have this character, Henry
VIII and Katherine are clearly entitled by their dramatic
importance to be put in the first class; Hotspur and Lady Percy
may be assigned to the second rank, and so may Capulet and
Lady Capulet, whereas Montagu and Lady Montagu must be
relegated to the third.

Working on these lines we may count altogether, in Shakespeare's thirty-seven plays, a total of 149 'positive relationships'.
Of these twenty-four appear to belong to the first class of
importance, and thirty-five to the second; making a total for
these two groups, the ones chiefly to be considered, of fifty-nine
out of the 149. It may be noted that very frequently the leading
relationships have originated before the start of the play, though

they may go on evolving during its course. Only eight out of the fifty-nine come about in the course of the plays they occur in; or, discounting previous marriages and other family connections, eight out of thirty-four. This helps us to feel that we are looking at *bona fide* beings at one critical point of their lives, instead of at puppets called into life only for a couple of hours. In general their relationships are healthy as well as life-like; they are oftener good than bad in their influence. Of thirty-nine out of the fifty-nine it may be said that they unite good people, and encourage goodness; of only four that they tend on both sides to the promotion of evil.

Of the 149 relationships taken all together, the lowest average number to be found is in the ten Histories, only 2.7 per play; the highest in the four Romances, 5.5. There is thus a notable increase of numbers as between Shakespeare's early and late work. Twelve Comedies show an intermediate average of 3.6. By way of comparison it may be remarked that Marlowe's seven plays, considered in the same manner, show fourteen analogous relationships, an average of only two, and with only four in the first class. In twenty-one of Shakespeare's thirty-seven plays, all of them except *Titus Andronicus* and *Timon* Histories or early Comedies, there are none of the first class. Taking the fifty-nine of the first and second classes, there are thirteen plays with none; nine with one; three with two; six with three; five with four (*J.C., K.L., A.C., W.T., T.*); one with six (*H.*). When the plays are arranged in their more or less accepted chronological sequence, five of the fifty-nine fall into the first third, twenty-seven into the middle third, twenty-seven into the last. But within each group and period we can perhaps distinguish plays where Shakespeare seems interested primarily in relationships, e.g. *As You Like It*, from those where his attention is fixed rather on situations, as in *A Midsummer Night's Dream*, or on problems, as in *All's Well That Ends Well*. The group of three late Comedies or 'problem plays' (*T.N., M.M., A.W.E.W.*) contains only three out of the fifty-nine; whereas the previous three plays (*J.C., T.C., H.*) contain fourteen, the richest vein in the whole collection.

The broadest dividing-line to be observed is between relationships in which the individual finds himself entangled willy-nilly, and those initiated or at least accepted by his free choice. A society of feudal cast, in Europe then as in Asia now, provides husband or wife just as Nature provides all other relatives. Love, in its modern romantic guise, breaks out from this ready-made circle; so does friendship, or loyalty to others besides friends, for example to a sovereign, when this loyalty is more than conventional or unavoidable. Various of Shakespeare's lovers turn into married couples; in what follows, marriages that have grown visibly and recently out of mutual love, like those of Romeo and Juliet or Othello and Desdemona, are treated as cases of love instead of matrimony. Of the fifty-nine most interesting relationships, then, twenty-five, or fewer than half, fall into the linked categories of marriage and other family ties (thirteen out of twenty-four however in the first class; in the third or lowest, about a third). Love contributes six relationships out of twenty-four in the first class and two out of thirty-five in the second; friendship, in a wide sense, three and fourteen; other loyalties, usually between ruler and subject or master and man, two and seven.

All the strains and tensions of an age of change set up vibrations inside the family, which is indeed the historian's most sensitive seismograph for detecting them. There was much to disturb the harmony of the Elizabethan family: disagreements over religion, politics, morality, and the financial jealousies that always become more obtrusive when 'the time is out of joint'. Hardships of younger sons condemned to poverty by the custom of primogeniture have been a stock theme of all the literature of western Europe. Property may be a bone of contention also between heads of families and impatient heirs. A play ascribed to Massinger, *The Old Law*, turns on an edict for the execution of all women at the age of sixty and men at eighty. Most of the sons and daughters, not realizing that it is a trick on the part of their ruler, are undisguisedly delighted; Cleanthes, who discourses virtuously on the bond between parent and child, looks a very odd young prig among them. This is satire, but it underlines a portrayal of the family by Massinger and others that forms part of their prevailingly gloomy picture of life.

Shakespeare's own view of it is far from rosy. But he, much more clearly than the others, can be said to have two families in mind: a traditional one, aristocratic or coloured by aristocratic prejudice, and an ideal one, the family as it might be – as it will be, he leaves us convinced, when his amiable young lovers have had time to grow up and to reclaim other husbands, wives, and parents by their example. The old family has been turning into a cage; Juliet complains of the 'bondage' it keeps her in. But the cage is crumbling. If England in the later Histories, respectable England outside the taverns of East-cheap, is becoming a grey sort of place, this is a good deal because the archaic household and its allegiances are crumbling, along with the feudal order of which they are an intrinsic part. In the rebellion that ends at Shrewsbury the loyalties of the Percies to their own clan ought to be the strongest binding force; instead uncle, brother, son are each led by his own interests or passions: Northumberland leaves son and brother in the lurch, Worcester deceives his nephew, Hotspur's reck-lessness takes no account of any wishes but his own. Shake-speare could not bring the desiccated family of the past back to life, but he never gave up the search for a 'new model', which led him further and further as time went on into the realm of inspired fantasy.

He has five married couples prominent enough to be put in the first class, and fourteen in the second, out of a total of thirty-five or about one per play. On the whole they represent the old unregenerate style of matrimony, now sinking into lifeless routine – the 'dull, stale, tired bed' that Edmund derides – if not into something worse; and as we go on through the plays marriage as an institution is not improving, but deteriorating. In them all, only a single marriage of any long standing impresses us as really authentic and wholesome, that of Brutus and Portia. Of the other seventeen leading instances (deducting Petruchio and his Katherine as mainly farcical) seven may be accounted tolerable or trivial; ten must be classed as, in point either of the relations between the couple or of their influence on each other, bad or very bad. We can discern more or less of genuine affection on both sides in only five of these nineteen cases; on one side alone in three; in eleven, on neither. (In eighteen extant plays attributed in whole or part to Massinger there is affection on both sides in four out of twelve comparable *ménages*.) More often than not there is temporary or chronic dissension, not brought about by external factors solely. Two marriages end in divorce or long, wilful separation; two in husband killing wife. Three of the wives commit or attempt or instigate murder. They are, to give them their due, seldom unfaithful; this is something that Shakespeare could not easily bring himself to accuse women of, whereas in much of Elizabethan drama – as in the Restoration Comedy that was growing out of it long before the Restoration – it is taken for granted.

There is broadly the same story about other family ties. The seven of these involving parents, children and siblings are represented in all (if we neglect a few infants and other shadows) 165 times; twenty-two times in the first class and forty-three in the second, an average for the two combined of two per play. Out of these sixty-five, fourteen may be dismissed as of no more than conventional interest; of the remaining fifty-one only nineteen qualify as 'positive relationships' in the sense indicated above. Estrangements befall no fewer than thirty-nine of the pairs (or groups), often of a serious nature; serious enough fifteen times to drive relatives to kill or desire to kill one another. It is true that twenty-two of the quarrels end in reconciliations, even if some of these (with Shakespeare as with the other playwrights, when happy endings have to be arranged) are not very convincing. Father and son appear fifty-six times, but no more than five times in the first class, and in only two of these cases is their relationship really attractive. Hotspur shows little respect or liking for his father, who deserves little better from him. Henry IV suspects his son of wanting him dead and out of the way, or even it would seem of contemplating his murder. Shakespeare's mothers are not ardently maternal, especially towards their daughters. Brothers find a great many reasons for falling out with one another. Between sisters things are worse still. The happiest relationship, by a long margin, is between brother and sister. But while there is not on the whole much positive affection or good-will within the existing family, there are many sighs over their absence. These regrets help to persuade us that men's feelings for one another *ought* to be filled with warmth and life, even if 'in this harsh world' we can think of no other answer than Hamlet's to his mother's chilling platitude about how common it is for us to lose and forget our nearest and dearest. 'Ay, madam, it is common.'

In the Comedies, where the new voluntary ties replace the stereotyped ones of the Histories, Shakespeare likes to relieve his people of family connections, except that the heroines must have parents or guardians to make trouble for them. Their detachment from kith and kin, accentuated by foreign settings and (as in Molière) outlandish names, seems meant not to isolate them, but on the contrary to allow their feelings and affections to sprout freely and follow their own bent. Love holds the first place here. To revitalize marriage, and with it the family, Shakespeare advocated freedom for young men and women to choose their own partners in life. He was doing so from very early days –

> For what is wedlock forced but a hell,
> An age of discord and continual strife?
>
> (*1 Henry VI*, v. 5. 62-3.)

The idea of such freedom has been in all societies of feudal mould a perennial expression of longing for a better life, betterment of the family and, by poetical implication, of mankind altogether. It inspired operas in medieval China, and Molière, as well as Shakespeare. It has glowed most brightly in times of transition like his, when windows open on to long vistas; it can then be a truly revolutionary impulse, a factor in a revolutionary transformation of society.

Shakespeare's point of view was close to that of the more humanistic Puritans, men like the young Milton who must have acquired it partly from reading his plays. It was in other words the point of view of the most enlightened and liberal section of the middle class then growing up – and growing up for a revolutionary trial of strength against the *ancien régime* – of which Shakespeare himself was a member. His 'freedom' here too is a new morality, not a discharge from morality. The choice once made is irrevocable. Heroines are at liberty to break with their parents, but not with their husbands, and equally Troilus declares that once a man has made his 'election' there can be no repenting of his bargain. Florizel promises Perdita to be 'constant': it is one of Shakespeare's great words, and embodies one of his great beliefs, to which he clung all the more closely as his world grew more harsh and storm-beaten. In his mind it went with that inner integrity of the individual which makes a firm alliance between him and others possible. This is the quality that Hamlet prized in Horatio, and that Cressida lacked: having no trust in herself or in the life about her, she was unable to be faithful to Troilus's trust in her. It went too with the antithesis Shakespeare was never tired of making between sincerity and pretence, between what a man really is and what he wants to be thought, or what he seems to be –

Out on thee! Seeming! I will write against it.
(*Much Ado*, iv. 1. 55.)

For European countries struggling to shake off the fetters of the past, romantic love had the same excitement of novelty then as in Asia today, and the recurrent Elizabethan image of love as a voyage of discovery was appropriate enough. But the atmosphere of Elizabethan London, tainted by the practice of mercenary or forced marriages, by prostitution flourishing on social distress, by puritanism reacting against aristocratic licence, was not one in which romanticism could breathe easily. Of this there is plenty of evidence in Shakespeare's own works, and his ability to suck up into his imagination all that was good and new in the age, and distil it into feelings like those of Beatrice and Benedick, or Perdita and Florizel, was an outstanding part of his achievement. Even for him it cannot have been easy. He has eighty-six cases of love, with fifteen in the first class and twenty-one in the second. In eleven of these thirty-six love is felt by one party only and not returned. Among the remaining twenty-five there are many strains and stresses; only fourteen of the couples end happily, and about half of the others have their own shortcomings to blame. Only eight of the twenty-five, or one third, qualify as 'positive relationships', and three of these eight belong to the world-beyond-the-world of the Romances. In the eighteen Massinger plays, it may be added, we find fifty-three cases of love, a higher frequency than Shakespeare's; but in as many as thirty-three of them, or eighteen out of the thirty more important ones, love is unrequited, and often amounts to no more than an unwelcome pestering of A by B.

Love in Shakespeare is a social, not an isolating force. Beatrice and Benedick are brought together initially by a trick played on them by their friends, but, much more seriously, by the impulse that moves them both to defend someone else against injustice. Love in other words is part of life, bringing with it concern and responsibility for others as well, not a substitute for social life as it becomes in later romantic literature. With the other playwrights it was becoming a substitute already. And with them love was not always, as it always was for Shakespeare, an individualized, personal bond: it was less a matter of free choice, more a survival in new guise from the kingdom of necessity, a mere freak or fatality. They fell back on sexual attraction as writers always do when they can think of no other means of bringing characters together and setting them in movement, because their society contains too little else that can bring human beings close to one another. Love made use of in this way, as a sort of magical force or conjuring trick, could not be woven into any pattern of real life; it was felt as part of the incalculability of everything in that age of disintegration. On the stage it was liable to grow freakish, unnatural, theatrical. One of its modes, and one of a number which did not interest Shakespeare, was incest. His lovers, it is worth noticing, seldom fall in love at first sight: this happens only half a dozen times among his thirty-six leading cases, only three times where there is love on both sides. In fifteen of them the lover or lovers are already head over heels when the play begins, so that we can allow them the benefit of the doubt and suppose them to have given some careful thought to what they are doing.

There are forty-one friendships in Shakespeare, and thirty-nine ties of loyalty; the two things tend more and more to merge, as he searches for a new moral cement to take the place of crumbling feudal affiliations. Only five of the total of eighty can be assigned to the highest class, twenty-four to the second. Friendship like love did not grow easily in the Elizabethan soil. 'Our age calls, erroneously, friendship but a name', says Farneze in Massinger's *Bashful Lover*, one of a pair of friends who set a worthy example by risking their lives for each other after a lost battle. Marlowe has only two 'positive' instances of friendship, one of them criminal. It is revealing both of him and of his failure to turn the Faust-myth into real drama that he embarks Faustus on his terrific adventure all alone, without human aid or counsel. His 'friends' Valdes and Cornelius, Wagner whom he makes his heir, the scholar whom he calls his 'sweet chamber-fellow' – all these are left remote spectators of his fate. Shakespeare would not have chosen this theme, but if he had he would have handled it very differently.

Friendship always meant much to him, as witness an early, touchingly ludicrous image in *King John* about hairs stuck together by a teardrop, 'in sociable grief',

> Like true, inseparable, faithful loves,
> Sticking together in calamity.   (III. 4. 65-7.)

And his friends, unlike many of those drawn by the other playwrights, lend small support to Dr. Johnson's dictum that friendships are usually partnerships in folly or confederacies in vice. But they suffer in the Comedies from a tinge of mawkishness, of self-conscious sentimentality, as in Antonio's devotion to Bassanio in Venice, or the other Antonio's to Sebastian in Illyria. Both these men insist on running themselves into danger without much rhyme or reason, and their choice of friends looks fanciful and unmeaning. In the mature plays friendship is more realistic, bringing men together in face of the problems of a real world: a world where they do well to choose their friends carefully and then 'grapple them to their souls with hoops of steel'. Words which from Polonius are a fossilized wisdom of the past possess a meaning that Hamlet learns through living experience. When the shock of his mother's marriage and knowledge of his father's murder drives him into self-isolation, he behaves somewhat like a 'Machiavel', or a Timon, solitary and embittered and distrustful. But this in him is so unnatural that he can only keep it up by pretending to others, and half-pretending to himself, to be mad; and it paralyses his faculty of action. Unable to trust anyone else, he at once discovers to his chagrin that he is unable to trust himself, or even to take himself and his grand mission seriously. It is through his recovered confidence in Horatio that he recovers faith in his world and what has to be performed in it, and with this the ability to prepare calmly for action.

An American radical, G. C. LeRoy, wrote lately of the 'new thinness of personal relationships' in the U.S.A. of today, and of the impediment it represents to any banding together of

citizens against reactionary pressures.[1] A similar 'thinness' is
to be looked for in the twilight of every social cycle, and we are
in the same phase of ours as the Elizabethans of theirs. In their
day as in ours moreover the individual was dwarfed and over-
shadowed by a towering political authority. It made use of
spying and delation, terrorism and corruption, and politics
included the suborning of great men's followers by their rivals,
or by the government. Shakespeare was acutely aware of this
growth of the State, a force in his eyes necessary perhaps,
terrible certainly. What Ulysses says about secret intelligence-
work as an instrument of the omniscient and therefore
omnipotent State has no conceivable relevance to the affairs of
a Greek camp, but very much to those of Tudor statecraft: it
is Burleigh and Walsingham all over. Under such conditions
there can be no combining for political action without strong
mutual trust, or what we may call a willing suspension of
disbelief in our fellow-men. Machiavelli the Florentine, his
hero Cesare Borgia, and the 'Machiavels' of the theatre were
all political failures, in spite of their boasted realism, because
trust was a thing not dreamed of in their philosophy.

Shakespeare would be one of the great political poets if he
had written nothing besides *Julius Caesar*, and his masterwork
there is the evocation of a group of men united by a truly
Roman blend of private friendship and devotion to a public
cause. When one of them is asked whether he means to betray a
dangerous confidence, and replies briefly

> You speak to Casca, and to such a man
> That is no fleering tell-tale,   (1. 3. 116-17.)

we feel as sure of him as his hearer does. Every man can rely on
all the others to go without flinching 'as far As who goes
farthest'. Brutus and Cassius call each other 'brother', and all
the conspirators are, more genuinely than Henry V and his army
of freebooters, a 'band of brothers'; much more than the
Percies, they are all one family. There is a striking contrast
to be observed between their plot and the *Conspiracy of Byron*
in Chapman, where the hero has no party and no programme
and goes to work on his own just as the hero of the popular
Revenge type of play usually did. There is an equally sharp

[1] G. C. LeRoy, *Monthly Review*, September 1962, pp. 268-9.

contrast with Chapman's Romans in his *Caesar and Pompey*, stonily statuesque personages with none of that mutual faith and regard that Shakespeare's conspirators are brimful of; and again, at the opposite pole, with the demoralized Romans in Ben Jonson's *Sejanus*, where evil bestrides the narrow world far more tyrannically than Shakespeare's mightiest Julius ever did, and goes unchallenged.

Brutus and his friends also fail, because their heroic qualities are not shared by the common people. They are 'noble Romans' in rank as well as in temper; and for Shakespeare human qualities above the level of the pedestrian, and with them the capacity for vital relationships, are still aristocratic, not yet the common property of mankind. English history in the half-century after his death, with the revolution and the New Model army and the rest, is from this standpoint the history of a partial democratizing of these virtues, a widening of the moral franchise; a complex process in which Shakespeare's plays are themselves one ingredient.

It has been often enough or too often said that Shakespeare had a horror of anarchy, of social disorder; what really horrified him was not any breakdown of 'order' in the policeman's understanding of the word, but something more fundamental, the destruction of men's faith in one another that is always liable to accompany the break-up of an old social pattern whether authority remains intact or not. He was always struggling to banish the chilling distrust that invaded his England in the later Histories and the following plays. Dis-loyalty and ingratitude are two of the sins he condemns most eloquently, and if he so habitually censures men by comparing them with brute beasts, what he has against the animals is, surely, their incapability of fellow-feeling. Tragic emotion in his plays springs, more generally than in those of other Eliza-bethans, from a sense of men's best feelings for one another being alienated or violated. Estrangement is one of his great themes; something that could not be said of Marlowe, in spite of his taking Dido and Aeneas for a subject. Of Shakespeare's fifty-nine leading 'positive relationships' twenty-four in all are disturbed by failings of the individuals concerned, only six by external accident alone. The quarrel of Brutus and Cassius is the classic 'quarrel-scene' of all literature because it combines perfectly the malign pressure of circumstances with the inner weaknesses that they bring out. And because the better selves of the two men rise superior to their weaknesses and reunite them, though to die together, the play ends tragically but triumphantly.

When Brutus tried to repel Portia's sympathy or risked a breach with Cassius he was coming close to the edge of a moral gulf. In the Tragedies this goes further. Lear capriciously throws away attachments and loyalties, to recover which he has to pay a fearful price. For Macbeth there is no recovery. He becomes odious to himself because he has cut himself off from humanity, and isolation and suspicion push him into indiscriminate crime; but to us he never becomes odious, or never altogether a lost soul, because he can still feel excruciatingly, what Iago and the 'Machiavels' would never feel, the value of all that he has sacrified to win the crown,

> As honour, love, obedience, troops of friends.
>
> (v. 3. 25.)

Macduff's lament over the murder of his wife and children by Macbeth –

> I cannot but remember such things were,
> That were most precious to me,   (IV. 3. 222-3.)

might have been spoken by the murderer himself.

Shakespeare's tragic climaxes are apocalyptic, because the human bonds that hold together his world of imagination are so close-knit and vital that their disruption seems portentous, far more than that of any 'social order' in the abstract. The hero's life is enmeshed with the lives of others, his fate implies the ruin or transformation of everything round him. The world breaks up, but at the same time it is, in a new way, reunited; its virtues and loyalties are liberated from what has warped or divided them, and death reconciles as well as destroying. Hamlet's dying response to the appeal of the dying Laertes –

> Exchange forgiveness with me, noble Hamlet,
>
> (v. 2. 321.)

is in the same accent as the last words we hear between Prince Henry and Hotspur, Antony and Brutus, Edgar and Edmund.

Tragedy is not softened, by any means, but it is saved by this
note of communion from ending in simple negation. In the other
playwrights there is no such knitting-together, no such density
of human feeling to be disrupted. Their tragic sense is concentrated on the life and fortune of a particular man or woman
coming to an end; it is allied to the besetting horror of death as
the extinction of individual existence which haunts the plays of
Ford and Tourneur and Webster, as it haunts men in all
crumbling societies where the cold winds of Time blow in
through every crack and chink. Shakespeare's firm attachment
to the universe of man, of mankind as one whole, and the freedom from religious glooms that it helped to give him, preserved
him from these other men's nightmare. 'Take any shape but
that!...' To his great characters death comes in a very different
shape, and they die thinking not of their own annihilation but
of one another, and of the life that is to go on.

SHAKESPEARE AND POLITICS

Kenneth Muir

Shakespeare was born only six years after the accession of Elizabeth I, when the religious strife which had divided England for nearly a generation entered a less violent phase. There had, of course, been martyrs during the reigns of Henry VIII and Edward VI, and there were many martyrs in the reign of Elizabeth; but it has been calculated that more people suffered in the five years of Mary's reign than in the forty-five years of her successor's, and many of the Catholic martyrs were priests who knew that they were risking their lives in attempting the re-conversion of England. When Shakespeare was eight years old, the massacre of St. Bartholomew's Eve was a terrible reminder to Englishmen of the results of fanaticism.

There is some evidence that Shakespeare's father retained Catholic sympathies, along with many of his countrymen,[1] but the views of the poet on religious matters are not known. One piece of gossip, recorded many years after his death, states that 'he died a papist'.[2] He seems, at least, to have lived a conformist. He echoes the Bishops' Bible (which he would have heard in church) and the Geneva version (which was a handier size) throughout his plays; but there are few probable echoes, and no incontrovertible one, of the Catholic versions.[3] He had an intimate knowledge of the Homilies appointed to be read in churches.[4] He had read Hooker's *Laws of Ecclesiastical Polity* and Harsnett's *Declaration of Egregious Popish Impostures*; but the former he may have read for its style, and the latter because a former acquaintance figures in it.[5] At least, if we are to judge from references in *Macbeth*, he had no sympathy with the Gunpowder conspirators.

[1] J. H. De Groot, *The Shakespeares and 'the Old Faith'* (1946).
[2] E. K. Chambers, *William Shakespeare*, II, p. 257.
[3] H. R. Williamson, *The Day that Shakespeare died* (1962).
[4] A. Hart, *Shakespeare and the Homilies* (1934).
[5] R. M. Stevenson, *Shakespeare's Religious Frontier* (1958).

The same ambiguity surrounds Shakespeare's political views. He had read, like everyone else, the propaganda on behalf of the Tudor settlement, but we do not know how far he accepted it. His plays could not be performed without a licence; and on one occasion when Shakespeare tried to satisfy the censorship by rewriting the riot scenes in *Sir Thomas More*, the ban was not lifted. His patron, the Earl of Southampton, was one of the Essex conspirators; and, on the eve of their fatuous insurrection, Shakespeare's company was persuaded to give a subsidised performance of *Richard II* because the play showed the deposing of a king. The actors got into serious trouble, in spite of the very orthodox views on rebellion expressed in the play. It is the only play, indeed, in which the theory of the Divine Right of Kings is expounded or assumed by sympathetic characters. In *Hamlet* the doctrine is put into the mouths of Rosencrantz and Guildenstern in support of the murdering usurper, Claudius: while the Bishop of Carlisle is depicted as a brave and honest man.

In the plays he wrote during the reign of Elizabeth, Shakespeare seems to have regarded civil war as an evil to be avoided at all costs. All the Histories (except *Henry V* and *Henry VIII*) are concerned with civil war; and even *Henry V* contains an abortive rebellion and a foreign war which is designed to bring internal harmony by pouring the oil of patriotism on the troubled waters. To busy people's minds with foreign quarrels was the standard recipe for curing internal dissension, expressed, for example, in a book by Shakespeare's neighbour at Stratford, Dudley Digges.[1] It is understandable that Shakespeare should stress the importance of avoiding civil war. The Wars of the Roses had been brought to an end by the uniting of the white rose and the red by Elizabeth's grandfather; but there had been rebellions in 1537 and 1555, and many plots against Elizabeth's life. No one fully realized that the destruction of the Armada had effectually banished the danger of Spanish invasion, even though it had proved the loyalty of English Catholics to their protestant Queen. The religious wars in France were a reminder of the miseries of civil war. Although Shakespeare's friendship with Southampton may have wilted before the end of the sixteenth century, he inserted a cordial reference to Essex in

---

[1] *Four Paradoxes.*

Henry V, and we must suppose that the Essex rebellion came as a shock to him, whether he deplored, or sympathized with, Essex's conduct.

It is well known from the writings of the late Dr. E. M. W. Tillyard and others[1] that Shakespeare was continually expressing a belief in Order, order in the state being linked, as it was in the Homilies, in Hooker's masterpiece, and in many other Elizabethan works, with the divine ordering of the universe and the laws of nature. We do not know, of course, whether Shakespeare was expressing his personal opinions, providing appropriate opinions for his characters, or making suitable choric comment in plays concerned with the evils of civil war; but from the way in which he harps on the theme, and from the intensity of the imagery connected with it, it has naturally been assumed that he felt strongly on the subject. But it is worth while to examine some of the contexts in which Shakespeare refers to the connection between order in the state and the divine ordering of the universe.

One of the first is in *King John* (III. I.) when Cardinal Pandulph, who has excommunicated John, demands that King Philip shall break the alliance he has just made with him. Philip urges Pandulph to offer a compromise:

> Out of your grace, devise, ordain, impose
> Some gentle order; and then we shall be blest
> To do your pleasure, and continue friends.

To which the Cardinal replies:

> All form is formless, order orderless,
> Save what is opposite to England's love.
>
> (III. I. 250-4.)

The sympathies of the audience are divided. On the one hand, John is a usurper, and the alliance between France and England, in defiance of Constance's pleas for Arthur, is described by the Bastard as 'a most base and vile-concluded peace'; on the other hand, Elizabeth had been excommunicated and Shakespeare arouses patriotic feelings against the intervention of the Pope – an 'Italian priest' with his 'usurp'd authority' – and the Bastard, acting as a chorus, baits Austria, who is urging Philip

[1] E. M. W. Tillyard, *The Elizabethan World Picture* (1943); L. B. Campbell, *Shakespeare's Histories* (1947).

to obey the Cardinal. Pandulph's use of order is therefore ambivalent.

In *Sir Thomas More*, the hero addresses the mob who are rioting against the refugees, and warns them that if their riot were to succeed,

> You had taught
> How insolence and strong hand should prevail,
> How Order should be quell'd, and by this pattern
> Not one of you should live an aged man;
> For other ruffians as their fancies wrought,
> With self-same name, self reasons, and self right
> Would shark on you, and men like ravenous fishes
> Would feed on one another.

He goes on to tell them that St. Paul had enjoined obedience to authority – an injunction which aroused Christopher Marlowe's scorn – and that they are in arms against God:

> For to the King God hath his office lent
> Of dread, of justice, power, and command,
> Hath bid him rule and will'd you to obey;
> And to add ampler majesty to this,
> He hath not only lent the King his figure,
> His throne and sword, but given him his own name,
> Calls him a god on earth.

This speech is entirely appropriate to the character and situation; but it is worth noting that the idea of men preying on each other like sharks was repeated several times in later plays. In *Troilus and Cressida*, Ulysses declares that the breakdown of degree would lead to a state of affairs when

> Appetite, an universal wolf,
> So doubly seconded with will and power,
> Must make perforce an universal prey,
> And last eat up himself;   (i. 3. 121-4.)

In *King Lear*, Albany says that if the savagery of Cornwall and Regan is not punished by divine intervention,

> Humanity must perforce prey on itself,
> Like monsters of the deep;   (iv. 2. 49-50.)

and, in *Coriolanus*, the hero says that the noble senate keeps the commons in awe,

                which else
Would feed on one another.   (I. I. 185-6.)

Similar sentiments have been traced back to Theodoretus:
Shakespeare could have read them in *Flores Doctorum* or, more
probably, in Ponet's *Short Treatise on Politic Power*, written in
exile during the Marian persecution, and defining the limits
of obedience to authority:

> The rich would oppress the poor, and the poor seek the
> destruction of the rich, to have that he had: the mighty
> would destroy the weak, and as Theodoretus sayeth,
> the great fish eat up the small, and the weak seek
> revenge on the mighty; and so one seeking the others
> destruction all at length should be undone and come to
> destruction.

But whereas in Ponet the great fish eat up the small – i.e. the
rich eat up the poor – in Shakespeare men prey on one another
indiscriminately.[1]

In the first scene of *Henry IV*, Part II, Northumberland, on
hearing of the death of his son at the battle of Shrewsbury, gives
expression to what Lord Bardolph calls 'this strained passion':

> Let heaven kiss earth! Now let not Nature's hand
> Keep the wild flood confin'd! Let order die!
> And let this world no longer be a stage
> To feed contention in a ling'ring act;
> But let one spirit of the first-born Cain
> Reign in all bosoms, that, each heart being set
> On bloody courses, the rude scene may end
> And darkness be the burier of the dead!
>   (I. I. 153-60.)

The same desire for universal destruction is to be found in what
is apparently a late addition in the last act of *Henry VI*, Part II.
Young Clifford begins by describing the defeat of his party:

> Shame and confusion! All is on the rout;
> Fear frames disorder, and disorder wounds
> Where it should guard.   (V. 2. 31-3.)

He dedicates himself to war, the son of Hell; and then, noticing

[1] K. Muir ed. *King Lear* (1952), p. 156.

the dead body of his father, he prays for the ending of the world:

> O, let the vile world end
> And the premised flames of the last day
> Knit earth and heaven together!
> Now let the general trumpet blow his blast,
> Particularities and petty sounds
> To cease!   (v. 2. 40-5.)

Clifford becomes a savage and inhuman avenger, dedicated to cruelty and disorder.[1]

In *Henry V*, one of the most famous speeches on order is put into the mouth of the Archbishop of Canterbury, a crafty politician who has protected church property by agreeing to back the King's war with France. The comparison of the ordered state to the kingdom of the bees, probably taken from Elyot's *The Gouernour* with some memories of Virgil, is a very strange and irrelevant prelude to the Archbishop's practical proposal, that the King should go to France with one quarter of his forces, leaving the remainder to protect England from a possible Scottish invasion. The honey bees are

> Creatures that by a rule in nature teach
> The act of order to a peopled kingdom.
>
>   (1. 2. 188-9.)

and Shakespeare may have wished to present a picture of an ideal society, a kind of corporate state in which everyone has a specific function, just as in a later scene he introduces a Scotsman, an Irishman and a Welshman to show the unifying effect of Henry's reign. But we should avoid any large deductions from this speech and remember that the Archbishop is crafty rather than wise or holy.

It is equally important to remember the speaker and the context of the great degree speech in *Troilus and Cressida*. The immediate context is the prolongation of the siege of Troy, caused largely by Achilles's refusal to fight, and Agamemnon's consequent lack of authority. Obedience is, of course, of paramount importance in an army; and Ulysses's stress on order and degree, and even his derivation of them from the natural

---

[1] The verse of this speech is more mature than that of the rest of the play.

laws obeyed by the stars in their courses, is quite natural in its context. The ideas of the speech are commonplaces, derived from Elyot, Hooker and the Homilies; but Ulysses relies, not as they did on the divine ordering of the universe, but on natural law. But we should not assume too readily that Ulysses, though a 'choric' character, is therefore Shakespeare's mouthpiece. His advice is determined by the situation and is, indeed, suggested by Homer's account. We should remember, too, that there was a strong dramatic reason for this impressive establishment of the idea of order, for, at the climax of the play, when Troilus witnesses Cressida's unfaithfulness, we witness the breakdown of order. As Othello puts it: 'When I love thee not, Chaos is come again.' The build-up of order by Ulysses is a necessary preparation for the chaos which seems to result from Cressida's unfaithfulness:

> If there be rule in unity itself,
> This is not she. O madness of discourse,
> That cause sets up with and against itself!
> Bifold authority! where reason can revolt
> Without perdition, and loss assume all reason
> Without revolt. (v. 2. 139-44.)

We should not feel the full force of this if Ulysses had not shown how

> The heavens themselves, the planets, and this centre,
> Observe degree, priority, and place,
> Insisture, course, proportion, season, form,
> Office, and custom, in all line of order.
> (1. 3. 85-8.)

The necessity of considering the dramatic context is borne out by reference to a speech in *All's Well that Ends Well*, written at about the same time. The King's speech (II. 3. 115 ff.) on virtue as the true nobility is a condemnation of Bertram's pride of birth and, by implication, of the whole hierarchical principle.[1] The King is a much more sympathetic character than either the Archbishop of Canterbury or Ulysses, and is at least as likely to express Shakespeare's personal views:

[1] Cf. M. C. Bradbrook, *Shakespeare and Elizabethan Poetry* (1951), p. 162-70.

> Honours thrive
> When rather from our acts we them derive
> Than our fore-goers. The mere word's a slave,
> Debauch'd on every tomb, on every grave
> A lying trophy; and as oft is dumb
> Where dust and damn'd oblivion is the tomb
> Of honour'd bones indeed.   (II. 3. 133-9.)

Ulysses, indeed, when talking to Achilles, warns him

> That no man is the lord of anything,
> Though in and for him there be much consisting,
> Till he communicate his parts to others.
>   (III. 3. 115-17.)

Here it is individual worth and individual deeds that are more important than a man's position in the hierarchy of order.

After *Troilus and Cressida* there are no passages which directly associate cosmic order with order in the state, although this association is implied in *Macbeth, Othello* and *King Lear*. The images of disorder in Macbeth, evoked by the hero's dedication to evil, and the restoration of order in Scotland at the end of the play, both assume that order in the state and order in the universe are interdependent. Macbeth's temptation to murder Duncan shakes his 'single state of man', as Brutus's temptation to assassinate Caesar makes the state of man, 'Like to a little kingdom', suffer

> The nature of an insurrection.

When Othello realizes after his murder of Desdemona that he has no wife, he says:

> Methinks it should be now a huge eclipse
> Of sun and moon, and that th'affrighted globe
> Did yawn at alteration.   (V. 2. 102-4.)

The storm in *King Lear* is partly a reflection of the tempest in his mind.

The insistence on order in the English Histories is a dramatic necessity, since all are concerned with the evils of civil war; and, as we have seen, there is an equal dramatic necessity for the speech of Ulysses. In *Measure for Measure*, however, written between *Othello* and *King Lear*, Shakespeare is more concerned with the abuses of authority than with the necessity of order. The word 'authority' is used six times in the course of the play, and in each case it is referred to not as a means of order, but as a synonym for tyranny, which may be defined as power without justice or mercy. Claudio, condemned to death for fornication, the result, as he admits, of 'too much liberty', speaks bitterly of 'the demigod Authority' who can

> Make us pay down for our offence by weight
> The words of heaven: on whom it will, it will;
> On whom it will not, so; yet still 'tis just.
>
> (I. 2. 115-17.)

He admits his guilt: his complaint is that he has been singled out from all the guilty ones for punishment. In the scene in which Isabella pleads for her brother's life she makes two references to authority, her whole plea being based on the necessity of tempering justice with mercy and on the fact that we are all sinners. She tells Angelo that

> man, proud man,
> Dress'd in a little brief authority,
> Most ignorant of what he's most assur'd,
> His glassy essence, like an angry ape,
> Plays such fantastic tricks before high heaven
> As makes the angels weep.   (II. 2. 117-22.)

She goes on to suggest that the same offence is treated differently according to the position of the offender, and she tells Angelo that

> Authority, though it err like others,
> Hath yet a kind of medicine in itself
> That skins the vice o'th' top.   (II. 2. 134-6.)

After Isabella has gone, Angelo confesses that she was right, that he has indeed 'a natural guiltiness' such as Claudio's, and that

> Thieves for their robbery have authority
> When judges steal themselves.   (II. 2. 176-7.)

The Duke speaks (IV. 2.) of the 'quick celerity' of offence,

> When it is borne in high authority.   (IV. 2. 105.)

and Angelo thinks he will escape exposure because his

>   authority bears a so credent bulk
>   That no particular scandal once can touch
>   But it confounds the breather.   (IV. 3. 24-6.)

The moral drawn by the Duke is that

>   He who the sword of heaven will bear
>   Should be as holy as severe;
>   Pattern in himself to know,
>   Grace to stand, and virtue go;
>   More nor less to others paying
>   Than by self-offences weighing.   (III. 2. 243-8.)

In *King Lear* the analysis of authority is carried a stage further. Kent, in disguise, tells the King:

>   You have that in your countenance which I would fain
>   [call master . . .
>   Authority.   (I. 4. 27-30.)

But in the first scene he had bluntly criticized Lear's exercise of his authority as madness, folly, and hideous rashness; and Lear himself, displaying what Edgar calls 'reason in madness', declares in Act IV that 'the great image of authority' is that 'a dog's obeyed in office'. George Orwell once criticized Shakespeare's timidity for putting his subversive statements only into the mouths of fools and madmen; but this criticism ignores the conditions under which Elizabethan dramatists wrote, the severity of the censorship, – 'Folly, doctor-like, controlling skill' – and the fact that Shakespeare's fellow-actors were likely to be more cautious than he was himself.[1] It ignores, too, the resemblance between the criticism of authority by the sane Isabella and that by the mad Lear. There are parallels in *Measure for Measure* to the thievish justice, the lustful beadle lashing the whore, and to the assertion that we are not all equal before the law:

>   The usurer hangs the cozener.
>   Through tatter'd clothes small vices do appear;
>   Robes and furr'd gowns hide all. Plate sin with gold,
>   And the strong lance of justice hurtless breaks;
>   Arm it in rags, a pigmy's straw does pierce it.
>   (IV. 6. 163-7.)

---

[1] George Orwell, *Selected Essays* (1957), p. 116.

The criticism of society apparent in these lines does not stand alone. Lear in the storm addresses the hypocrites whose crimes have so far been concealed:

> Tremble, thou wretch,
> That hast within thee undivulged crimes
> Unwhipp'd of justice. Hide thee, thou bloody hand;
> Thou perjur'd, and thou simular man of virtue
> That art incestuous; caitiff, to pieces shake,
> That under covert and convenient seeming
> Hast practis'd on man's life. Close pent-up guilts,
> Rive your concealing continents, and cry
> These dreadful summoners grace.   (III. 2. 51-9.)

Lear deplores the inequalities of society, both in general terms, when he prays to the 'poor naked wretches', and later, in particular terms, when he pities Poor Tom. His injunction to Pomp to take physic –

> Expose thyself to feel what wretches feel,
> That thou mayst shake the superflux to them,
> And show the heavens more just.   (III. 4. 34-6.)

is repeated in the next act, when Gloucester too pities Poor Tom:

> Heavens, deal so still!
> Let the superfluous and lust-dieted man
> That slaves your ordinance, that will not see
> Because he does not feel, feel your power quickly;
> So distribution should undo excess,
> And each man have enough.   (IV. I. 67-72.)

The same idea is expressed, this time by one of the victims of inequality, in the first scene of *Coriolanus*:

> We are accounted poor citizens, the patricians good. What authority surfeits on would relieve us; if they would yield us the superfluity while it were wholesome, we might guess they relieved us humanely; but they think we are too dear. The leanness that afflicts us, the object of our misery, is as an inventory to particularize their abundance; our sufferance is a gain to them.
>   (I. I. 14-24.)

This cannot be brushed on one side as the irrational envy of the starving mob, or as the expression of Lear's insanity: it is a protest against the immorality of inequality, which allows some to have too much and others to have too little.

The mock trial of Goneril and Regan before a bench of magistrates consisting of the Fool, Caius (Kent in disguise) and Poor Tom – although Lear complains that they have been bribed – is another means of showing up the imperfections of justice in a class society.

The exact date of *Coriolanus* is unknown. It was probably the last of the tragedies and may have been written in the middle of Shakespeare's last period. Some critics have supposed that it reflects the terrified reactions of a man of property at the time of the Midlands insurrection of 1607 against the enclosures. But the parallels between the address to the Warwickshire Diggers and the speeches of the citizens in the first act of *Coriolanus* are of doubtful validity, since the extant copy of the address dates from the middle of the seventeenth century, and it may not have any connection with the 1607 insurrection; and in any case Shakespeare's sympathies during the insurrection cannot be deduced from the play. Although Hazlitt asserted that Shakespeare leaned to the arbitrary side of the question, he had for purely dramatic reasons to preserve some sympathy for his hero. Yet it is clear from a study of Plutarch that Shakespeare whittled down some of Coriolanus's excuses; that he made him more insolent than Plutarch had done; that he gave the people genuine grievances; that, though they are less courageous in battle than Coriolanus, they resented being treated as mere cannon fodder; that the war was a means of disposing of the surplus population, what Coriolanus shockingly calls 'our musty superfluity'; that it is Coriolanus, not they nor the Tribunes, who wishes to overturn the constitution; and that when Rome is besieged they exhibit more genuine patriotism, and much greater objectivity, than the patricians. Even the Tribunes, who have been described as 'comic and detestable villains', are depicted by Shakespeare as shrewd politicians who are much less unscrupulous than their opponents. Their greatest mistake is to commute the death-sentence on Coriolanus to one of banishment. Their conviction that he would have made a tyrannical consul, and that he was a threat to the liberties of the people, is justified by every word he utters.

Shakespeare appears to display more sympathy for the citizens' point of view than any previous writer on Coriolanus, with the single exception of Machiavelli.[1] Dudley Digges tells with approval of the way the Senate resolved on a war with the Volsces to cure internal dissension; Bodin and Fulbeck tell the story to show the disadvantages of democracy; Goslicius deplores the creation of the Tribunes; and Sidney and other writers recount Menenius's fable and accept its dubious moral without questioning.[2] There is something to be said for the view that *Coriolanus* is a 'tragical satire'. The hero's character has been warped by his dependence on his domineering mother, by his upbringing with its monstrously perverted values, and by his environment. We are clearly meant to associate his character with that of his young son who is described early in the play:

> O' my word, the father's son! I'll swear 'tis a very pretty boy. O' my troth, I look'd upon him a Wednesday half an hour together; has such a confirm'd countenance! I saw him run after a gilded butterfly; and when he caught it he let it go again, and after it again, and over and over he comes, and up again, catch'd it again; or whether his fall enrag'd him, or how 'twas, he did so set his teeth and tear it. O, I warrant, how he mammock'd it!
> (I. 3. 57-65.)

Volumnia comments, without irony: 'One on's father's moods'. Coriolanus behaves through much of the play as a boy who has never learnt to control himself; and Aufidius's final insult, in calling him a boy, leads him to lose his temper for the last time.

But Coriolanus is nevertheless superior to his environment, though his upbringing makes him half-ashamed of the tenderness he feels for his wife. He is brought to his ruin not merely by his excessive pride, but also by his inability to play the hypocrite, as his mother and the patricians urge – this is

---

[1] Although Machiavelli was regarded with horror by the Elizabethans because of the cynical realism of *The Prince*, his *Discourses on Livy* are often substantially democratic.

[2] K. Muir, *Shakespeare's Sources* (ed. 1961), pp. 219 ff.

brought out by the frequent imagery drawn from the stage – and by his sacrifice of his hatred of Rome to his love for his family. Although he believes that he renounces vengeance because of his mother's pleadings, Shakespeare makes it clear that he is more affected by the tears of his wife and son.[1]

Democracy in the modern political sense was not a practical issue in 1608, as it would have been a generation later; and it is futile to complain that Shakespeare probably accepted the monarchy as the best form of government. Neither the plebeians nor the patricians are idealized; and the play illustrates not Shakespeare's distrust of the common people, but rather, as Coleridge said, 'the wonderfully philosophic impartiality of Shakespeare's politics'.

In *Timon of Athens* the only genuinely sympathetic characters are the servants. The senators are all corrupt and ungrateful; the Poet deserts Timon when he can no longer act as a patron; Alcibiades is little more than a scourge of the corrupt Athenians; Apemantus is not much better than Thersites; and Timon's prodigality is succeeded by an equally excessive bitterness. But all his servants display a genuine love for their master – a love which is not affected by his loss of wealth and status. Flavius is a faithful steward who does his best to avert Timon's ruin, who follows him into exile, and offers to support him on his own meagre savings, some of which he has already shared with his fellow-servants. Flaminius, one of the servants, is disgusted at the ingratitude of Lucullus, throwing his bribe in his face:

> Let molten coin be thy damnation,
> Thou disease of a friend, and not himself!
> Has friendship such a faint and milky heart
> It turns in less than two nights? O you gods,
> I feel my master's passion!   (III. 1. 51-5.)

Another servant of Timon's, similarly horrified at the ingratitude of Sempronius, calls him a 'goodly villain'; and after Timon's first great curse of the inhabitants of Athens at the beginning of Act IV, Shakespeare deliberately inserted a scene to demonstrate the perversity of his hero's absolute

---

[1] H. C. Goddard, *The Meaning of Shakespeare* (1951); U. Ellis-Fermor, *Shakespeare the Dramatist* (1961).

misanthropy. Four of his faithful servants lament the fall of a
noble master, and inveigh against the ingratitude of his false
friends:

> *2 Serv.*   As we do turn our backs
> From our companion, thrown into his grave,
> So his familiars to his buried fortunes
> Slink all away; leave their false vows with him,
> Like empty purses pick'd; and his poor self,
> A dedicated beggar to the air,
> With his disease of all-shunn'd poverty,
> Walks, like contempt, alone. . . .

> *3 Serv.*   Yet do our hearts wear Timon's livery;
> That see I by our faces. We are fellows still,
> Serving alike in sorrow.

> *Flav.*   Good fellows all . . .
> Let's yet be fellows; let's shake our heads and say,
> As 'twere a knell unto our master's fortune,
> 'We have seen better days'.   (IV. 2. 8-27.)

Even if we were tempted to see in the play a reflection of some
personal bitterness on Shakespeare's part – for which there is
no direct evidence – it is clear that this bitterness did not
extend to the common people. Once again we see the way
in which the poet's feelings and opinions seem to be evoked
by the dramatic situation. Just as it was necessary to show the
fickleness of the people in dramatizing the story of Coriolanus,
so it was necessary to show the disequilibrium of Timon by
presenting characters who were not ungrateful. But it may
be significant that Shakespeare made no exception in the
ingratitude of the upper classes.

   Timon of Athens, as it stands, is an unsatisfactory play, and
it is probably a fragmentary draft of which only about half
has been revised.[1] It was written, presumably, either just
before or just after *Antony and Cleopatra*, although its theme of
ingratitude makes it close in spirit to parts of *King Lear*. Shakespeare's intentions are less ambiguous than they are in many
of his plays. For once he states his theme openly in the
form of the fable of Fortune put into the mouth of the Poet

---

[1] U. Ellis-Fermor, op. cit.

in the first scene – that when Fortune changes, flatterers desert
the ruined man. This meaning is reinforced by the image-
cluster of flatterers, dogs and melting sweets, often used before
by Shakespeare, but dominant in this play alone.

Wilson Knight has called attention[1] to the importance of
gold symbolism – the gold Timon dispenses with such prodigality and the gold he discovers when digging for roots. But
the gold is not, as Wilson Knight argues, the symbol of Timon's
golden heart. He is nearer the truth when he suggests that
there is

> a contrast between gold and the heart's blood of passion-
> ate love of which it is a sacrament: the association of the
> metaphorical value of gold and the value of love.

Timon tries to buy love with gold, but he buys not friends but
flatterers. Gold is a symbol of the way in which gross inequality
in society destroys disinterestedness in love. Timon's love for
his fellow-men is warped and poisoned by their ingratitude.
It is significant that the only women in the play are performers
and harlots. In the society which Shakespeare depicts love is a
commodity like everything else. We cannot imagine a married
Timon. This accounts for the sex nausea apparent in several of
his speeches. He curses the Athenians with syphilis, partly
because he assumes that all love has a sexual basis, and partly
because it is the appropriate plague for those to whom everything can be bought and sold. Timon's initial flaw is that he
expects disinterested love at the same time as he is using his
gold to make himself beloved.

Shakespeare chose for his hero, not a king or a great warrior,
but a man whose eminence depended entirely on his wealth.
It is as though he realized at the dawn of the capitalist era that
power was beginning to shift from one class to another, and
that authority would be decreasingly invested in the nominal
rulers. The new domination of gold was clearly a threat to the
old hierarchical conception of order, for it substituted for it an
order in itself divorced from morality – although many puritans
would be moral for religious reasons – an authority without
responsibility, a power animated entirely by self-interest. The
full horror of this situation is expressed by Timon when he

[1] G. Wilson Knight, *The Wheel of Fire* (1930).

discovers gold and meditates on the way it can overturn the moral order, making

> . . . black white, foul fair,
> Wrong right, base noble, old young, coward valiant.
>
> (IV. 3. 28-9.)

knitting or breaking religions, elevating thieves to the senate, embalming and spicing 'the wappen'd widow' and the syphilitic; destroying chastity, serving as the 'common whore of mankind' and as the 'visible god'. Marx's commentary on these lines in *Capital* was condensed, as I have shown elsewhere,[1] from an earlier commentary in an unfinished work, only recently translated into English.[2] This commentary brings out Shakespeare's insight into the nature of developing capitalism in which everything is a commodity; but we should not, of course, take it to imply that his own point of view was the same as Marx's three hundred years later.

We have seen how order and authority were the thesis and antithesis of the Shakespearian dialectic, and that in *Timon of Athens* the power of gold is seen as a terrifying threat both to order and authority. It may be noted that Jonson's exposures of the acquisitive principle were written at about the same time.[3] In his last unaided play, *The Tempest*, Shakespeare made a final comment on the political problem. Prospero, the philosopher prince, has been deposed by the 'politicians' who sacrifice morality to their pursuit of power; but by acquiring power over nature he is enabled to overcome his enemies and regain his throne, as well as defeat the new rebellion against his authority by Caliban and his drunken associates. The good old politician, Gonzalo, is allowed to day-dream about his ideal commonwealth, a return to the golden age. It is based on one of Montaigne's essays, although Shakespeare selects only the pleasanter features of the primitive society there described. Nature's abundance is such that there are no economic problems and no need for the arts of civilization; and human nature is such that no laws or armaments are required. The state has withered away:

---

[1] K. Muir, '*Timon of Athens* and the Cash-Nexus' in *Modern Quarterly Miscellany* (1947).

[2] K. Marx, *Economic and Philosophic Manuscripts of 1844*, (1959).

[3] L. C. Knights, *Drama and Society in the Age of Jonson* (1937).

I'th'commonwealth I would by contraries
Execute all things; for no kind of traffic
Would I admit; no name of magistrate;
Letters should not be known; riches, poverty,
And use of service, none; contract, succession,
Bourn, bound of land, tilth, vineyard, none;
No use of metal, corn, or wine, or oil;
No occupation; all men idle, all;
And women too, but innocent and pure;
No sovereignty— . . .
All things in common nature should produce
Without sweat or endeavour. Treason, felony,
Sword, pike, knife, gun, or need of any engine,
Would I not have; but nature should bring forth,
Of its own kind, all foison, all abundance,
To feed my innocent people.   (II. I. 141-58.)

Shakespeare shows that a return to primitive communism is neither possible nor desirable. For the primitive reality is represented by the savage Caliban who desires freedom without morality; and human nature as it is, is represented by the murderous plots of Antonio and Sebastian and the drunken villainy of Trinculo and Stephano. The nature of the good society, as envisaged by Shakespeare himself, is hinted at in the love-scenes between Ferdinand and Miranda, who find freedom in bondage to each other, and in the clemency of Prospero who is not corrupted by his power. It is no doubt significant that in depicting a kingdom in which a philosopher-prince is able to control threats from within and without, Shakespeare went to an enchanted island. But even so, he was not guilty of an easy Utopianism. Half the characters of the play are evil.

Shakespeare was often concerned with problems of power and with the difficulty of maintaining the personal virtues in public life. He realized instinctively that the proper function of politics was to enable people to lead a good life; and he was keenly aware of the obstacles to the good life – pride, the love of power, avarice, ingratitude and hatred. His villains are all individualists. But his mind, in Keats's phrase, was a thorough-fare for all thoughts, not a select party. He was so essentially a dramatist that each of his characters speaks for himself and not for him; and because of this negative capability he seems to have an almost universal sympathy. We cannot, therefore, deduce Shakespeare's opinions from his characters, since they are not his mouthpieces: but we can tell something about his own attitude from the material to which he was drawn, from his treatment of that material, and especially from his recurrent themes and images.

Shakespeare was obviously inspired by the ideas of humanism, though he was also conscious of its dangers. He accepted the traditional Christian ethical values, but showed comparatively little interest in its dogmas. He was suspicious of puritanism and, it would seem, strongly opposed to usury. He believed that men should be stewards of their wealth; and that wealth should be used to relieve poverty. In the last words he wrote, at the end of *The Two Noble Kinsmen*, he makes Theseus say:

> Let us be thankful
> For that which is.

But this, in its context, is not an expression of conservatism, but of wonder at the mystery of life.

HENRY V AND HISTORY

Zdeněk Stříbrný

The Life of Henry V is hardly the greatest play in Shakespeare's cycle of ten dramas of English history. Yet it may certainly be considered as central, or at least helpful in revealing his artistic approach to politics, politicians, world-order, kingship, the people, the Elizabethan nation-state, and more generally to war and peace – in a word, to history. It has the unquestioned distinction of crowning the second, and more mature, group of his 'histories' which stretch from the very beginnings to the actual close of his writing career.

For a clearer understanding of its place among these national historical plays a list of all of them, in the order in which they were probably written, may be useful:[1]

3 Parts of *Henry VI* (written about 1590-2)	The first historical tetralogy
Richard III (written about 1592-3)	
King John (about 1595-6)	
Richard II (about 1595-6)	The second historical tetralogy
2 Parts of *Henry IV* (about 1597-8)	
Henry V (1599)	
Henry VIII (about 1612-13).	

There is no need to suppose that Shakespeare had such an extensive and neat pattern in his mind when he decided to try his hand at the English chronicle play. Nevertheless, the outcome of his endeavours was commanding enough. With the exception of *King John* and the late *Henry VIII*, all his histories are grouped in two tetralogies, culminating respectively in *Richard III* and *Henry V*. This gives these two plays a special

---

[1] The list can only be tentative because the chronology of Shakespeare's plays is a vexed problem of long standing. For our purposes, however, there is no need to go into the innumerable discussions of Shakespearian scholars. Two important and sound views are presented in E. K. Chambers' *William Shakespeare: A Study of Facts and Problems* (Oxford 1930), I, 243-74, and in James G. McManaway's 'Recent Studies in Shakespeare's Chronology', *Shakespeare Survey 3* (1950), 22-33.

position and perhaps a special appeal, even in our day: they are so far the only histories that have been filmed and thus brought to millions of modern spectators. Laurence Olivier's choice may also have been due to the fact that they present, in mutual contrast, supreme examples of a bad and a good king, of a tyrant, as the humanist thinkers of the Renaissance conceived and condemned him, and of an ideal ruler, aspiring to the high place awarded by Thomas More to his King Utopus, or by Thomas Elyot to his Governor.

It is a commonplace that it has always been easier for an author to create a negative character, ranging up to a thorough-going villain, than an accomplished hero. This applies even to Shakespeare who, of all the world's great writers is only the nearer to us for his normal share in our common frailties. Nobody has any doubts about the crushing impact of his *Richard III*. But his *Henry V* has been subjected to much discussion and has been both extolled and execrated with considerable vehemence.

The main attack against Henry has been launched since the nineteenth century by liberal-minded critics who have tended to see in him a jingoist – not to say imperialist – conqueror destroying all he could not enslave. Their first, and not least effective, spokesman was William Hazlitt. Branding the historical king for his practice of 'brute force, glossed over with a little religious hypocrisy', Hazlitt enjoyed him in the play with ironic reservation as 'a very amiable monster', 'as we like to gaze at a panther or a young lion in their cages in the Tower, and catch a pleasing horror from their glistening eyes, their velvet paws, and dreadless roar'.[1] With similar half-amused and half-indignant irony Bernard Shaw, by the end of the century, could not forgive his old rival Shakespeare 'for the worldly phase in which he tried to thrust such a Jingo hero as his Harry V down our throats'.[2] This brisk dismissal has been carried well on into the twentieth century by such liberal critics as Bradley, Granville-Barker, Mark Van Doren, and John Palmer, to name the most typical.

In more recent years, however, a pronounced contrary

[1] W. Hazlitt, *Characters of Shakespear's Plays*, in *Complete Works* (London 1930), IV, 285-6.
[2] G. B. Shaw, *Our Theatre in the Nineties*, Standard edition (London 1948), II, 128.

trend has been noticeable. It has crystallized in the two representative modern English editions, The New Cambridge (1947)
and The New Arden Shakespeare (1954). The Cambridge
editor, John Dover Wilson, writing under the immediate
impact of the Second World War, was quick to appreciate the
'heroic poetry' of the play. He used all his resources of erudi-
tion and style to show Henry in his proper historical setting as
a national leader, the 'star of England', outshining Marlowe's
Tamburlaine in his magnanimity, justice, mercy, heroic faith,
sense of humour and other human qualities which, in Wilson's
view, represent the essence of an English happy warrior.[1] With
a different accent, but with no less enthusiasm in his general
appraisal, J. H. Walter continued the exoneration of Henry,
carrying on, in this point at least, the tradition of the old
Arden edition of 1903. Walter's apotheosis rests mainly on the
assumption that Shakespeare created his Henry as a 'mirror of
all Christian kings', as 'the epic leader strong and serene, the
architect of victory' whose remarkable self-restraint, magnificent
courage, royal clemency, gay and gallant spirits and, above all,
piety, can be matched only by Virgil's Aeneas.[2]

How are we to deal with these clashing critical contradictions?

There can be no doubt that Shakespeare wanted his *Henry V*
to become a triumphal account of the English victory against
overwhelming odds at Agincourt in 1415. As the historical
events, described in chronicles and sung about in ballads,
afforded, apart from the battle itself, rather little dramatic
matter, he was both forced and inspired to create a new dramatic
genre, what we might almost call an epic drama, certainly the
most epic of all his plays. Accordingly, he introduced every act
by an epic prologue and closed the whole piece by an epilogue
in the form of a narrative sonnet. In the opening lines of the play
he invoked his Muse to 'ascend the brightest heaven of
invention': the final play of his two historical cycles was to be
a lavish parade of mellow poetry both epic and dramatic, of
richly varied prose and of good-humoured parody on affected
and outmoded dramatic styles, not excepting the 'mighty line'
of Marlowe.

---

[1] Introduction to *King Henry V*, New Cambridge edition (Cambridge 1947),
vii-xlvii.

[2] Introduction to *King Henry V*, Arden edition (London 1954), xi-xxxiv.

Stylistic analysis certainly suggests that Shakespeare was anxious to marshal and display all the formal resources he had thus far mastered. The blank verse in *Henry V* reaches the highest standard of his middle phase. Far from confining every idea to a single line, as is the tendency in the early plays, the verse runs majestically on, yet within a firm discipline and without breaking under the pressure of heavy thought or overflowing into the freedom of the later tragedies and final romances. It makes use of all the bold images and ornamental devices of Renaissance poetry, without piling them up or showing them off. Youthful exuberance gives way to measure, balance and harmony:

> Suppose within the girdle of these walls
> Are now confin'd two mighty monarchies,
> Whose high upreared and abutting fronts
> The perilous narrow ocean parts asunder.
> Piece out our imperfections with your thoughts:
> Into a thousand parts divide one man,
> And make imaginary puissance;
> Think, when we talk of horses, that you see them
> Printing their proud hoofs i' th' receiving earth; . . .
>
> (1. Prologue, 19-27.)

The prose presents an even greater fullness. It ranges from passages highly rhetorical and refined in the manner of the university and court wit John Lyly (most of the speeches of the French courtiers) to passages almost naturally colloquial (e.g. Henry's discourse with the good soldiers Bates, Court and Williams) and to pieces still more homespun and spiced with farcical gags. Perhaps the best example of the latter type of prose comes up in the scene where our hostess Pistol, *quondam* Quickly, tells about the death of Sir John Falstaff. Already at the beginning of the second act she has prepared us for the worst by her announcement that 'he'll yield the crow a pudding one of these days' because 'the King has killed his heart'. After the contrasting effect of the ensuing scene in the King's council-chamber at Southampton, full of solemn poetry, she comes again, this time to deliver her famous comic dirge on Falstaff's end:

> Nay, sure, he's not in hell: he's in Arthur's bosom, if ever man went to Arthur's bosom. 'A made a finer end,

and went away an it had been any christom child; 'a
parted ev'n just between twelve and one, ev'n at the
turning o' th' tide; for after I saw him fumble with the
sheets, and play with flowers, and smile upon his finger's
end, I knew there was but one way; for his nose was as
sharp as a pen, and 'a babbl'd of green fields. 'How
now, Sir John!' quoth I. 'What, man, be o' good cheer'.
So 'a cried out 'God, God, God!' three or four times.
Now I, to comfort him, bid him 'a should not think of
God; I hop'd there was no need to trouble himself with
any such thoughts yet. So 'a bade me lay more clothes
on his feet; I put my hand into the bed and felt them,
and they were as cold as any stone; then I felt to his
knees, and so upward and upward, and all was as cold
as any stone.   (II. 3. 9-26.)

This old wife's tale is typical of the way Shakespeare transformed the farcical prose of his dramatic predecessors. He
retained something of the clownish fooling which was expected
from characters of low life when they appeared on the pre-
Shakespearian stage, yet at the same time he permeated their
speech with genuine popular idiom and imagination, with
sharply observed comparisons, with strong epic narrative and
pithy dramatic dialogue, as well as with pungent humour.
Mistress Quickly's high-explosive style, compounded of convention and originality, of old cliché and realistic vision, of
broad farce and unaffected feeling, was bound to give her an
even stronger appeal than that of her older relative, the Nurse
in *Romeo and Juliet*.

The great variety of style, climbing from the depth of
London taverns up to the flights of court poetry, is in full
accord with the basic idea-content of the play. No pains are
spared to present an imposing panorama of Britain's unity
in arms, including every 'kind and natural' citizen, whatever
his rank and his nationality, English, Welsh, Irish, or Scottish.
All the sons of Mother England are called upon to do their
duty, which is apportioned according to their social 'degree',
yet is in each case important and responsible. Moreover, when
it comes to the decisive battle, everybody who sheds his blood
is gentled in his condition while any gentlemen who shun
fighting must 'hold their manhood cheap'.

The English nobility of action stands in sharp contrast to the nobility of blood among the French who look down upon the English 'beggared host' as well as on their own 'superfluous lackeys' and 'peasants'. Even after their defeat they send their herald Montjoy to ask King Henry to allow them

> To sort our nobles from our common men;
> For many of our princes – woe the while! —
> Lie drown'd and soak'd in mercenary blood;
> So do our vulgar drench their peasant limbs
> In blood of princes; . . .   (IV. 7. 71-5.)

The essential difference between the two nations is perhaps best reflected in their different conceptions of honour. The French conceive of honour in the old feudal sense as an aristocratic virtue *par excellence*, based on class superiority and hereditary privilege. For the English, on the contrary, honour is much more of a national ideal, attainable by all those who deserve it by their deeds. Here again the progressive social thinking of Thomas More and his humanistic circle comes to full flowering. Thus the whole conflict between France and England is presented as an encounter between the surviving feudal order and the English nation-state as it developed in Shakespeare's own time, especially during the years of struggle against the repressive power of Catholic Spain. Shakespeare lays special stress on the fact that the French lords at Agincourt refuse to lean upon their own people and rely solely on their own chivalric bravery. Whereas in the English host gentlemen fight side by side with their yeomen as one compact national army.

The leader of this 'band of brothers', King Henry, quite naturally assumes the place of a real father of his country and grows into a symbol of British unity and glory. Quantitatively speaking, he is the most voluminous of all Shakespeare's characters. As early as in *Richard II* he is spoken of as a young loafer who, despite his recklessness, harbours 'a spark of hope' in his bosom. The spark is fanned (not without tricky moments) in the next two plays in the cycle until, in *Henry V*, it bursts out into festive fireworks. We may therefore illuminate the whole play by centring our critical attention on Henry's character and career as well as on his relations both to his friends and his enemies.

One of the essential virtues of an ideal ruler, according to Thomas Elyot and other humanist thinkers, was concern for justice. Consequently, Shakespeare did not spare place or poetry to show right from the start that Henry's war against France was just and justifiable. Already at the end of *Henry IV* we saw him repudiate the wild company of Falstaff and choose the Lord Chief Justice for his main counsellor. In the exposition of our play another grave man, the Archbishop of Canterbury, is invited by the King to unfold 'justly and religiously', without fashioning or bowing his reading, whether the English claim to the French crown and territory is lawful. The Archbishop's answer is certainly too long-winded for our modern taste in tempo; however, Dover Wilson is probably right in assuming that not only Henry but also Shakespeare's audiences, being rhetorically minded and litigious, loved to hear a good pleader proving that France belonged to them.[1] Only when the Archbishop and all the English peers unanimously persuade the King of the righteousness of his action, does he give the final signal for the French expedition.

At the same time he insists, and keeps on insisting during the whole campaign, that he does not forget God as the supreme judge in whose name he puts forth his 'rightful hand in a well-hallowed cause'. On the eve of the Agincourt battle he prays the Lord not to remember the sin committed by his father in compassing the English crown, and repeats for himself, and for his audience, what he has done in the way of penitence. After the miraculous victory, when he hears about the French holocaust, while English losses are only some thirty, he ascribes it all to the arm of God and forbids anybody under threat of death to boast and so to take the praise from the only One to whom it is due. Taken in all, Henry may well claim the epithet of 'the complete Christian monarch' attributed to him by J. H. Walter, since piety appears as his second cardinal virtue.

We might go on pointing out Henry's virtues for a good while longer. Most of them have been extolled by his sympathetic critics: his magnanimity, modesty, bravery, coolness and

[1] New Cambridge *Henry V*, xxiv.

high spirits in the face of danger. His sense of humour is what every Englishman likes to think of as typically English: he can even enjoy a joke or two against his own anointed person.

To close this part of our analysis, let us consider for a moment one trait in Henry's character which has not always been fully appreciated. I mean his plainness, his soldier-like bluntness, his dislike of social pretence and his striving for simple and honest relations between himself and all his subjects. Some American scholars[1] have observed how the blunt soldier had come to be a striking type in life and on the stage by the end of the Elizabethan period and how he was often placed in opposition to courtly fops or intriguers. Shakespeare developed and enriched this type in many of his characters, starting with the Bastard in *King John* and culminating tragically in *Coriolanus*. Surely the warlike Harry deserves to be admitted to this military brotherhood. Already his wild youth in the company of Jack Falstaff may be explained, at least in part, by his instinctive dislike of courtly falsity and foppery, because every court breeds flattery and dissimulation, and the court of Henry IV, the 'king of smiles', had been full of it. On this basis we are permitted to sympathize with Prince Hal's escapades in the less decorous yet more wholesome air of the London world, or underworld. What he learns there stands him in good stead later. Hardly any other king would be able to mix with his common soldiers as freely as Henry does the night before Agincourt. Not only does he have a reassuring chat with them. He shows himself as eager to cut through the official hierarchy by means of his disguise and to learn the plain, even bitter, truth directly from their rank-and-file point of view, without trimmings. Moreover he thinks it proper to stress right at the beginning of his discussion that 'the king is but a man' to whom the violet smells the same as it does to anybody else. The ideal monarch of the sixteenth century must base his position on some sort of sense of essential human equality.

A similar candour informs his attitude to the woman of

---

[1] This observation already appears in the classic book of the American historian, E. P. Cheyney, *A History of England from the Defeat of the Armada to the Death of Elizabeth*, 2 vols., (1914, 1926). It has been developed by the literary historians, notably by Lily B. Campbell *Shakespeare's Histories: Mirrors of Elizabethan Policy* (San Marino 1947), P. A. Jorgensen *Shakespeare's Military World* (Berkeley and Los Angeles 1956), and H. J. Webb.

his heart. When he comes to woo the French Princess Katharine, he does not choose to speak in the vein of a mighty conqueror, however much he would be entitled to the pomps of a Tamburlaine. Nor does he 'mince it in love' like so many sonneteering and capering courtiers. Although his courting speeches are stylistically much more deliberate and cultivated than they may seem at first sight, essentially he remains true to himself as a 'plain soldier' and a 'plain king'. Many critics[1] have felt rather baffled, if not disgusted, when Henry playfully suggests, instead of love-lorn rhyming and dancing, that he buffet for his love, or bound his horse for her favours and 'lay on like a butcher, and sit like a jack-an-apes, never off'. However inelegant such words may sound, we should not close our eyes to the simple truth and beauty of what they really imply and lead up to:

> . . . What! a speaker is but a prater: a rhyme is but a ballad. A good leg will fall; a straight back will stoop; a black beard will turn white; a curl'd pate will grow bald; a fair face will wither; a full eye will wax hollow. But a good heart, Kate, is the sun and the moon; or, rather, the sun, and not the moon – for it shines bright and never changes, but keeps his course truly. If thou would have such a one take me; and take me, take a soldier; take a soldier, take a king.   (v. 2. 158-66.)

It is certainly to Henry's credit that he keeps his course throughout the whole play as 'the best king of all good fellows'. He detests the courtly 'fellows of infinite tongue, that can rhyme themselves into ladies' favours' only to 'reason themselves out again'. Instead, he prefers quickly to 'leap into a wife' whom he likes in the rough but honest manner of a real soldier-king. Only such a soldier could win the sympathy and support of *all the people* in his national army, as well as in Shakespeare's national theatre. Only such a king could gain victory over the terrifying odds commanded by the French princes and, to cap it all, get the French princess.

---

[1] E.g. Samuel Johnson, or, to give a modern instance, E. M. W. Tillyard, *Shakespeare's History Plays* (London 1944). Dr. Tillyard considers Henry's speech to Katharine to be 'a piece of sheer writing down to the populace' (309). Later on he adds a highly sophisticated speculation: 'The coarseness of Henry's courtship of Katharine is curiously exaggerated; one can almost say hectic: as if Shakespeare took a perverse delight in writing up something he had begun to hate.' (313).

So far so good. Yet there are more things in *Henry V* than
are dreamt of in the kind of philosophy most of his eulogists
go in for. However fervently Henry's ideal qualities are ham-
mered home, they represent only half of the poet's whole
truth about the King and his holy war. A deeper analysis,
probing under the shining surface, will find that the highlights
in Henry's portrait are thrown into relief by dark shades.

We need not take back anything that has been said and
quoted so far in Henry's favour. There is no doubt, first of all,
that he *is* shown as a just ruler and defender of the faith and
international law. At other moments, however, we may discover in his character quite different features and motives.
For the first hint we may look again at the end of *Henry IV*
where the hidden motive of his French campaign shows up.
'Therefore, my Harry, / Be it thy course to busy giddy minds /
With foreign quarrels' (2 *Henry IV*, IV. 5. 213-15.): thus does
the dying king, anxious to divert the attention of his subjects
from the drops of Richard's blood which stain his crown, advise
his son. And the young Harry faithfully follows this course from
the very beginning of our play, being only too loyal to his
dead father and his lion-and-fox policy. After all, a foreign
war, as every Renaissance politician knew, has always certain
advantages for rulers in difficulties at home. To camouflage
his aims, Henry leaves the Archbishop of Canterbury to do
most of the propaganda and goes so far as to exhort him before
God to take heed how he awakes the 'sleeping sword of war'.
And yet he knows better than anyone that the Archbishop has
his own urgent reason for advising foreign quarrels if he
is to save the better part of the Church's property from
the attacks of the Commons who are striving to pass a bill
against it.

It should be remembered that Shakespeare, in his usual
way, based the Archbishop's warlike speech on the Elizabethan
chronicler Raphael Holinshed who, in his turn, took it over
from the anti-Catholic chronicle of Edward Hall, where any
sign of corruption in the old unreformed Church was seized
upon with great gusto. However, the remarkable fact remains
that Shakespeare, in his fanfare introducing the glorious
Henry, did not suppress but gave full vent to the bass tones
of his French policy. When Henry succeeds in manoeuvering

the Archbishop into a willing enough oath 'The sin upon my head, dread sovereign!', his typical knack of policy is completed. He always proves extremely ingenious in putting the blame for his actions on somebody else: on Falstaff, on the Archbishop, on the Dauphin, on the besieged citizens of Harfleur, on whoever comes in handy, not excluding God himself.

In this light, the second of Henry's cardinal virtues, his piety, does not emerge untarnished. The more devout the words on his lips, the more humble his glances towards Heaven, the more he falls under suspicion of hiding the bad conscience of an aggressor under constant references to God, as so many of his historical predecessors and successors were in the habit of doing. If we judge his piety not only by his words but also by his works, the result is more disquieting. It is true that he does ostentatious penance for the crime committed by his father upon Richard II. Nevertheless, the fruit of this crime, the English crown, rests firmly in his hands and is being stained by much more blood in the war against France. Now nobody would expect Henry to give up his crown in a fit of belated penitence. Such things seldom happen in practical politics and, moreover, Shakespeare had his Holinshed and the main historical facts, not to mention the position of the Tudors, to consider. Yet would it not have been much better for Henry, then, simply to leave Richard, as well as God, at rest, without taking their names repeatedly in vain? As it is, it would seem as though the poet had penetrated too deeply into the King's soul not to see there an incessant strife between political exigencies and human feelings, between the call of power and glory and the urge towards genuine simplicity and piety.[1]

Let us recall, in this connection, what a really pious king, Henry's successor Henry VI, created by Shakespeare some eight years earlier, had to say about his father's actions:

> But, Clifford, tell me, didst thou never hear
> That things ill got had ever bad success?
> And happy always was it for that son
> Whose father for his hoarding went to hell?

---

[1] Derek Traversi, in his recent monograph, *Shakespeare from Richard II to Henry V* (Stanford University Press 1957), arrives at somewhat similar conclusions: 'The inspiration of *Henry V* is, in its deeper moments (which do not represent the whole play), critical, analytic, exploratory . . . .' (197-8).

I'll leave my son my virtuous deeds behind;
And would my father had left me no more!
(3 Henry VI, II. 2. 45-50.)

Shakespeare must have kept these considerations in his mind and imagination throughout both his historical cycles. Otherwise he would not have closed his fervently patriotic Henry V with an epilogue summing up unobtrusively, yet firmly, the whole historical frame and outcome of Henry's famous victories:

Henry the Sixth, in infant bands crown'd king
   Of France and England, did this king succeed;
Whose state so many had the managing
   That they lost France and made his England bleed;...
(Epilogue, 9-12.)

After these apprehensions, there remains the image of Henry as a hearty soldier-king to be re-examined. Again his qualities as a good mixer and blunt wooer need not be denied. Only they need to be qualified and supplemented by some less engaging features. Henry, as we know from both parts of Henry IV, had acquired the art of free-and-easy intercourse with all sorts of people while playing truant from the court and painting London red in the company of Jack Falstaff. He was well aware all that time that as soon as he ascended the throne he would have to cut out the Falstaff side of his life, including Falstaff himself. This is quite understandable, and we cannot criticize it, without blaming Henry for doing what was, for a king, politically inevitable. What we do find hard to swallow, though, is the coldly self-righteous way he chooses to reject his former boon companion and win the approval of respectable society; and it is hard to believe that an Elizabethan audience, however ardently monarchist, would not also have had divided feelings at this point. We should not be too much surprised, therefore, to find similar streaks of hypocrisy and opportunism in Henry's character during his French expedition. However friendly, even brotherly, he appears during his incognito conversation with his common soldiers, as soon as he is alone again, he complains of his 'hard condition . . . subject to the breath of every fool'. And he goes on philosophizing plaintively until he finds that his wretched subjects enjoy their simple pastoral lives much better than he his ceremony, because he must keep watch day and night 'to maintain the peace, whose hours the peasant best advantages'.

This does not come altogether convincingly from a king whose main aim and occupation we have seen to be the waging of war and is bound to raise some doubts about the arguments he has used to convince the soldiers of the righteousness of his cause. Coming from the home of the good soldier Schweik, I appreciate with immense relish the spirit of deflated heroism and ironic common sense entertained by Court, Bates and Williams in the face of the war hysteria shared by both the English and the French aristocrats. Not that the soldiers are afraid of fighting. They go to it lustily enough when they see no other way of defending themselves and their country. But before that they give the disguised king a gruelling time, asking him some really sticky questions about the welfare, both physical and spiritual, of soldiers who die in an unjust war. Even when in the end they seem reasonably pacified, it is not difficult to perceive that the King's answers leave much to be desired. Above all, they avoid any direct answer to the most delicate point: whether the war against France is really just or not. The contradictions within this telling scene are, in fact, not resolved by Shakespeare, only stated.

Nor are the implications of Henry's courtship of Katharine beyond criticism. Although we have clarified his offending bluffness as behaviour fit for a soldier, there is a seamy side to his wooing that cannot be so easily explained away. I mean the fact that Katharine is regarded by everybody (including herself), and by Henry in the first place, as part of the war spoils resulting from the Agincourt victory. Henry puts it again quite bluntly when Katharine coyly expresses her doubts whether it is possible for her to love the enemy of France. Says Henry in a cock-sure tone: 'No, it is not possible you should love the enemy of France, Kate, but in loving me you should love the friend of France; for I love France so well that I will not part with a village of it; I will have it all mine. And, Kate, when France is mine and I am yours, then yours is France and you are mine.' (v. 2. 169-75.)

It would not be fair to take Henry's humorous love-making too seriously. His lady-killing attitude somewhat resembles the cracking of a good-humoured Petruchio's whip over another Kate. More clearly than in the early comedy we can see here the amorous play of a pair of Renaissance lovers who use the old crude farce of the taming of a shrew as a background for both concealing and surprisingly revealing their own feelings, abounding in passionate intensity and new human dignity. Also we should bear in mind the often very practical and business-like character of Elizabethan marriages in general. But for all that it has to be conceded that Henry's marriage is essentially political, with all the implications such marriages bring as their dowry, and that Shakespeare sees it as such with all his penetrating truthfulness.

Henry, in fact, unlike his creator, is often content with half-truths. He uses them with so much readiness and rhetorical convincingness that he often succeeds in persuading both his friends and his enemies, as well as, one suspects, himself. That is perhaps why he is also able to persuade so large a proportion of his modern audience.

But to less idealistic interpreters Henry reveals a less comforting but perhaps more rewarding dramatic character of a conquering king who has to pay a heavy human toll for his success. His good qualities are seen as reaching their richest and most interesting point by being both contrasted with, and dynamized by, equally potent qualities of the opposite tendency. The result is a double triumph: that of Henry and of truth. In the very act of apotheosis Shakespeare tears down Henry's godlike aureole and shows that 'in his nakedness he appears but a man'. A man with victorious laurels – and bleeding wounds.

A similar polarization may be observed in Shakespeare's vision of the French war as a whole. The most poignant contradiction here is that between the glory and the horror of war. To get an insight into the contradictory structure of the play, it is enough to compare the fiery, school-room-resounding poetry of the King before Harfleur

> Once more unto the breach, dear friends, once more;
> Or close the wall up with our English dead.
>
> (III. I. 1-2.)

with the chilling prose of Private Bates commenting upon the King's bravery on the eve of Agincourt:

He may show what outward courage he will; but I
believe, as cold a night as 'tis, he could wish himself
in Thames up to the neck; and so I would he were, and
I by him, at all adventures, so we were quit here.

(IV. I. 112-16.)

Still more chilling are the comments of Private Williams
who reminds the King of 'all those legs and arms and heads,
chopp'd off in a battle' that are going to 'join together at the
latter day, and cry all "We died at such a place" – some swear-
ing, some crying for a surgeon, some upon their wives left
poor behind them, some upon the debts they owe, some upon
their children rawly left.' (IV. I. 134-40.)

The contrasting of war heroics with suffering human beings
is only one of Shakespeare's strands in his realistic panorama
of war. He goes further to introduce into it, against all the
patriotic fervour, some very unflattering portraits of the
English gentlemen-rankers out on a French spree. Lieutenant
Bardolph, Ancient Pistol, and Corporal Nym, all three the
brightest buds of London brothels, do very little fighting,
except in their bombastic words. They are experts in quite
another branch of soldiering, that of looting. Their actual
leader is Pistol and their war-cry is his fustian on their leave-
taking:

Let us to France, like horse-leeches, my boys,
To suck, to suck, the very blood to suck.

(II. 3. 55-6.)

Of course, they are not as bloodthirsty as all that. They
know easier methods by which their 'profits will accrue'.
They are extremely lightfingered with regard to all kinds of
'chattels and movables', not excepting Church sacraments.
And even though Bardolph and Nym do not get away with their
'Loo! loo! Lulu! Loot!' and are hanged in the end, Pistol
survives all calamities and steals back to England to steal
there anew with added experience.

Finally, one more contrast appears in the complex unity
of the play, being displayed again not so much perhaps out of
premeditated purpose as out of true observation of reality. This
is the different approach to war by the statesmen and generals,
both English and French, and by the common soldiers. The

statesmen, and King Henry above all, start war in great style primarily to divert internal dissension and to acquire new corners in foreign lands. The Courts, Bateses and Williamses go to war willy-nilly, with a good deal of grumbling. Yet once they are in it, they fight tooth and nail for their country and their king. To them war is not an arena for winning honour, or profit, but an altar before which they confess their love for England. And the king saves his soul and human face only when he comes to know and accept their standpoint, when he leads them as the brother and father of the whole nation.

Thus one of the essential features of Shakespeare's humanism emerges. It consists in the fusion, both in form and content, of the advanced social thinking of the sixteenth-century European humanists, who had set up the example of an ideal, though utopian governor, with the attitudes and feelings of the English people, particularly their moral integrity and sharp sense of reality. This fusion represents one of Shakespeare's greatest achievements.

The contradictions, contrasts and fusion that we have noticed within *Henry V* can be understood still better if we see the play not only in the context of the tetralogy of which it is the climax but in the light of (and indeed as the expression of) Shakespeare's whole vision of history.

Professor Jan Kott has recently remarked that Shakespeare's Histories are all concerned with the struggle for power and 'always, with Shakespeare, the struggle for power is divested of all mythology, presented in its purest form', and he goes on to suggest that the image of history that emerges from the plays is one of an unchanging mechanism, a great stairway leading to an abyss.

> It has a powerful impact on us, this image of history, repeated so often by Shakespeare. History is a great staircase which a line of kings endlessly ascends. Each step, each pace towards the summit, is marked by murder, perjury and treason. . . . The kings change. But the staircase remains the same.[1]

There is much that is true and telling in such an analysis, yet it surely leaves out something essential, perhaps because

[1] Jan Kott, *Shakespeare Notre Contemporain* (Paris 1962), 17.

Kott, in his chapter on the Histories, concentrates on the Richards to the virtual exclusion of the Henries. What is left out is Shakespeare's acute realization of the emergence of the national monarchy of the Tudors as a new force which in some way or other resolves the contradictions of the English historical past.

The tetralogy consisting of *Richard II*, *Henry IV* and *Henry V* is the nearest thing in Elizabethan literature to a realistic national epic. It is set in the past, yet more than any other group of Shakespeare's plays, it tells us what Tudor England was actually like. We watch the events of late fourteenth and early fifteenth century England and we see the England of Shakespeare's own time coming to life before our eyes.

In *Richard II* we witness the passing of the medieval world, a world of stable values and ceremonial actions. The structure of the play, the very language of it, reflects, not without sympathy and even a lyrical nostalgia, a past world, whose tone is set by the formal challenges and decorums of the opening scene. One might almost say that whereas the episode of the tennis balls in *Henry V* already points towards the modern world of popular international sport – test matches and Davis cups – the gages in *Richard II* look back to the sport of the medieval tournament, or even beyond. And when Richard II is deposed and conducted to prison we know in our bones that the new men are indeed new, different in some fundamental way. Bolingbroke, though a feudal baron among feudal barons, belongs to a different world from Richard and will be a different king.

Henry IV, in its two marvellous parts, is in ˙this sense a transition play. The old world, reincarnated for a moment in the chivalric Hotspur, is on the way out; but the new world has yet to be born. The crown he has usurped sits very uneasily on Bolingbroke's head: he is tormented by the past (Richard) and fears the future (Hal). And *Henry IV*, amidst so much else, tells us, almost in the terms of a Morality, of the making – the education and testing – of the new king who is to replace the transitional figure of Bolingbroke. Hal must defeat Hotspur (the knightly past) and understand – even, up to a point, identify himself with – Falstaff and his cronies (the Commons).

Like Elizabeth herself he must get a whiff of the people, not as they ought to be but as they are.

The contradiction which Henry IV cannot solve is that he has seen the necessity of doing away with Richard, yet feels at the same time that he himself is a usurper. It is not a contradiction that can be resolved in abstract terms within the ideology and sanctities of the old world which Henry IV still accepts. Yet it has to be resolved, historically by England and the Tudors, artistically by Shakespeare the Elizabethan dramatist. And it is resolved by Henry V, though not, as we have seen, without human cost.

The sin of usurpation is forgotten and the *bona fides* of the new monarchy established by the act that links Henry most firmly with the future, with the Tudor state in general and in particular with the Elizabeth who has defeated the Spanish Armada. The sin which has tormented Henry IV is exorcized, not by time or argument, but by his son's victory over the French at Agincourt. Hal's education has not been in vain. Henry V is the hero of the tetralogy and able to settle its haunting problems for one reason above all – he is the new *national* king, the herald of the Tudor monarchy which is no longer a monarchy of the old type, but something different and necessary.

It adds to Shakespeare's greatness that he can divine, at the very moment of reaching his historical synthesis, the destructive and ultimately self-destructive nature of the new men and their new ways. This divining glimpse in *Henry V* points forward to some of the conflicts in the great tragedies.

MACBETH

J. K. Walton

Macbeth, which was probably the last written of the four great tragedies, is the play where Shakespeare gives his fullest presentation of the individualist, in the sense of the person who consciously and unvaryingly puts what he conceives to be his own interests before those of his fellow men.[1] An early treatment of individualism is to be found in *Richard III*. Its comic possibilities are developed in Falstaff, while in the later tragedies other than *Macbeth* it is to be found portrayed in a number of secondary characters, most notably Edmund and Iago. But of all the later tragedies, it is only *Macbeth* in which the central role is allotted to such a person. Antony, Timon, and Coriolanus all have some individualist features; they all largely cut themselves off from their fellows; but none of them can be said to make his supposed self-interest the main motive for action. Ultimately Antony loves Cleopatra more than himself, and likewise her love is ultimately not self-centred. Coriolanus, when it comes to a crisis, submits his will to the appeal of his mother and his family. Timon shuns mankind but only because his generosity to his friends has been betrayed.

The presentation of individualism in *Macbeth* involves the presentation of its opposite, the putting first of the interests of the community as a whole; and we have, in fact, in this play Shakespeare's most direct working out of a conflict between two opposing views of man. This conflict finds its first explicit expression immediately after Macbeth's great soliloquy in I. 7., in which he sees not only the possible retribution of 'judgment here' but has a vision of Duncan's virtues, which

> Will plead like angels, trumpet-tongu'd, against
> The deep damnation of his taking-off;

[1] It is in this sense that I use the words 'individualist' and 'individualism' throughout the chapter.

and of how

> pity, like a naked new-born babe,
> Striding the blast, or heaven's cherubim hors'd
> Upon the sightless couriers of the air,
> Shall blow the horrid deed in every eye,
> That tears shall drown the wind.   (I. 7. 19-25.)

The soliloquy concludes with Macbeth's sense that he has no motive for proceeding but ambition, which he is aware only defeats itself:

> I have no spur
> To prick the sides of my intent, but only
> Vaulting ambition, which o'er-leaps itself,
> And falls on th' other.   (I. 7. 25-8.)

He thus declares to Lady Macbeth, who enters at this point, that 'We will proceed no further in this business'. She succeeds in making him change his mind by proposing the individualist view that he has a right, even a duty, to act according to his desires and to sweep aside any obstacles to their fulfilment. She asks,

> Art thou afeard
> To be the same in thine own act and valour
> As thou art in desire? Wouldst thou have that
> Which thou esteem'st the ornament of life,
> And live a coward in thine own esteem . . . ?
>   (I. 7. 39-43.)

Macbeth replies:

> I dare do all that may become a man;
> Who dares do more is none . . .

and his wife retorts,

> What beast was't then
> That made you break this enterprise to me?
> When you durst do it, then you were a man;
> And to be more than what you were, you would
> Be so much more the man.   (I. 7. 46-51.)

She reinforces her argument by recalling an oath he had sworn on an earlier occasion to kill Duncan; and Macbeth, without further ado except about the practical question whether they may fail, is won over to her view of what it is to be a man, and is ready to undertake 'this terrible feat'.

The view of man implied in Macbeth's 'I dare do all that may become a man; / Who dares do more is none' is indicated in the earlier part of the play and is at first associated with feudalism but is by no means limited to it. One aspect of what he understands by what it is legitimate for a man to dare is demonstrated in the account we are given of his heroic actions in defeating both rebellion and external aggression. These actions are undertaken as part of his feudal duties. This is emphasized by Macbeth himself, although we are already aware that one part of his mind is working in a very different manner, when he replies to Duncan's words of gratitude by declaring that

> The service and the loyalty I owe,
> In doing it, pays itself. Your Highness' part
> Is to receive our duties; and our duties
> Are to your throne and state children and servants,
> Which do but what they should by doing everything
> Safe toward your love and honour.   (I. 4. 22-7.)

Another aspect, however, of Macbeth's understanding of 'man', when he says 'I dare do all that may become a man; / Who dares do more is none' is indicated by Lady Macbeth when she has received his letter telling her what has happened.

> Glamis thou art, and Cawdor; and shalt be
> What thou art promis'd. Yet do I fear thy nature;
> It is too full o' th' milk of human kindness
> To catch the nearest way.   (I. 5. 12-15.)

In order to understand the full meaning of 'human kindness', we have to remember that both words had in early seventeenth century usage a more extended meaning than they have today. 'Human' (which was usually spelt 'humane', as it is, in fact, in the Folio text[1]) could mean 'belonging or pertaining to a man or mankind' but also 'befitting a man, kindly . . . kind, benevolent'[2] – that is to say, it combined the meanings now usually given to 'human' and 'humane'. On the other hand,

---

[1] There is only one text of *Macbeth*, that of the First Folio, 1623.

[2] See C. T. Onions, *A Shakespeare Glossary*, s.v., 'human, humane'. The differentiation of spelling did not take place until the early eighteenth century.

'kindness' could mean both 'kinship' and the 'natural affection arising from this'[1] as well as its more limited present day sense of 'kind feeling . . . affection, love'. We should therefore take the phrase 'the milk of human kindness' as meaning the gentle[2] qualities which arise from a sense of community with other men. This sense in Macbeth finds its supreme expression in his vision of 'pity, like a naked new-born babe'.

The killing of Duncan involves a struggle within Macbeth's mind between the two opposing views of man, the view of man as an individualist whose primary loyalty is to his own interests, and the view of man as a member of society whose primary loyalty is to the interests of his fellow men. This struggle gives rise to the terrible hallucinations Macbeth experiences, which are summed up in his feeling that 'nothing is but what is not' (I. 3. 141), and to his agonized remorse, which finds its most direct expression when he tells how 'Methought I heard a voice cry "Sleep no more; / Macbeth does murder sleep" ' (II. 2. 35-6.). Critics have been perplexed by the fact that Macbeth, for all his spiritual anguish, never actually says that the killing of Duncan is wrong. This has led some critics, such as E. K. Chambers, to hold that Macbeth has in fact no conscience. The most generally favoured explanation is the Coleridge-Bradley view that he has a conscience but is unaware of its existence since it disguises itself as fear. This view, however, fails to explain why his conscience should disguise itself as fear. A more adequate explanation would seem to be that Macbeth has not one conscience but two, each conscience corresponding to one of the opposing views of man, and that while his individualist conscience prevails and thus prevents him from saying that what he has done is wrong, the other conscience continues to torment him until the banquet scene, where, as we shall see, the individualist view of man wins a complete victory in his mind.

That Macbeth in killing Duncan is acting in accordance with a view of man is emphasized by the sense of duty with which he would seem to perform the deed. As A. C. Bradley remarks, 'the deed is done in horror and without the faintest desire or sense of glory, – done, one may almost say, as if it

---

[1] See *N.E.D.* s.v., 'kindness'.
[2] Cf. *King Lear*, I. 4. 342, 'This milky gentleness'.

were an appalling duty'.[1] Macbeth in the murder scene would appear to act not so much out of a desire for the crown as in keeping with a theory that he has a duty to act according to his desires. His exhortation to the company after the murder of Duncan has been discovered, 'Let's briefly put on manly readiness' (II. 3. 132.), is an uncanny echo of what he has felt as his real – or at least immediate – motive for action, just as are his words explaining why he killed the grooms –

> Who could refrain,
> That had a heart to love, and in that heart
> Courage to make's love known?
>
> (II. 3. 115-17.)

– an echo of Lady Macbeth's

> Art thou afeard
> To be the same in thine own act and valour
> As thou art in desire?

The issue of the nature of man is again brought forward before the murder of Banquo. To Macbeth's question to the Murderers whether they are prepared to pray for Banquo, 'Whose heavy hand hath bow'd you to the grave / And beggar'd yours for ever?', the First Murderer replies, 'We are men, my liege', and Macbeth answers,

> Ay, in the catalogue ye go for men;
> As hounds, and greyhounds, mongrels, spaniels, curs,
> Shoughs, water-rugs, and demi-wolves, are clept
> All by the name of dogs. The valued file[2]
> Distinguishes the swift, the slow, the subtle,
> The housekeeper, the hunter, every one
> According to the gift which bounteous nature
> Hath in him clos'd; whereby he does receive
> Particular addition, from the bill
> That writes them all alike; and so of men.
> Now, if you have a station in the file,
> Not i' th' worst rank of manhood, say't . . .
>
> (III. 1. 91-102.)

Macbeth here, in general terms which are applicable to himself as well as to the Murderers, propounds the individualist view

---

[1] *Shakespearean Tragedy* (1904; ed. 1905), p. 358.
[2] The 'valued file' is a list giving the value of each item.

that murder may help to distinguish a man according to his gifts. This development of the man theme is accompanied by a development of the animal imagery, which has an important role in associating individualism with the qualities of a beast. The association is first introduced by Lady Macbeth herself when, in reply to her husband's 'I dare do all that may become a man; / Who dares do more is none', she asks, 'What beast was't then / That made you break this enterprise to me?'. Her question is of course ironical; far from believing that he will become a beast by murdering Duncan, she believes that he will be 'so much more the man'. Her question, however, contains a truth of which she is unaware. Macbeth's use of the dog analogue, which is given a predatory emphasis by the final item in the list, 'demi-wolves', suggests that, with an experience which neither he nor Lady Macbeth possessed before the murder of Duncan, he now sees manhood, in his wife's sense of the word, as entailing the acquisition of bestial qualities. In other words, he already has an incipient awareness that the initial plan is working out in a manner contrary to intention. During the following scene this awareness is shown as further developed, in a different way, in Macbeth's speech beginning, 'We have scotch'd the snake, not kill'd it', with its terrible realization,

> Better be with the dead,
> Whom we, to gain our peace, have sent to peace,
> Than on the torture of the mind to lie
> In restless ecstasy . . .   (III. 2. 19-22.)

which is preceded by the individualist conjuration,

> But let the frame of things disjoint, both the worlds
> [suffer,
> Ere we will eat our meal in fear and sleep
> In the affliction of these terrible dreams
> That shake us nightly.   (III. 2. 16-19.)

The man theme next appears at the climax of the dramatic action, the banquet. This is where Macbeth decisively realizes that he has lost control of the situation which he has created. The realization comes with the news that, although Banquo has been killed, Fleance has escaped, and is given an added dimension by the appearance of the Ghost. This scene is also

where the individualist view of man, which up to now has been
opposed in Macbeth's mind by a still existing view of man as a
member of society, irrevocably gains the upper hand and so
brings Macbeth past the point of no return. The banquet is
likewise marked by a constant transmutation of Macbeth's
intentions into their opposite. This transmutation is given an
added irony by the fact that his publicly expressed wishes,
which are contrary to his real wishes, achieve a macabre fulfilment.

The scene, which signifies Macbeth's final separation from
the rest of mankind, begins with his hearty welcome of his
guests and his announcement that

> Our self will mingle with society
> And play the humble host.   (III. 4. 3-4.)

There follows the news from the Murderers at the door of
Banquo's death and Fleance's escape, which means that, in
addition to having lost control of the situation, Macbeth is
now subjectively a prisoner – 'cabin'd, cribb'd, confin'd,
bound in / To saucy doubts and fears' (24-5.). At the very
time when his powerlessness has been revealed by the news from
the Murderers his publicly expressed wishes are promptly
carried out. When Macbeth is lamenting the absence of
Banquo,

> Here had we now our country's honour roof'd,
> Were the grac'd person of our Banquo present;
> Who may I rather challenge for unkindness
> Than pity for mischance . . .   (III. 4. 40-3.)

his Ghost appears,[1] and a few lines later Macbeth becomes
aware of its presence ('Which of you have done this?'). After
Lady Macbeth has attempted to explain to the company her
husband's strange behaviour, she asks him in an aside, 'Are you a
man?' (58.). The answer is, ironically, 'yes'; he is still, in a
part of his being which is now momentarily uppermost, a man

---

[1] The Folio text (followed by Alexander) gives the entry of the Ghost a few
lines earlier (after Lady Macbeth's speech ending at l. 37). However, as
Kenneth Muir points out, 'this may be either a premature direction to give
plenty of warning to the actor, or it may merely indicate that on the Elizabethan
stage the ghost would have some distance to walk . . . The Ghost appears when
summoned' (*New Arden* ed. p. 94).

in the opposite sense to that accepted by his wife – hence his
fear and remorse represented by his seeing the Ghost. When
Macbeth gives expression to this fear –

> If charnel-houses and our graves must send
> Those that we bury back, our monuments
> Shall be the maws of kites –   (III. 4. 71-3.)

the Ghost vanishes. After Lady Macbeth exclaims, 'What,
quite unmann'd in folly?', Macbeth explicitly reveals the
sense of man opposed to his wife's which he still possesses:

> Blood hath been shed ere now, i' th' olden time,
> Ere human[1] statute purg'd the gentle weal;
> Ay, and since too, murders have been perform'd
> Too terrible for the ear. The time has been
> That when the brains were out the man would die,
> And there an end; but now they rise again,
> With twenty mortal murders on their crowns,
> And push us from our stools.   (III. 4. 75-82.)

Here Macbeth, 'unmann'd' in his wife's sense of the word, takes
a view of murder which is in keeping with an awareness of
man as a member of society. The line 'Ere human statute
purg'd the gentle weal' recalls Lady Macbeth's description of
his nature as 'too full o' th' milk of human kindness'. In both
passages the word 'human' means, as we have seen, 'humane'
as well as 'human'. Thus the phrase 'human statute', especially
when taken in conjunction with 'gentle weal',[2] means both a
statute made by men and one which manifests the feeling
for others which arises from being human.

Macbeth, however, prompted by his wife, remembers that
he has a role to play in keeping with the other, individualist
view of man, from which his acts have made it increasingly
difficult for him to escape, and, with an excuse for his 'strange
infirmity', he gives a toast:

---

[1] Alexander here adopts the Folio spelling 'humane'. Since, however, 'humane'
included both the present meanings 'human' and 'humane' (see above, p. 104),
we may, following a number of editors, modernize it here to 'human', as in
fact do all editors in I. 5. 14. The more specialized 'humane' obscures the
connection of this passage with the man theme.

[2] 'Weal' means 'society, commonwealth'.

> I drink to the general joy o' th' whole table,
> And to our dear friend Banquo, whom we miss.
> Would he were here!   (III. 4. 89-91.)

The Ghost reappears in fulfilment of his expressed wish.[1] On
its reappearance the climax of the dramatic action of the
play is reached, with a final struggle in Macbeth's mind
between the two views of man, a struggle that is expressed in
a speech in which the first appearance (I. 7. 46 ff.) of the man
theme is recalled:

> What man dare, I dare.
> Approach thou like the rugged Russian bear,
> The arm'd rhinoceros, or th' Hyrcan tiger;
> Take any shape but that, and my firm nerves
> Shall never tremble. Or be alive again,
> And dare me to the desert with thy sword;
> If trembling I inhabit, then protest me
> The baby of a girl. Hence, horrible shadow!
> Unreal mock'ry, hence! [*Exit Ghost.*
>   Why, so; being gone,
> I am a man again.   (III. 4. 99-108).

The development of Macbeth's thought is indicated partly by
the beast images. Macbeth, himself become bestial through
his acts, sees the beast as representing, in comparison with
the Ghost, what is normal. He begins to doubt the reality of
the Ghost, and so of the fear and remorse which it symbolizes;
the words 'be alive again' provide a transition to what he now
sees as the deadness – the unreality – of the 'horrible shadow'
and what it stands for; and, ordering the Ghost to depart, he
is able to call it an 'Unreal mock'ry'. The Ghost as always
obeys, this time because the individualist view of man has
absolutely triumphed in Macbeth's mind. He is 'a man again'
but in the opposite sense to what he implied when he declared
in I. 7. 'I dare do all that may become a man; / Who dares
do more is none'. From this moment he is single-minded in
his individualism, declaring, after announcing his intention
of visiting the Witches in order to know 'By the worst means
the worst', that

---

[1] In the Folio text (followed by Alexander) the entry is marked earlier (after
l. 88.); but cf. above, note 1, page 108.

> For mine own good
> All causes shall give way. I am in blood
> Stepp'd in so far that, should I wade no more,
> Returning were as tedious as go o'er . . .
>
> (III. 4. 135-8.)

and that 'My strange and self-abuse / Is the initiate fear that
wants hard use' (142-3.).

The man theme has a central place in Macbeth's meeting
with the Witches. His demand that they answer his questions
is preceded by the most ferociously individualist of his utterances, which concludes with the conjuration,

> though the treasure
> Of nature's germens[1] tumble all together,
> Even till destruction sicken – answer me
> To what I ask you.   (IV. 1. 58-61.)

In the instructions of the Apparitions which the Witches summon
up, Macduff, who is to slay Macbeth in personal combat, is
clearly indicated as the chief of his adversaries. As we shall see,
the anti-individualist view of man comes largely to be typified
by Macduff in the latter part of the play. Associated especially
with him is the 'babe' symbol – symbol of both pity and 'human
kindness' as well as of the all-powerful future[2] – which first
appears in Macbeth's great simile (I. 7. 21-5, quoted above,
page 103). The first Apparition, 'an Armed Head',[3] instructs
Macbeth to 'beware Macduff'. The second Apparition, 'a
Bloody Child', representing Macduff untimely ripped from his
mother's womb, instructs Macbeth,

> Be bloody, bold, and resolute; laugh to scorn
> The pow'r of man, for none of woman born
> Shall harm Macbeth.   (IV. 1. 79-81.)

Here the word 'man' has both its opposing meanings. The
instruction 'laugh to scorn / The pow'r of man' may mean

---

[1] 'Nature's germens' means Nature's germs or seeds.

[2] For a view of the ramifications of the 'babe' symbolism see Cleanth Brooks, *The
Well Wrought Iron* (1947; London, 1949), chap. 2, 'The Naked Babe and the
Cloak of Manliness'.

[3] Most critics think that the '*Armed Head*' represents Macbeth's head cut off and
brought to Malcolm by Macduff; some (e.g. G. L. Kittredge) hold, however,
that the armed head represents Macduff himself.

'laugh to scorn the power of other men, men in society'; and so interpreted the instruction encourages Macbeth in his individualism. The instruction, however, may mean, 'laugh to scorn the power of the individual man, of the individualist, of yourself in fact'. The third Apparition, *a Child Crowned, with a tree in his hand* (Malcolm), gives an instruction which, while obviously encouraging Macbeth in his individualism, is, as we shall see, also connected with the view of man with which Macduff is increasingly associated:

> Be lion-mettled, proud, and take no care
> Who chafes, who frets, or where conspirers are;
> Macbeth shall never vanquish'd be until
> Great Birnam wood to high Dunsinane Hill
> Shall come against him.   (IV. I. 90-4.)

The result of the instructions of the Apparitions, as interpreted by Macbeth, is that he reaches the extreme point of the philosophy indicated by his wife when she asked him, 'Art thou afeard / To be the same in thine own act and valour / As thou art in desire?'. He now declares, having heard Macduff has escaped to England, that

> From this moment
> The very firstlings of my heart shall be
> The firstlings of my hand . . .   (IV. I. 146-8.)

and he orders the first of the insensate crimes which seal his doom, the slaughter of Macduff's 'wife, his babes, and all unfortunate souls / That trace him in his line'.

The association of Macduff with the opposing view of man is further developed in the following Act. When Macduff is appalled by the news that his wife and all his children have been slaughtered, Malcolm tells him, 'Dispute it like a man', to which Macduff replies,

> I shall do so;
> But I must also feel it as a man.
> I cannot but remember such things were
> That were most precious to me.   (IV. 3. 220-3.)

In this way, Macduff is shown to possess the instinctively human feelings which Macbeth's individualism has outraged. But Macduff also disputes it 'like a man', and when he prays that he will have the opportunity of confronting Macbeth in personal combat, Malcolm replies, 'This tune goes manly' (235.). The particular qualities which go to make up Macduff's kind of manhood are clearly indicated. He is altogether unselfcentred, being ready to attribute to himself responsibility for the deaths of his family:

> Not for their own demerits, but for mine,
> Fell slaughter on their souls.   (IV. 3. 226-7.)

His outburst when he hears Malcolm accuse himself of the most terrible crimes makes Malcolm speak of his 'noble passion, / Child of integrity' (IV. 3. 114-15.). Macduff's manhood, moreover, contains qualities which are not in keeping with the orthodox theory of the relationship of a subject to his ruler as laid down by the Tudors and James I, despite the fact that the play was probably in the first instance written for performance before him.[1] In the testing of Macduff, Malcolm, after cataloguing the evil qualities of which he accuses himself, asks

> If such a one be fit to govern, speak.
> I am as I have spoken.

Macduff replies,

>   Fit to govern!
> No, not to live!   (IV. 3. 101-3.)

and he proceeds to bid Malcolm farewell and declare that 'These evils thou repeat'st upon thyself / Hath banish'd me from Scotland'. Irving Ribner has pointed out that

> though a usurper is on the throne, Malcolm is, according to orthodox Tudor theory, the actual king of Scotland. He is so recognized by God, and he retains all of the rights and prerogatives of that office. Yet Macduff bids him farewell. He will not serve him, no matter how just his title. Instead he offers to exile himself from his beloved Scotland, since neither its usurping ruler nor its actual king in the eyes of God is worthy of his allegiance. [2]

---

[1] The commonly held view that the play was written for performance before James is most fully argued in H. N. Paul, *The Royal Play of Macbeth* (New York, 1950).

[2] *The English History Play in the Age of Shakespeare* (Princeton, 1957), p. 258.

Moreover, in declaring that not merely is Malcolm unfit to govern but unfit to live, Macduff is clearly going beyond orthodox doctrine. His earlier behaviour towards Macbeth has already shown signs of his independent and politically rebellious nature. He has refused to attend his coronation at Scone, and at the banquet denied 'his person / At our great bidding' (III. 4. 128-9.), though at the time he can only have had suspicions rather than proof that Macbeth had usurped the throne by killing Duncan[1] – even Banquo, who has more information than Macduff tending to incriminate Macbeth,[2] has only suspicions, and, less daring than Macduff, fails to act on them.

The concept of man as owing his chief duty to the well-being of his fellow men is further developed in the battle scenes at Dunsinane. In the first of these scenes, Caithness asks 'if Donalbain be with his brother?', and Lennox replies:

> For certain, sir, he is not; I have a file
> Of all the gentry. There is Siward's son,
> And many unrough youths that even now
> Protest their first of manhood.   (v. 2. 8-11.)

The reference to 'a file / Of all the gentry' and 'manhood' recalls Macbeth's exhortation when he speaks of 'the valued file' which distinguishes the dogs according to their various qualities and suggests to the men he is addressing that, if they have 'a station in the file, / Not i' th' worst rank of manhood', he will give them an opportunity to establish their worth by murdering Banquo. This particular aspect of the contrast between two kinds of manhood is completed in the account of the manner of the death of Siward's son killed in combat with

---

[1] James I in *The Trew Law of Free Monarchies* (reprinted in C. H. McIlwain (ed.), *The Political Works of James I*, Harvard U.P., 1918) observes (p. 60), that Jeremiah threatened the people of God with utter destruction for rebellion against Nebuchadnezzar, who was 'an idolatrous persecuter, a forraine King, a Tyrant, and vsurper of their liberties'. The reason, according to James, was that 'they had . . . receiued and acknowledged him for their king', and thus were bound not only to obey him but to pray for his prosperity.' Macbeth was, of course, crowned king at Scone. It is true that Macduff, in accordance with James's belief in hereditary right could have refused Macbeth allegiance, but in fact neither he nor anyone else refuses to recognize his coronation on this ground. We do not hear anything of Macbeth's depriving Malcolm of his right until iii. 6. 25., when an anonymous lord mentions it incidentally in speaking of Malcolm's residence in the English court.

[2] Banquo is present at Macbeth's first meeting with the Witches, and Macbeth makes darkly worded overtures to him (II. 1. 22-6.).

Macbeth and the only one of the file of gentry whom Lennox mentions by name. Ross tells Siward,

> Your son, my lord, has paid a soldier's debt:
> He only liv'd but till he was a man;
> The which no sooner had his prowess confirm'd
> In the unshrinking station where he fought,
> But like a man he died.   (v. 8. 39-43.)

Young Siward, killed in a communal effort to destroy the tyrant, has used 'the gift which bounteous nature / Hath in him clos'd' in a manner altogether opposed to that employed by the murderers of Banquo.

The main working out of the man theme occurs, however, in Macbeth's conflict with Macduff who tells him that 'Macduff was from his mother's womb / Untimely ripp'd' (v. 8. 15-16.), thus recalling the 'Second Apparition, *a Bloody Child*' of VI. I, who instructs Macbeth to 'laugh to scorn / The pow'r of man, for none of woman born / Shall harm Macbeth'. Macbeth replies to Macduff:

> Accursed be that tongue that tells me so,
> For it hath cow'd my better part of man;
> And be these juggling fiends no more believ'd
> That palter with us in a double sense,
> That keep the word of promise to our ear,
> And break it to our hope! I'll not fight with thee.
>   (v. 8. 17-22.)

Macbeth's words, 'my better part of man' must refer to the part which depended on the 'juggling fiends', since he is now cowed when he hears of their deception; he therefore here is referring primarily to himself as an individualist. Nevertheless, he also means his courage and determination, those qualities which he is described as displaying on the battlefield at the beginning of the play and which now for the moment fail him. We thus have here an indication of the nature of Macbeth's tragedy. His individualist side has absorbed and transformed his good qualities. It has turned his courage and determination into a fanatical perseverance in bloodshed, just as it has turned his pity and 'human kindness' into 'these terrible dreams / That shake us nightly' and finally into a sense of the meaninglessness of life, which he comes to see merely as 'a tale / Told by an idiot' (v. 5. 26-7.).

The meaning and implications of the two views of man, the conflict between which provides the main theme of the play, are deepened by the presentation, on the one hand, of the increasing isolation which Macbeth's individualism involves and, on the other, of the achievement of unity by those suffering under his tyranny, by which it is overcome. In choosing the individualist path, Macbeth chooses also its concomitant, isolation. His isolation goes through a series of stages the first of which is his isolation from his former self, the self that existed before the murder of Duncan. When Macbeth commits the murder he is already aware of an increasing self-estrangement, that he has created a new self by his deed which is for ever separated from his former being. This realization is summed up in his last speech of the scene: 'To know my deed, 'twere best not know myself'. The next stage in his isolation is the increasing distance which separates him from his wife. This separation, which is first suggested by the differing ways in which they react to the killing of Duncan, undergoes an important development in the following scene (II. 3.), where Lady Macbeth faints.[1] Lady Macbeth faints when she realizes that her husband has lost control of himself. This realization occurs at the point when she hears him explain his killing of the Grooms of Duncan's chamber – which was no part of the original plan – by bizarrely re-echoing an important part of her earlier exhortation to him in such a way as to suggest that he killed them partly as a vicarious punishment on himself. The gulf between Macbeth and his wife becomes greater when he does not take her into his confidence in planning the murder of Banquo. Shortly afterwards, Macbeth's isolation from his subjects, as well as from his former self and his wife, reaches its climax in the banquet scene, where he alone sees the Ghost and where the individualist view of man completely triumphs in his mind. At this point when all his human contacts have failed, he seeks out the Witches, and the double-edged advice he is given only encourages him in the path of increasing isolation from

---

[1] There has been much discussion whether Lady Macbeth really faints or only pretends to. As I try to show, when we judge the question bearing in mind the man theme, we can see that her faint is real.

all human kind. He finally sees man's life as lacking any individual personality whatever; it is merely a depersonalized actor,

> a poor player,
> That struts and frets his hour upon the stage,
> And then is heard no more . . .   (v. 5. 24-6.)

Thus Macbeth's individualism leads him not only to a sense of self-estrangement but also to a total loss of any sense of personal identity.

Lady Macbeth also undergoes a process of isolation, which reaches its final stage in the sleep-walking scene, where, cut off from the present and the surrounding world, she lives fragmentarily and only in the past.

The individualism of Macbeth and Lady Macbeth, however, brings isolation not only on themselves but on the other characters as well. The first to be affected are the sons of Duncan, Malcolm and Donalbain. They leave Scotland, 'where our fate, hid in an auger-hole, / May rush and seize us' (II. 3. 121-2.), Malcolm going to England and Donalbain to Ireland, so that their 'separated fortune' will keep them 'both the safer'. The disappearance of Malcolm removes the centre for a movement against Macbeth, and provides a reason for the inactivity and consequent death of Banquo. Macduff's leaving of his wife and children is yet another instance of the isolation which overtakes everyone in the play. When Ross is explaining to Lady Macduff that her husband may have good reason for leaving her, he gives an account of the general process of isolation which has taken place. In doing so, he reintroduces the concept of not knowing oneself which first appeared in Macbeth's 'To know my deed, 'twere best not know myself'. Thus Ross tells Lady Macduff that

> cruel are the times, when we are traitors
> And do not know ourselves; when we hold rumour
> From what we fear, yet know not what we fear,
> But float upon a wild and violent sea
> Each way and none.   (IV. 2. 18-22.)

The beginning of the contrary process, that of the overcoming of isolation and the integration of the forces opposing Macbeth, consists of Macduff's meeting with Malcolm (IV. 3.), which

Macduff has been able to achieve only at the cost of abandoning his wife and children. The later part of the play presents the growing unity of these forces. Soon after the testing of Macduff by Malcolm, Ross arrives, and Malcolm says, 'My countryman; but yet I know him not'. After Macduff has recognized him, Malcolm exclaims,

> I know him now. Good God betimes remove
> The means that makes us strangers!   (IV. 3. 162-3.)

In answer to Macduff's question, 'Stands Scotland where it did?', Ross replies, 'Alas, poor country, / Almost afraid to know itself!'. A little later, however, after describing its state of desolation, Ross tells how, before he left Scotland, there were rumours of signs of rebellion: 'there ran a rumour / Of many worthy fellows that were out' (182-3.). The culmination of this achievement of unity occurs when Malcolm and Macduff join forces with the rebels 'near Birnam wood', and Malcolm gives the order, 'Let every soldier hew him down a bough / And bear't before him' (v. 4. 4-5.). As John Holloway has observed, this would suggest to an early seventeenth-century audience a May procession representing a communal celebration: 'the single figure, dressed in his distinctive costume (one should have Macbeth in his war equipment in mind) pursued by a whole company of others carrying green branches, was a familiar sight as a Maying procession, celebrating the triumph of new life over the sere and yellow leaf of winter'.[1] The final stage of the battle takes place when Malcolm orders, 'your leavy screens throw down, / And show like those you are' (v. 6. 1-2.). Those opposing Macbeth have already by unity come to know themselves and each other; now Macbeth is made likewise to know the forces against him and realizes, 'I cannot fly, / But bear-like I must fight the course' (v. 7. 1-2.), while his remaining hope is destroyed a little later when he encounters Macduff.

Enriching the presentation of the central conflict of the play is the imagery relating to growth and sterility. The first major occurrence of this imagery is when Banquo asks the Witches,

---

[1] *The Story of the Night: Studies in Shakespeare's Major Tragedies* (London, 1961), p. 66.

If you can look into the seeds of time
And say which grain will grow and which will not,
Speak then to me . . .   (I. 3. 58-60.)

Throughout the play individualism is associated with what is
sterile or withered. Lady Macbeth asks, 'you spirits / That
tend on mortal thoughts, unsex me here' (I. 5. 37-8.). Macbeth
himself has a premonition of what is to come when he speaks of
'wither'd murder' (II. 1. 52.), and sees himself as having murdered sleep, 'Chief nourisher in life's feast' (II. 2. 40.). He
remembers, in thinking of the Witches' prophecy, that 'Upon
my head they plac'd a fruitless crown / And put a barren
sceptre in my gripe' (III. 1. 60-1.), and rather than that this
should be is ready to challenge fate 'to th' utterance'. As we
have seen, the most extreme statement of Macbeth's individualism occurs when he asks the Witches to answer him 'though
the treasure / Of nature's germens tumble all together, / Even
till destruction sicken'. At the end of the play, however, it is
not 'nature's germens' but Macbeth that is destroyed; and
he himself is aware that

> My way of life
> Is fall'n into the sear, the yellow leaf . . .
>
> (v. 3. 22-3.)

On the other hand, the united community is associated with
fertility and growth, symbolized especially in the 'babe'
imagery and in the 'moving grove' of the soldiers bearing
branches.

Related to the images of growth and sterility is the clothing
imagery.[1] One of its main functions is to emphasize the point
that Macbeth, in following the individualist view of man, is
not 'more the man' but less. When Macbeth, after the murder
of Duncan has been discovered, says to the assembled company,
'Let's briefly put on manly readiness', he is ostensibly speaking
of the need to fight treason, but also, as elsewhere in the same
scene, he is re-echoing the earlier conversation with his wife
(I. 7.) when he put on manly readiness in a very different

---

[1] See Caroline Spurgeon, *Shakespeare's Imagery* (Cambridge, 1935), pp. 324-7.
Cleanth Brooks, op. cit., deals with some aspects of the clothing imagery not
touched on by Caroline Spurgeon.

sense. At the end of the play Angus, using a clothing image, says of Macbeth,

> Now does he feel his title
> Hang loose about him, like a giant's robe
> Upon a dwarfish thief.   (v. 2. 20-2.)

In this play there is a constant turning of intentions into their opposite. While the chief instance is provided by Macbeth and Lady Macbeth, whose acts invariably bring about the contrary of what they intend, we are elsewhere reminded of this process. The Porter, in speaking of the effects of drink, explains that

> lechery, sir, it provokes and unprovokes: it provokes the desire, but it takes away the performance. Therefore much drink may be said to be an equivocator with lechery: it makes him, and it mars him; it sets him on, and it takes him off; it persuades him, and disheartens him; makes him stand to, and not stand to; in conclusion, equivocates him in a sleep, and, giving him the lie, leaves him.   (II. 3. 28-33.)

This contradictory quality of the world of *Macbeth* is also directly expressed in the theme of equivocation, touched on by the Porter, and given its fullest expression in the utterances of the Witches, 'these juggling fiends' that

> palter with us in a double sense,
> That keep the word of promise to our ear,
> And break it to our hope!   (v. 8. 20-2.)

The Witches, as J. Dover Wilson has remarked, proceed by contraries;[1] the concluding instruction for the preparation of the contents of their cauldron is 'Cool it with a baboon's blood' (IV. 1. 37.), the baboon being reputedly one of the most lustful of animals. In general, encouraging as they do Macbeth in his individualism, they represent the quintessence of the main contradictions of the play, seen predominantly in their most negative aspects.

Despite the fact that *Macbeth* presents a tremendous force of evil, it is the most optimistic of the four great tragedies. This optimism consists not only in the fact that a united people

---

[1] *Macbeth*, ed. J. Dover Wilson (Cambridge, 1947), p. 148.

overcome the tyrant, but is also to be found in the presentation of Macbeth himself. Macbeth can set out on his career of total destruction, which begins after the banquet, only after he has destroyed a large part of himself. The fact that he is confronted with what are in effect two views of man and that initially, in his murder of Duncan, he acts not from an immediate ambitious greed but from a misconceived sense that he should act according to his desires makes it possible to see his initial choice, despite all its terrible consequences, as arising from an error of judgement rather than from any ingrained propensity to evil. In *Macbeth* evil itself is unnatural. This aspect of the play is summed up in the choric comment of the Old Man on the darkness of the day after Duncan's death, ' 'Tis unnatural, / Even like the deed that's done' (II. 4. 10-11.), and throughout the play it is constantly implied in the imagery. L. C. Knights points out that in *Macbeth* analogies for human good are found in the general process of nature, 'whereas evil is defined solely in terms of what is perverse or abnormal in nature, and is constantly described as " 'gainst nature" or "unnatural". Nature, we are made to feel, is on the side of good and disowns evil'.[1] This view of Nature is contrary to the traditional medieval belief that physical nature was involved in the Fall of Man and is therefore corrupt and to be associated with Satan. Here *Macbeth* is in conformity with a general trend of Renaissance humanism, such for example as is to be found, in different forms, in the writings of Montaigne and Bacon.

To what extent should we associate the two views of man, the conflict between which forms the dramatic structure of *Macbeth*, with feudal and bourgeois modes of thought?[2] We have seen that even at the beginning of the drama the view of

---

[1] *Some Shakespearean Themes* (London, 1959), p. 178.

[2] In considering this question we should remember that Shakespeare's presentation of events is quite unhistorical It carries still further the distortions of his main source, Holinshed's *Chronicles*, and bears little relation to the Scotland of the eleventh century, when the historical Macbeth was king. One main difference is to be found in the fact that the form of succession to the crown in the earlier part of the eleventh century, when the historical Macbeth began his reign, was by election within a small group of kinsmen (tanistry), and the historical Malcolm was in fact the first of a line of kings who established the principle of primogeniture. It is arguable that 'from the eleventh-century standpoint Duncan was the usurper, and Macbeth the vindicator of the true line of succession' (Dover Wilson, ed. cit., p. ix.).

man as a member of society is given a more than merely feudal connotation; and, in the course of the play, as Macbeth's individualism becomes wider in its effects and implications, so correspondingly does the opposing view of man represented in the later scenes primarily by Macduff, despite the fact that at the end there is a formal restoration of the disrupted feudal order.[1] Nor should we entirely associate the individualist view of man with bourgeois ways of thinking, though it is true that the raising of self-interest – or what is conceived to be self-interest – into a view of life is especially characteristic of the epoch of capitalism, and Macbeth may be seen to have some affiliations with the early 'heroic' days of capitalism, tragically conceived.[2] What Shakespeare has done is not so much simply to depict a conflict between feudal and bourgeois ideas as to write a tragedy which, while embodying this conflict, has a relevance to the historical development of Britain as a whole.

[1] This restoration was inevitable, given the high degree of royal control over the stage, and the added fact that *Macbeth* was probably written in the first instance for performance before James I (see note 1, page 113).

[2] Cf. Christopher Caudwell, *Illusion and Reality: a Study of the Sources of Poetry* (1937; ed. 1946), p. 74. Caudwell, quoting the advice of the second Apparition to Macbeth, argues that 'intemperate will, "bloody, bold and resolute", without norm or measure, is the spirit of this era of primitive accumulation. The absolute-individual will overriding all other wills is therefore the principle of life for the Elizabethan age. Marlowe's Faust and Tamburlaine express this principle in its naïvest form'. Though Caudwell's argument does not depend on their existence, there are a few references in *Macbeth* suggesting the growth of a money economy which may be noted. There is the farmer 'that hang'd himself on th' expectation of plenty' (II. 3. 4-5.); the reply of young Macduff to his mother's remark that she can buy twenty husbands at any market, 'Then you'll buy 'em to sell again' (IV. 2. 41.); and Macduff's despairing remark about Scotland when he thinks that Malcolm suspects him and that there is no hope of resistance to Macbeth, 'The title is affeer'd' (IV. 3. 34.). Here 'affeer'd' means 'confirmed' but 'affeer' was originally a commercial term meaning 'fix the market price'.

OTHELLO AND THE DIGNITY OF MAN

G. M. Matthews

The most important feature of *Othello* is the colour of the hero's skin. This is superficially obvious enough, but most critics have avoided treating Othello's colour as the essence of the play for two good reasons: first, that it is unhistorical to suppose that 'colour', as we understand the term, had much meaning for the Elizabethans or early Jacobeans; and second, that to interpret *Othello* as a play about race would be like saying that *Henry IV* is a play about fatness. The real pre-occupations of the tragedy, critics say, are incomparably wider and deeper than the nationality assigned to the characters, and sooner or later Dryden is quoted on the subject of Shakespeare's comprehensive soul.

I agree about Shakespeare's soul, and that racial differences were, ultimately, irrelevant to it; but I do not think this irrelevance was a premise which the dramatist took for granted in taking over the hero of this play, nor is the irrelevance easy to deduce from the events of the play, which suggest that Desdemona might have done better to marry a white man. For the example chosen is inescapably specific. Shakespeare had no need to borrow Cinthio's original story if all he wanted was a tragedy of jealous love; it was not a very good story, and nobody in the audience would have known it except a few highbrows who read Italian. In borrowing, he had to alter it more fundamentally than the originals of his other tragedies. One change he made was to modernize: the events dramatized in *Othello* took place in 1544, Cinthio's account of them appeared in 1565, but Shakespeare based the threatened Turkish attack which takes Othello to Cyprus on a historical event of 1570. This sharply distinguishes *Othello* from the earlier *Hamlet*, set in ancient Scandinavia, and from the later *King Lear* and *Macbeth*, both set in ancient Britain; the time of action corresponds roughly to that of a present-day play based on Mussolini's invasion of Ethiopia. *Othello* is not a vaguely timeless story of jealousy, but a modern instance of a black man's love for a white woman.

R. B. Heilman has shown how strongly the imagery, and even the structure of the play, emphasize the contrast between light and dark.[1] Othello is far more fair than black, because his visage is in his mind; Iago will make the blonde Desdemona begrimed and black by turning her virtue into pitch: 'Iago's business is to confuse the opposites'. The first and last Acts are set in darkness, broken in one case by torches and in the other by Othello's fatal candle as he speaks the soliloquy 'Put out the light, and then put out the light'. 'While Iago is trying to bring darkness into the happy light of Othello's life, there is an opposing force which tries to bring light into the surrounding darkness.' The bearing of this symbolism on the moral opposition between 'good' and 'evil' is obvious, but Shakespeare does not start with symbols and then attach complexions to them, and the inevitable effect of this opposition (though Heilman does not make the point) is to stress the racial contrast between Othello and his associates. I believe it is right, therefore, to see this contrast as the core of the play, its ultimate determinant (which is not, of course, to say it is the whole of the play), and the present essay will try to show that in Shakespeare's hands this determinant is not a limiting one.

Naturally it would be wrong to approach *Othello* as if it had been written after several centuries of imperialist relations with Africa. 'Colour-prejudice' could not possibly have been a current problem in Shakespeare's day in the modern sense of economic, political, and sexual rivalry within a competitive society, conditioned by the hangover from slavery and by movements for African independence. Elizabethans would, however, have had firsthand contact with Moors. Trade with North Africa had long flourished; and on two occasions when there was an expulsion of Moors from Spain, in 1598 and 1609, they were carried back to Africa in English ships, apparently with much sympathy from the crews.[2] As England

---

[1] 'Light and Dark in Othello', *Essays in Criticism*, Oct. 1951.

[2] C. J. Sisson, *Shakespeare's Tragic Justice*, 1961, p. 37.

backed the Moors against a common enemy, Spain, it is perhaps significant that the form of Iago's name is Spanish. In 1600, only four years before the first recorded performance of *Othello*, many theatregoers would have seen 'noble Moors' lodging in London, members of an embassy from the Barbary Coast to Queen Elizabeth.[1] There is little doubt that Moors were generally credited with savagery as well as splendour. Elizabethan processions might be lent magnificence by a 'King of the Moors',[2] but many of the words associated with 'Barbary' (1596) are also Elizabethan: for instance, *barbarity* (=uncivilized condition, first recorded in 1570), *barbarism* (same meaning, 1584), *barbarous* (=cruelly savage, 1588). Shakespeare's earlier Moor, Aaron in *Titus Andronicus*, had been an atheist and an 'inhuman dog' (in some respects interestingly like Iago), who went to death by torture saying defiantly,

> If one good deed in all my life I did,
> I do repent it from my very soul.   (v. 3. 189-90.)

There was evidently a contradiction between the theory of 'order and degree', which enjoined the marriage of class-equals, and a deep suspicion of the alien. Although the Prince of Morocco in *The Merchant of Venice* is eligible to marry Portia, she is glad to get rid of him and 'all of his complexion'; and the King of Naples in *The Tempest* is bitterly reproached for marrying his daughter to the King of Tunis after the whole court had begged him not to 'loose her to an African'. Again, the force of Hamlet's pun when he is making his mother compare her first husband with her second,

> Could you on this faire mountaine leaue to feede,
> And batten on this Moore; ha, haue you eyes?
>   (text from Second Quarto)

depends on the double antithesis not only between *mountain* and *moor*, but between *fair* and *Moor*. All these are reasonable tests of audience-response. The unfamiliarity of the colour-problem would even tend to increase its impact: marriage between Othello and Desdemona must have been very startling to an

---

[1] Bernard Harris, 'A Portrait of a Moor', *Shakespeare Survey* 11, 1958.
[2] Malone Society *Collections*, Vol. III, 1954, pp. xvii-xviii, xxv.

audience that had never even seen a coloured boy walking out with a white girl. Professor Dover Wilson goes further and says: 'If anyone imagines that England at that date was unconscious of the "colour-bar" they cannot have read *Othello* with any care'.[1] Tension, it is clear, could quickly be generated by confronting white with black under certain conditions, although *Othello* cannot be a product of existing tension in Elizabethan society.

It looks as though the colour-difference in *Othello*, while topical and even prophetic in form, may draw some of its emotional intensity from other antagonisms, not necessarily racial, for example those involving puritan, heretic, and crypto-Jew, and even those created by the hierarchical system itself. Othello's royal lineage was not valid in Venice, and it is notable that his enemies (even discounting Iago) tend to assimilate him with the lower orders, as in Roderigo's complaint that Desdemona had been conducted

> with a knave of common hire, a gondolier,
> To the gross clasps of a lascivious Moor.
>
> (I. I. 126-7.)

Othello presents, in extreme form, the situation of the alien (including the class-alien) in a hierarchical, predatory and therefore not yet fully human society. Othello's colour is thus representative of a much wider human protest than concerns race alone, and Paul Robeson was right in maintaining that

> Shakespeare meant Othello to be a "black moor" from Africa. . . . But the color is essentially secondary – except as it emphasizes the difference in *culture*. This is the important thing. . . . Shakespeare's Othello has learned to live in a strange society, but he is not *of* it – as an easterner today might pick up western manners and not be western.[2]

In another way, however, the colour is of crucial importance in focusing the irrational feelings associated with that difference, as a remarkable footnote by A. C. Bradley illustrates. He is agreeing with Coleridge that Othello should be 'sunburnt' rather than black on the modern stage:

[1] *Othello* (New Cambridge Shakespeare), 1957, p. xi.
[2] Quoted from Marvin Rosenberg, *The Masks of Othello*, Berkeley, U.S.A., 1961, p. 195.

Perhaps if we saw Othello coal-black with the bodily eye, *the aversion of our blood, an aversion which comes as near to being merely physical as anything human can, would over-power our imagination* and sink us below not Shakespeare only but the audiences of the seventeenth and eighteenth centuries.[1]   (my italics.)

Whatever we make of this, it reminds us that Shakespeare forced his audience to see Othello first with the 'bodily eye' of Iago. This hero is a great human being who, differing *physically* as well as *culturally* from the community he has entered, recognizes (within the limits of his social role) only universal humane values of love and loyalty; but when in his equalitarian innocence he assumes full human rights in a society where other values are dominant, he makes himself and his personal relationships vulnerable to irrational, un-human forces, embodied in Iago, that try to reduce him to a level as irrational as themselves and almost – but not quite – succeed.

Othello's commanding personality and the glamour of his poetic idiom tend to make his actual social position seem much higher than it really is. He is employed by the Venetian republic as a professional soldier, a mercenary, and has become its most reliable and popular general. In his own country he was descended 'From men of royal siege', and he can say without boasting that he merits the position he has reached. Yet in Roderigo's words he is 'an extravagant and wheeling stranger' (where *extravagant* means 'straying outside his proper place'), who has lived in Venice, as distinct from the camp, for less than a year (I. 3. 83-5.). The precarious anomaly of Othello's status is vividly dramatized in what are perhaps the most brilliant opening scenes in any Shakespeare play. In the second scene two parties of men are searching for him independently through the streets of Venice: one from the Duke's senate to require his urgent service against the 'enemy Ottoman', the other to imprison him for marrying a senator's daughter. Ironically, one party is at first mistaken for the other in the darkness. Othello himself, not without irony, comments on the paradox; if I obey the prison party, he says, 'How may the duke be therewith satisfied?'. Othello's prestige rests on his indispensability, but being indispensable does not make him

---

[1] *Shakespearean Tragedy*, 1904, p. 202n.

socially acceptable in governing circles. Brabantio invited him home and 'loved' him while he recounted his past adventures, but as a future son-in-law he is decidedly *persona non grata*, a 'thing' that no Venetian girl could possibly look at with affection except by some preposterous error of nature. Brabantio never does reconcile himself to the match, the grief of which kills him. There were, of course, 'fortunes' at stake, and the runaway marriage (in contrast to Cinthio's version, which takes place with the reluctant consent of the girl's parents) signifies not rashness but purity of motive. Their secret union, in contempt of the 'many noble matches' available to Desdemona, is to make it quite clear that no material interests were involved in what was a free love-match. Othello gets nothing from it, while as Desdemona says:

> That I did love the Moor to live with him,
> My downright violence and scorn of fortunes
> May trumpet to the world. (I. 3. 248-50.)

Desdemona affirms her choice in public and with devastating simplicity – devastating because when her father asks her to say where her obedience lies, she answers:

> here's my husband,
> And so much duty as my mother show'd
> To you, preferring you before her father,
> So much I challenge that I may profess
> Due to the Moor, my lord. (I. 3. 185-9.)

She makes no distinction whatever, that is, between her parents' marriage and her own. Brabantio retorts in effect that in that case he is no longer related to her: 'I had rather to adopt a child than get it'. And Desdemona finds, without dismay, that her act has isolated her with Othello, for her father will not admit her into his house, even alone. Desdemona's childlike simplicity, dramatically so effective at the end of the play in heightening the pathos of her helpless isolation, has the effect in this scene of positing the spontaneous, instinctive naturalness of her love for Othello (to Iago her act means the opposite: 'If she had been blest she would never have loved the Moor'). Unlike her father, Desdemona entertains no consideration 'of years, of country, and of credit', only of direct human relationships: parents, lover, husband, friend.

Othello's commitment complements hers. Shakespeare shows that this is the first relationship he has experienced since childhood (Cassio's friendship apart) that was not based on military or political expediency but purely on human feeling. Yet in staking his emotional life on Desdemona he has put his free condition into a 'circumscription and confine' which makes him vulnerable, and that is why the supposed loss of her love exhausts his capacity for suffering. There is nothing egotistical in this attitude; on the contrary. Disease, poverty, slavery, even public disgrace – the loss of all he has valued up to now – he could bear 'well, very well',

> But there, where I have garner'd up my heart,
> Where either I must live or bear no life,
> The fountain from the which my current runs,
> Or else dries up – to be discarded thence!
>
> (IV. I. 58-61.)

Thus both lovers assert 'humane' values against the conventions that debase them; but 'humaneness', so isolated, is itself an abstraction and reliance on it leaves them fatally vulnerable. The emotional innocence of the hero and heroine (like the extreme youth of Romeo and Juliet) reflects both their protest against the social environment and their ultimate helplessness before it.

It is of course between Othello and Iago that the main issue is fought. Here Shakespeare made another significant change in Cinthio's original story. Cinthio's equivalent of Iago did not hate the Moor at all, but deceived him in order to revenge himself on his wife for her refusal to commit adultery. It was only after having her murdered that the Moor, regretting the deed, turned on its instigator and demoted him, and they then began *to hate each other*. In Shakespeare Iago's hatred, which fills the entire play from line 7 to the end, is one-sided, obsessive, and single-minded. Yet Othello, like all the other characters, has no reason to suspect its existence. Cassio and Roderigo are of marginal importance to Iago, and when he actually has Desdemona at his mercy in Act IV Scene 2 he is perfectly indifferent to her suffering and makes no attempt either to prolong or to exploit it. It looks as if Iago's interest in Desdemona is solely on account of her relationship with

Othello. 'Peradventure' lust has something to do with it, he says, but his chief anxiety is to get even with the lusty Moor for supposed adultery with Emilia, the thought of which

> Doth like a poisonous mineral gnaw my inwards;
> And nothing can or shall content my soul
> Till I am even'd with him, wife for wife.
>
> (II. I. 291-3.)

Indeed, revenge by proxy would do just as well; he tells Roderigo, whom he keeps going 'For his quick hunting' as well as for the money in his purse, 'If thou canst cuckold him, thou dost thyself a pleasure, me a sport'. Desdemona is simply the best means of getting at Othello; and Roderigo, like Cassio, a means of getting at Desdemona. To Cassio, Othello's only friend, Iago extends the same fantastic suspicion of adultery with Emilia: 'For I fear Cassio with my night-cap, too'. That *too* is revealing. If Iago has an obsession about sex it is clear that Othello is somewhere at the centre of it.

Why does Iago hate Othello? This has always been the crux of the play. The characters themselves are baffled by hatred of such intensity; the dying Roderigo calls Iago an 'inhuman dog', and to Lodovico he seems 'More fell than anguish, hunger, or the sea' – more implacable than the blind forces of nature. Yet when Othello asks him point-blank why he acted as he did, he shuts up completely. Not that Iago has ever been unwilling to talk, indeed he has just 'part confessed his villainy': all he refuses to explain is the motive of his hatred. 'What you know you know'. What could he possibly say? 'I was passed over for the lieutenancy'? 'Some people thought Othello had seduced my wife'? The possible rational motives are so ludicrously incommensurate with the effects. But although the quick-witted Iago cannot explain his conduct rationally, Coleridge's verdict of 'motiveless malignity' overlooks the first scene of the play, which shows that his conduct was powerfully motivated. He is no devil from hell, except metaphorically. We learn within twenty lines that he is sensitive to aliens, because one of his first objections to Cassio is that he is a foreigner, 'a Florentine'. And although Iago's avowed policy is to thrive by Othello until he has lined his coat, his first dramatic action is to stir up an unprofitable

racial riot against Othello merely in order to 'poison his delight'
in his marriage, which is described to Brabantio in bestially
obscene language:

> *Iago.*   Even now, now, very now, an old black ram
> Is tupping your white ewe. . . .
> . . . you'll have your daughter cover'd with a Barbary
> horse; you'll have your nephews [=grandchildren]
> neigh to you; . . . your daughter and the Moor are now
> making the beast with two backs.
> *Brabantio.*   Thou art a villain.
> *Iago.*   You are – a Senator.
>
> (I. I. 89-119.)

The moment is crucial. The profane wretch and the magnifico
suddenly recognize, behind their hostile confrontation, a kind of
mutual identity: Brabantio is face to face with his own un-
confessed reaction to the news of his daughter's elopement with
a black man. Before the Duke that reaction becomes explicit,
and Iago afterwards uses it as an invaluable source of quotation
in baiting Othello. When Brabantio's 'loved' visitor is also
loved by Desdemona he is immediately regarded as a heathen
dealer in witchcraft and aphrodisiacs, and the senator's class-
prejudice and religious intolerance are revealed in his horrified
fear that if such unions are permitted, 'Bond-slaves and pagans
shall our statesmen be'. These early scenes demonstrate, therefore, that Iago's view of Othello is not – except in pathological
intensity – a unique aberration, but an attitude held by the
Venetian ruling class when forced into human relationship with
a Moor. The Duke and the rest of his council who are concilia-
tory and tolerant cannot afford to be otherwise, 'cannot with
safety cast him': they need Othello's professional services.

Iago hates Othello because he is a Moor. This irrational but
powerful motive, underlying the obsessive intensity of his
feeling and the improvised reasons with which he justifies it,
continually presses up towards the surface of his language. It
breaks through into action at the opening of the play in order to
give the audience the key to his character; after this its energies
go into the intrigue that will bring the hated object and all
its associates to destruction; but it often nearly betrays itself.
Iago's 'motive-hunting' has been much discussed, but the
fact is that he never gives a direct reason of any kind for his

hatred. He tells Roderigo the story of Cassio's appointment and then asks whether this gives him any reason to *love* the Moor? Later he reflects: 'I hate the Moor; And it is thought abroad that twixt my sheets He's done my office' – the hatred and its possible cause are unconnected. Again he tells himself: 'The Moor, howbeit that I endure him not, Is of a constant, loving, noble nature', where this phrase *I endure him not* ('I just can't stand him') is even more revealing than *I hate*, especially when accompanied by an acknowledgment of his true qualities. 'I have told thee often, and I re-tell thee again and again, I hate the Moor'. Iago's mind broods constantly over Othello's colour. After the disembarkation at Cyprus, when Cassio drinks 'To the health of our general' Iago drinks 'to the health of black Othello'. But it is in conversation with Othello himself that the hidden disgust most nearly betrays itself. One exchange is of particular importance. Othello's trust in Desdemona is just beginning to waver:

> *Othello.*   And yet, how nature erring from itself –
> *Iago.*   Ay, there's the point: as – to be bold with you –
> Not to affect many proposed matches
> Of her own clime, complexion, and degree,
> Whereto we see in all things nature tends –
> Foh! one may smell in such a will most rank,
> Foul disproportion, thoughts unnatural.
> But pardon me –   (III. 3. 231-8.)

Othello has been judged stupid for failing to see that this is an open insult, but it is *not* an open insult; Iago is repeating what Brabantio had said in council:

> she – in spite of nature,
> Of years, of country, credit, every thing –
> To fall in love with what she fear'd to look on!
> It is a judgment maim'd and most imperfect
> That will confess perfection so could err
> Against all rules of nature   (I. 3. 96-101.)

The point lies in two antithetical interpretations of 'nature'. For Othello, as for Desdemona, what was 'natural' was a marriage between two lovers, involving the same duties as their parents had owed each other, and by *nature erring from itself* Othello meant 'a wife forgetting her proper loyalty'. To

Brabantio it was against all rules of nature for a Venetian
girl to love a Moor, and Iago therefore inverted Othello's
phrase *nature erring from itself* to mean 'a woman flouting the
laws of colour and class' ('clime, complexion, and degree').
The tragedy is epitomized in this exchange. Human love is
what Othello stands by. But for Iago Othello is not a human
being at all, he is an animal: a ram, a horse, an ass; his sexual
union with Desdemona will produce not children but colts.
Since Iago himself admits Othello's qualities ('a constant,
loving, noble nature'), he is involved in complete irrationality,
forced to argue that it is the very virtues of men that make them
beast-like:

> The Moor is of a free and open nature
> . . . And will as tenderly be led by th' nose
> As asses are.   (i. 3. 393-6.)

This particular beast is loved by his wife and honoured as a
brilliant military commander. The real relationship between
him and Iago was established at the beginning of the play
when Othello quelled the uproar Iago had raised by saying:
'For Christian shame put by this barbarous brawl'; Othello is
the civilized man, Iago the barbarian. Iago's task is to reduce
him in actuality to a shape that at first exists only in Iago's
fantasy, that of an irrational beast, by

> making him egregiously an *ass*,
> And practising upon his peace and quiet
> Even to *madness*.   (ii. 1. 303-5; my italics.)

So when Othello exclaims, at the beginning of his ordeal, that
Iago would have to 'exchange [him] for a goat' before he would
make jealousy the business of his soul, he is describing with
unconscious irony exactly what Iago proposes to do. This is not
a study of a civilized barbarian reverting to type (for Othello
has never been a barbarian, though he has been a slave), but
the more subtle one of a white barbarian who tries to make a
civilized man into his own image.

The psychology of the Nazi underlings who ran the con-
centration camps has been similarly explained. By reducing
intelligent human beings to the condition of animals they could
enjoy a superiority that inverted the real relation between them:

it was a fantasy enactment, resembling magic as magic has been defined by Professor Gordon Childe, 'a way of making people believe they are going to get what they want'.[1] The element of fantasy and the reliance on magic is one of the 'realist' Iago's most striking characteristics. Some of his logic, even when it is not designed to mock the half-witted Roderigo, shows an opportunism that is simply bizarre. He will postulate almost anything for immediate effect, not just on others but even on himself, and then back it up with moralizings that sound shrewd only because they are cynical, like a sort of lunatic Polonius. It is a superb study of an irrational mind, lucid and cunning on the surface but mad just underneath; and in this it contrasts directly with Othello's, which is deeply rational but guileless on the surface.

Other characters find Iago's surface convincing, but when they describe him as *honest* they are in effect confessing that all they see in him is surface. The main function of the famous epithet is of course ironic: the pitiless deceiver is the man everybody turns to for help and everybody trusts. But the word *honest*, constantly repeated, is eventually felt to express a definite limitation; Iago is imprisoned within the boundaries of the epithet as a modern commodity is imprisoned within the slogan advertising it. When Othello says 'Iago is most honest', the honesty is that of an N.C.O. who is thoroughly reliable at his own job but never in the running for a commission. Iago seems to recognize the limiting force of the description so automatically attached to him by the savage way he quotes it himself when undertaking to make discord of the lovers' harmony:

> O, you are well tun'd now!
> But I'll set down the pegs that make this music,
> As honest as I am.   (II. 1. 197-9.)

Thus there is an ironical parallel between Iago who, though lavishly praised for honesty, is not in fact able enough even for minor promotion, and Othello, the truly 'noble Moor', who is not considered good enough to marry into the Venetian ruling class. And the parallel almost converges in the end, for Othello's nobility deceives everyone and becomes, in its effects, practially indistinguishable from Iago's honesty.

[1] *History*, 1947, p. 37.

The weapon Iago uses is systematic unreason, magic. Brabantio's first assumption on learning that his daughter had fallen in love with a Moor was that she must have been corrupted by sorcery:

> thou hast practis'd on her with foul charms,
> Abus'd her delicate youth with drugs or minerals . . .

> For nature so preposterously to err, . . .
> Sans witchcraft could not.   (I. 2. 73-4, 62-4.)

The Duke's council soon realizes that mutual love was the only 'witchcraft' in the case. Shakespeare is careful to show that the advances came equally from both sides, though at first he plays down the sensual element in Othello's love because men from hot climates were traditionally hot-blooded and this must not be supposed of Othello. The perfect equality of the lovers is symbolized in their playful exchange of roles on arrival in Cyprus, where Othello is Desdemona's 'dear' and Desdemona is Othello's 'fair warrior', while the imagery of Cassio's benediction on them is rich with fertility-feeling:

> Great Jove, Othello guard,
> And swell his sail with thine own powerful breath,
> That he may bless this bay with his tall ship,
> Make love's quick pants in Desdemona's arms,
> Give renew'd fire to our extincted spirits,
> And bring all Cyprus comfort!   (II. 1. 77-82.)

It is hard to see how Shakespeare could have made the case clearer. It is not their union but their disunion that is effected by 'drugs or minerals', as the imagery now begins to demonstrate. Iago curbs Roderigo's impatience by reminding him that 'we work by wit and not by witchcraft', meaning 'the job can't be done without planning'; but in this most ironical of Shakespeare's tragedies the statement carries an opposite implication: 'I work by witchcraft, not by reason'. The degrading of Cassio in Act II is a kind of symbolic rehearsal of the method Iago will use with his principal victim. Betrayed into drunkenness and senseless violence Cassio cries in self-disgust: 'To be now a sensible man, by and by a fool, and presently a beast!' The 'medicine' that so 'unwitted' Cassio was alcohol; the drug used on Othello will be more subtle and instead of wine into his mouth Iago will pour pestilence into his ear, but the sequence of results is to be identical. 'The Moor already changes with my poison', Iago says after his first insinuations, and for this the victim has no counter-drug:

> Not poppy, nor mandragora,
> Nor all the drowsy syrups of the world,
> Shall ever medicine thee to that sweet sleep
> Which thou owed'st yesterday.   (III. 3. 344-7.)

This poetry, it has been noticed, is in Othello's own style: Iago is putting on the verbal habits of his victim, as Othello's later 'Goats and monkeys!' will adopt Iago's; but its *content* is quite alien to Othello's thinking, who is not a drug-addict. Othello's characteristic images are of achieved perfection: Desdemona is a pearl, she is as smooth as monumental alabaster, he would not exchange her for a world made of chrysolite; and it is this integrity of love that Iago attacks with the solvents and corrosives of unreason.

The two exceptions are Othello's description of the handkerchief, and his request for poison in order to kill Desdemona. The *actual* virtue of the handkerchief is simply that both lovers valued it as Othello's first remembrance and to lose it might have been interpreted as a 'symptomatic act' (even Desdemona fears that such a loss might put some men to 'ill thinking'), but Iago's plot loads it with fictitious *mana* as a symbol of infidelity. Naturally Desdemona cannot see it like that, and Othello, mentally unbalanced after his latest interview with Iago, piles more and more on to the supposed properties of the handkerchief in order to scare her into some sense of the enormity of her offence. She feels his urgency but is sceptical of the details ('Sure there's some wonder in this handkerchief' is the furthest she will go), which are evidently new to her; all Othello's previous stories have been factual. Thus it is Iago's magic that went into the web, the absurdity of the hallowed worms and maidens-heart dye corresponding to the irrational significance he has made Othello attach to it. Iago's refusal to agree to the use of poison has been explained as reluctance to implicate himself, but more is implied than mere caution. If Romeo could get poison without signing a register Iago certainly could. Othello surely thinks first of poison because he wants to do the right thing: isn't this the way (his request implies) in which good Italians dispose of unfaithful wives? But Iago cannot allow him to kill Desdemona at a distance, like a civilized Venetian; he must 'strangle her in her bed' with his bare hands, like a savage. Poison is Iago's speciality. 'Work on, my medicine, work!' Just before advising Othello to strangle Desdemona, Iago succeeds in goading him to the point of complete mental breakdown; in the Folio text he 'falls in a trance', and Iago has the satisfaction of telling Cassio that he sometimes 'breaks out to savage madness' and foams at the mouth. As he recovers his reason, it is with loss of manhood that Iago taunts him. 'A passion most unsuiting such a man'; 'Good sir, be a man'; 'Would you would bear your fortune like a man!'. *Like a man* in this context carries a double irony because the fortune Othello is being advised to bear is that of cuckoldry, so it really means 'like a monster'. From this point on, Othello is absorbed more and more into Iago's mental world. His vicious 'I will chop her into messes' shows him becoming as barbarous as Iago wishes.

How is it that what is rational and human, personified in the hero, is so nearly turned into its opposite by this medicine-man? The classic dilemma of *Othello* criticism has been that if the hero is as noble as he seems, a villain of superhuman intelligence would be needed to break him down. There are therefore critics who make Iago superhuman: a symbol or embodiment of Evil. Alternatively, if Iago is as ignoble as he proves, the hero must be a very poor type to be taken in by him. This (broadly speaking) is the line followed by critics from F. R. Leavis to Laurence Lerner. Both views depend ultimately on the Aristotle-Bradley doctrine of the 'tragic flaw' – a doctrine that has obscured the true nature of Shake-spearian tragedy far more than any over-emphasis on 'character'. Indeed, it is only when a man's 'character' is pictured as a sort of hard, fixed core somewhere inside him (rather as the essential particles of matter were once pictured as miniature billiard-balls) that looking for 'flaws' in it makes any sense. The idea is that if a dramatic character changes into something different from what he was, he must really have been like that all along; or, at least, he must always have shown some incipient weakness which could lead to that result. In one way this is a truism, for a man obviously cannot develop in any direction unless he is capable of doing so; but the theory is a nuisance because the potentialities of men are infinite, and whatever the greatness of a dramatic hero, any number of potential 'flaws' can be found, or invented, to account for his downfall. Yet in all Shakespeare's tragedies except, perhaps, *Macbeth*, the determining 'flaw' is in society rather than in the hero's supposed distance from perfection. Tragedy does not occur in *Hamlet* because the hero has a bad habit of not killing people at once, but because the power of the Danish court is founded on violence and adultery. No personal idiosyncrasy can alter the tragedy inherent in this situation, though it may of course affect the special form the tragedy takes. The 'tragic flaw' theory means that it is a punishable offence to be any particular kind of man. Moreover it shifts the emphasis from *men in conflict* to the *private mind*; J. I. M. Stewart has even interpreted *Othello* as a debate in which Iago and Othello are at times the two halves of one mind, 'abstractions from a single and, as it were, invisible protagonist'.[1] This seems perversely un-Shakespearian.

Far from being self-centred or stupid, Othello is not presented as having any particular moral or intellectual weakness, though he is fully individualized. Certainly Othello has very different qualities of mind from Hamlet. But Hamlet's superiority lies mainly in the other meaning of the word intelligence. Hamlet is equipped to face the treachery around him because all the facts have been revealed to him, so that throughout the play the dramatic irony works entirely on his side. If Claudius had told the audience the facts, and not the Ghost Hamlet, would Hamlet seem so very bright when his uncle patronized him?

Some impression of cleverness in a plotter and of stupidity in his victim is inevitable when the dramatic irony works the other way. Iago knows something essential that Othello does not know; the audience share the knowledge and so are implicated with Iago whether they like it or not. Iago's knowledge is not objective knowledge of real human relations, which Othello ought in reason to share, for Iago has invented the situation that puts Othello at a disadvantage; but the power

[1] *Character and Motive in Shakespeare*, 1949, p. 108.

it confers is real enough, and this is why the audience find themselves tied to Iago by a bond of complicity. The effect is intentional; *Othello* is not a play for making consciences comfortable. A rather similar effect occurs in Patrick Hamilton's thriller *Rope*, where a young moron who has committed a motiveless killing gets the victim's father to share a meal with him on top of the box containing his son's body. This gruesome situation inevitably causes the father's perfect ignorance to appear as stupidity and his own knowledge (which the audience share) to appear as wit. Hamilton is said to have been thinking of the psychology of fascism when he wrote *Rope*.

Even if Othello's 'stupidity' is partly a dramatic illusion, it would still seem a paradox to say that because he was rational he failed to notice that he was being led by the nose, and this needs explanation. Some recent criticism has blamed Othello's credulity on his immature attitude towards his wife, or on some inadequacy in their relationship. A marriage that ends in murder certainly ends inadequately, but again it would be wrong to deny the fact of change, especially in a play where change is constantly stressed; and if the marriage was inadequate from the beginning, its destruction is not so very regrettable. But 'immature', in modern critical jargon, often turns out to mean 'not adjusted to the existing social order', and in this sense both the lovers were emphatically immature, since they disregarded the convention of the arranged marriage as well as the 'natural' laws of clime, complexion, and degree, and married for love. It is the flaw in society that breaks Othello down and destroys the marriage. In purely human terms his bond with Desdemona is strong, and it is hard to imagine any of the wealthy curlèd darlings of Venice forging a stronger one, but the phrase 'purely human' is an admission of the price paid in isolation and vulnerability. Othello's pathetic defence in the last Act, sword in hand, of a dead body in an empty bedroom – in fact, the whole claustrophobic movement of the play – reflects this isolation and confinement. *Socially* speaking, the union of what Iago called 'an erring barbarian and a supersubtle Venetian' was genuinely frail, and although his words were a parody not a description of the difference between them, he was accurately foreshadowing his line of attack. *Supersubtle*, the opposite of what Desdemona really

is, comes from Iago's sardonic fantasy, but it is fantasy he makes
Othello share; *erring* in its primary sense means 'wandering',
for Othello is a soldier of fortune, but *erring barbarian* also
suggests a savage who has strayed from his proper station in
life by embracing Christianity and a white wife. Iago puts it
to him, after some preliminary softening-up, that he is un-
familiar with the local customs:

> *Iago.*   I know our country disposition well:
> In Venice they do let God see the pranks
> They dare not show their husbands . . .
> *Othello.* Dost thou say so?
> *Iago.*   She did deceive her father, marrying you;
> And when she seem'd to shake and fear your looks,
> She lov'd them most.   (III. 3. 205-12.)

The deadliness of these first reasonings lies in the fact that
they are not Iago's, but endorsements of what Desdemona's
own father has said; they voice a social attitude already expressed to Othello. For example: 'She has deceiv'd her father,
and may thee' (I. 3. 293.), and 'To fall in love with what she
fear'd to look on!' (I. 3. 98.). Only now, when Iago quotes
Brabantio as saying: 'He thought 'twas witchcraft –', he imputes
the witchcraft to Desdemona's skill in deceit, not Othello's
power of attraction as Brabantio had done.

Under this combined pressure, Othello discovers very quickly
that he has overrated his own emotional security. However
well he knows his wife, this difference of race is the one factor in
their relations in which he is necessarily ignorant, and through
this irrational door the prompting of a Venetian supposed to be
experienced in 'all qualities of human dealings' gains entry.[1]
Consequently the first and principal thing Othello considers in
weighing the possibility of Desdemona's unfaithfulness is his
own colour: 'Haply, for I am black . . . She's gone'. He is
persuaded, in fact, that he *cannot* know her, and all his tragic
blindness stems from that persuasion.

Iago's aim has been not Othello's overthrow but his total
degradation as a human being: that he should kill what he loved

---

[1] Iago would seem still more convincing if, as Paul A. Jorgensen maintains
(*Redeeming Shakespeare's Words*, Berkeley, U.S.A., 1962, pp. 14-19) the audience
took him to be posing to Othello as Honesty, a professional smeller-out of
knaves.

most, in jealous madness, with his bare hands. This aim is almost realized. At least once Othello has broken down into actual madness under Iago's mental drugs; he has solemnly dedicated his heart to hatred and vengeance; and in his insults to Desdemona he has become indistinguishable from the bond-slave Brabantio once compared him to: 'a beggar in his drink Could not have laid such terms upon his callet'. Yet he does not actually commit the murder in jealous revenge but as an act of objective justice, even of civic and religious duty. In a way this makes it worse; but it means that Iago has already partly failed. Othello kills in persisting love, not hate ('O balmy breath, that dost almost persuade Justice to break her sword!'), and even against his will: for every two lines of the soliloquy 'It is the cause, it is the cause my soul' there is a word of negation or qualification, *not, nor, yet, but*. Action has restored his self-command and reasserted his public respon-sibility at the expense of his private inclination. In Desdemona's actual presence, instead of behaving like a mad beast he has to force himself to go through with it. When he says, weeping over the girl he intends not to murder but to sacrifice,

> this sorrow's heavenly;
> It strikes where it doth love.   (v. 1. 21-2.)

he is recognizably trying to administer the same impersonal justice as when he dismissed Cassio:

> Cassio, I love thee;
> But never more be officer of mine.   (II. 3. 240-1.)

There too, ironically enough, he had been tricked into his act of justice, and here it is a horrible delusion, as Desdemona tries to tell him with her unanswerable 'That death's unnatural that kills for loving'; but from now on Othello is deluded but responsible, capable of summing himself up with complete self-awareness after his enlightenment as 'an honourable murderer'.

This second change in Othello raises one question of impor-tance for an Elizabethan audience at least. Iago has not only destroyed all that Othello valued on earth but has consigned him to eternal punishment by trapping him into murder and suicide. Othello was a Christian convert, and by killing himself he knowingly accepts the fate of being 'damned beneath all depth in hell' for what he has done; to the dead Desdemona he says:

> When we shall meet at compt,
> This look of thine will hurl my soul from heaven,
> And fiends will snatch at it.   (v. 2. 276-8.)

If Shakespeare as an orthodox Christian believed the same, what can be the point of emphasizing Othello's recovery of human integrity? Speculation on Shakespeare's religious beliefs is of course unprofitable, but the text does make one broad hint. Some thirty lines after Desdemona has been left for dead, she speaks again, and her last words, in answer to Emilia's question 'O, who hath done this deed?' are: 'Nobody: I myself . . . Commend me to my kind lord: O, farewell!' This attempt to take the blame for her own murder (which provokes Othello into a furious avowal of responsibility: 'She's like a liar gone to burning hell. 'Twas I that killed her') is so piteously absurd that its dramatic point has been queried; but the point is surely obvious. There is a precedent for Desdemona's absurdity in the Christian doctrine of the Atonement. This does not mean that Desdemona is a 'Christ-figure'. In letting her speak as it were from beyond the grave, Shakespeare is suggesting to his audience that whatever might happen 'at compt', one voice at least – his victim's – was unlikely to be raised against Othello.

It is Emilia who, after the murder, takes over from Othello as representative of common humanity. Deluded herself for most of the play (like every single character in it), once she sees the truth she refuses to compromise either with the misleader or the misled, and her magnificent outbursts first against Othello and then against her husband reassert what is human and rational in a world almost completely given over to unreason. The human relation was valid after all: 'she loved thee, cruel Moor'. For the last time Iago tries to control the course of events by witchcraft:

> Iago.   Go to, charm your tongue.
> Emilia. I will not charm my tongue; I am bound to
> [speak.
>   (v. 2. 186-7.)

So he silences commonsense by another murder; but it is too late: she has brought the issues into the plain light of day, and Othello's judges as well as Othello himself have at least partly understood them.

Othello's behaviour in the final scene is governed by the way Lodovico discriminates between him and Iago in allotting punishment. Iago has been unmasked, and the Venetian delegation joins with Othello in execrating him. He is sentenced out of hand to be tortured to death – the most savage punishment in Shakespeare, or indeed, anywhere else. Othello is relieved of his post and remanded in custody 'Till that the nature of [his] fault be known To the Venetian state'. The customary Elizabethan class-distinction whereby, for example, noble traitors were gracefully beheaded while commoners were hanged, drawn, and quartered may have something to do with this. But the truth is that among the Venetians as in the audience there is strong sympathy for him, and some reluctance to condemn:

> O thou Othello, that was once so good,
> Fall'n in the practice of a damned slave,
> What shall be said to thee?   (v. 2. 294-6.)

While Iago is called 'demi-devil', a 'hellish villain', Othello is a 'rash and most unfortunate man'. In Cinthio's story, where the Moor's deed is far less excusable, he escapes with his life. The deferment of judgment, when the facts are so plain, clearly implies that Othello's life may well be spared in view of the circumstances and of his own past merit. So at least Othello understands the position, for as soon as Lodovico's decision is announced he says:

> I have done the state some service, and they know't–
>   (v. 2. 342.)

an ironic repetition of his confidence in Act I that his usefulness to the state would outweigh Brabantio's objections to his marriage: 'My services which I have done the signiory Shall out-tongue his complaints'. He can hardly be 'cheering himself up', as T. S. Eliot oddly interprets; he is recognizing, and rejecting, the possibility of avoiding the death-penalty. He refuses to throw himself on the mercy of the Venetian senators,

even though the most powerful of those that might seek vengeance on him, Brabantio, is known to have died. Instead he
repudiates the deed – for which his sterile tears flow like the
secretions from trees in his native Africa that can restore life to
the phoenix – and also dissociates himself from those who would
judge him for the deed. They are offered, almost contemp-
tuously, 'a word or two before you go'. Othello is now seeing
himself and his social environment with complete objectivity:
'Speak of me as I am; nothing extenuate, Nor set down aught
in malice,' and his own comments are not expressed subjectively but in detached clear-cut images. Whether it is to the
'base Judean' of the Folio or to the 'base Indian' of the Quarto
that he compares himself (v. 2. 350.), Othello's final image of
his relationship with Desdemona is of a white pearl in a black
hand. And his self-assessment just before he pronounces
sentence on himself broadens the implications of the play in an
image that brings its ironies into sharp focus:

> say besides that in Aleppo once,
> Where a malignant and a turban'd Turk
> Beat a Venetian and traduc'd the state,
> I took by th' throat the circumcisèd dog
> And smote him – thus.   (v. 2. 355-9.)

Overtly Othello presents himself as a servant of the State,
avenging an insult by a foreigner: he is the Turk, the heathen
barbarian Iago has tried to make him, who has committed
violence on a Venetian citizen and betrayed a public trust,
having defiled his human relation with Desdemona and his
soldier's honour alike. But the words *malignant, turbaned,* and
circumcisèd dog are bitterly ironic, because *turbaned* and *circumcisèd* tend to identify the Turk with Othello rather than
provide an insulting analogy (for circumcision could be a
mark equally of Christian, Moor, Turk and Jew), while
malignant and *dog* do not fit Othello at all, only Iago. Hence
Othello's apparent tit-for-tat in killing the Turk can also be
taken in the opposite sense: that he had acted to suppress
racial violence in the trading-centre of Aleppo, just as when
the play opens we see him suppressing Iago's 'barbarous
brawl'. As a final irony, Othello's analogy reminds the Venetians that in dealing with himself as he dealt with the Turk he is

in fact depriving them of their main bulwark against Turks. Some of Shakespeare's audience might have remembered that the historical Turkish attack on Cyprus in 1570 had been successful.

Othello's final speech, therefore, though it cannot mitigate what he has done, demonstrates the complete recovery of his integrity as a human being. He will not beg for mercy on the strength of his past greatness, but sums up himself and others with objective self-knowledge, and carries out his own sentence, offering himself by his last gesture as a sacrifice to his victim, since this is the only act of reunion open to him:

> I kiss'd thee ere I kill'd thee. No way but this –
> Killing my self, to die upon a kiss.   (v. 2. 361-2.)

All that Iago's poison has achieved is an object that 'poisons sight': a bed on which a black man and a white girl, although they are dead, are embracing. Human dignity, the play says, is indivisible.

FROM *HAMLET* TO *LEAR*

Arnold Kettle

I will first put, as a hypothesis, a description of *Hamlet* which, though obviously oversimplified, I think gets somewhere near the heart of the play, what it is about.

Hamlet is a sixteenth-century prince who, because of certain extremely disturbing personal experiences, the death of his father and his mother's marriage to his uncle, comes to see his world in a different way. This new vision affects everything: his attitude to his friends and family, his feelings about sex, his view of the court and its politics, his image of himself. The experience is so all-embracing and so shattering that he is not at first sure that his new vision can be true or, if it is, whether he can endure it. But as the situation clarifies he becomes convinced of its validity and comes to understand its implications better. In this he is helped by two things: his education, which has predisposed him towards a humane and rational approach to life, and his friendship with Horatio, another young man who, though much less brilliant than Hamlet, is also a humanist scholar and who stands firm in loyalty and affection when the rest of the world treats him as a pitiable or dangerous neurotic.

At first Hamlet, though of an active disposition, is almost overwhelmed by the difficulty of solving his problems – especially with regard to his uncle – in terms of his new way of looking at things. He more or less deliberately prolongs the business of testing-out his well-founded suspicions and allows his uncle to get back the initiative and ship him out of the country. At this point, however, he comes to the conclusion that he cannot avoid acting, even if the actions he takes cannot satisfactorily meet all the problems he has unearthed. He acts very decisively therefore on the voyage to England, returns to Denmark and, moved beyond measure by the suicide of Ophelia and the reactions of her stupid but not ineffectual brother, puts on once more the bearing and responsibilities of a prince and solves the situation in action in the only way he can, by killing the king, leaving Prince Fortinbras to reign in his place, and begging Horatio to live on to tell the tale.

The degree to which Hamlet, in the last act, capitulates to the values he has previously rejected – the extent to which he gives up the battle to act as a man rather than as a prince – corresponds, I suggest, to the actual possibilities in the year 1600 of putting into practice the ideas of the new humanism or, perhaps more accurately, holds the mirror up to nature in the sense that certain limitations in sixteenth-century humanism and discrepancies between humanist theory and practice are revealed.

Hamlet's new view of the world he lives in is, essentially, the view of the world of the most advanced humanists of his time. It rejects as intolerable the ways of behaviour which formed the accepted standards of the contemporary ruling class. The basic view of man of the feudal ruling class had been, in theory, a metaphysical one which saw man as a fallen creature seeking to win redemption through submission to and service of God, in practice a highly conservative one which saw each man as having a specific, appointed place within existing society, and wisdom as acceptance of this fact. Within this view abuses of responsibility – tyranny, cruelty, murder – were theoretically condemned but in practice sanctioned by political custom. There was no lack of all three in Elizabethan England. The revolutionary nature of Hamlet's view of the world is that he sees tyranny and murder and inhumanity not as unfortunate abuses but as the norm and essence of the court of Denmark, not as blots on a society he can accept but as integral parts of a way of life he now finds intolerable.

In other words, Hamlet can no longer base his values and actions on the accepted assumptions of the conventional sixteenth-century prince. He ceases to behave as a prince ought to behave and begins behaving as a man, a sixteenth-century man, imbued with the values and caught up in the developing and exciting potentialities of the new humanism. The words which Hamlet comes back to in his deepest moments of need and trouble are the words man and friend.

He was a man, take him for all in all   (I. 2. 187.)

is the best he can say of the best of men, his father. And when, dying, he stretches out his hand to Horatio it is with the words 'As thou art a man, Give me the cup'. He scarcely speaks, even in the two great soliloquies most relevant to his public position and behaviour ('O, what a rogue and peasant slave am I!' and 'How all occasions do inform against me') of his duties and obligations as a prince, except in so far as he happens to be the son of a murdered father who was also a king; always the question is, what should a *man* do? He scarcely refers to what, in any of the Histories, would have been uppermost in the thoughts of a prince whose father has been murdered: his own claims to the throne.

Throughout the play he is obsessed by the contradiction between his own desperate unease and his vital sense of the potentialities of man, so noble in reason, infinite in faculty, 'the beauty of the world, the paragon of animals'. (II. 2. 292ff.). It is this contradiction that provides the underlying dramatic and verbal tensions of the soliloquies and makes them so much more than exercises in melancholic introspection. It is Hamlet's optimism and vitality that give his pessimism and misery their unique power to move us. He is so unbearably horrified by a man like Claudius because he has recognized the possibility of being a different kind of man. What most disgusts him about Rosencrantz and Guildenstern is their betrayal of friendship, but when Horatio uses the conventional 'your poor servant ever' he at once replies

> Sir, my good friend. I'll change that name with you.
>
> (I. 2. 163.)

When Polonius is asked to see the players well bestowed, he says, thinking to please the Prince who has been expatiating on their virtues,

> My lord, I will use them according to their desert

and Hamlet cuts back with

> God's bodykins, man, much better. Use every man after his desert, and who shall scape whipping?
>
> (II. 2. 525.)

Obviously Hamlet is not a twentieth-century democrat; his thinking remains deeply sixteenth-century in its flavour. But

within the context in which he is operating his humanism has
very definite democratic implications – as any able actor doing
the part before a modern audience quickly discovers – especially
when it is contrasted with the social and political attitudes of
Claudius, Laertes, Polonius and Fortinbras.

At the centre of any discussion of *Hamlet* must always be what
he himself calls his 'mystery'. I think it is important to recognize
that this mystery, though it includes a psychological 'state',
cannot be adequately described in purely psychological terms.
It involves not only Hamlet but the world he lives in. If his
view of that world had no real basis, if it were at bottom a
delusion, then one would be justified in seeing Hamlet, as his
interpreters on the stage often seem to see him, as a 'case', a
neurotic. But Shakespeare is at pains to show that Hamlet's
view of his world in the opening scenes of the play is not a
delusion. It is the worldly-wise of the play, in particular the
Queen and Polonius, who are time and time again shown to be
deluded. In his very first speech, after his three sardonic puns,
Hamlet states the problem. The King and Queen are trying
to persuade him to be sensible about his father's death. Everyone dies. To die is common.

> If it be,
> Why seems it so particular with thee?

asks his mother, immediately treating Hamlet as the queer one.
But he, whose experience has made him aware of the double
edges of words as well as deeds, immediately seizes on her
least-considered assumption and throws it back:

> Seems, Madam! Nay, it is; I know not seems.

It is not his superficial behaviour, the forms, moods and shows
of grief, that can denote him truly.

> These, indeed, seem;
> For they are actions that a man might play;
> But I have that within which passes show –
> These but the trappings and the suits of woe.
>   (I. 2. 74-86.)

The contrast between 'seems' and 'is' is a key question in
the play. And it is not treated metaphysically. The contrast
between appearance and reality which Hamlet at once

emphasizes is not at all an abstract philosophical problem: it is a problem of behaviour and human values. When he cries out agonizingly

> That one may smile, and smile, and be a villain;

he adds at once

> At least I am sure it may be so in Denmark.
>
> (1. 5. 108-9.)

The phrase 'I have that within that passes show' means not only 'I cannot express what I feel' but 'What I have experienced makes further pretence at conformity impossible'. Hamlet is putting the issue quite bluntly: which way of feeling and behaving corresponds most fully to the situation? The Queen's and the court's, or his? Who is putting on a show? Is it the conventional, 'normal' behaviour of the court that 'is', so that he 'seems' the odd man out, or is it *their* behaviour that involves dissimulation and self-deception, the rejection of reality?

Hamlet, at the beginning of the play, is on the verge of suicide, seeing life as entirely weary, stale, flat and unprofitable. The delineation of this state of mind is so convincing and indeed so clinically precise that it immediately entitles Shakespeare to an honoured place in the history of psychology. But the limitation of Freudian interpretations of the play[1] is that, though they can throw light on the nature of Hamlet's experience and reactions – the effects on him of his father's murder (which he already half-suspects) and his mother's marriage – they tend to draw attention away from the real dramatic significance of that experience, that it makes him see the world differently in ways which have little to do with the experience itself. The personal crisis Hamlet has been through is the *occasion* of his new vision but does not explain it or help us to judge its ultimate validity. We are so used to separating 'personal' from 'public' issues in our thinking that is not easy for us to recognize that Hamlet's discontent is not merely private: on the contrary, it is deepened and validated by his perception that the values and attitudes which corrupt personal relationships are essentially the same values and attitudes which reside at the corrupt core of the public world.

[1] As, for instance, Ernest Jones, *Hamlet and Oedipus* (1949).

Shakespeare goes out of his way to emphasize that what Hamlet is up against is not a problem of personal relationships simply but a whole society. 'Something is rotten in the state of Denmark'. The rottenness is not psychological (though it has its psychological manifestations all right) but social. This is stressed right through the play. The King and the state are reflections of one another.[1] It is the *time* that is out of joint, not Hamlet. The difficulty of his dilemma is that he sees all too clearly for his comfort that it is only by setting the time right that he can set himself right. This and not some metaphysical mole is the 'cursed spite' behind his mystery.

That is why it is unforgiveable to act Hamlet as though he were a neurotic instead of a hero and why one must reject as hopelessly on the wrong track any interpretations of the play which offer us a 'negative' Hamlet skulking in the wings of a sanity represented by the Court of Denmark.

What Hamlet has come to see, as a result of the goings-on in his family, is, I would suggest, nothing less than what, from the point of view of an advanced sixteenth-century humanist, the Renaissance court of Denmark is actually like. The King, whom a generous-minded modern critic like Professor Wilson Knight can describe as 'a good and gentle king'[2] he sees as a drunken, lecherous murderer. The Queen is 'stew'd in corruption'. The politicians are time-servers and machiavels, without a decent principle between them, to whom the lives of the common people mean nothing except as a factor in personal struggles for power. The women are mere pawns in the intrigues of the court, generally willing pawns reducing themselves to the status of whores. Friends cannot be trusted. The values of love are those of the stud or the stock-market.

And all this does not 'seem' but 'is'. Shakespeare makes sure that we are in a position to check up on Hamlet's judgments, to see whether he is deluded or not. It is not only the authenticity of the Ghost and the conscience of the King that are tested out in the play scene but also the moral values of the

---

[1] This is brought out particularly in Act I. Sc. 4.

[2] *The Wheel of Fire* (1930). Professor Knight recognizes, of course, that this is only one side of Claudius; but he argues that Claudius is presented as being 'human', Hamlet 'inhuman'. Hamlet is no doubt in the right but his philosophy is the negation of life. I think Professor Knight grants Claudius far too much and underemphasizes Hamlet's realism.

Danish court. Shakespeare leaves much to the imagination but nothing to chance, permitting no escape into metaphysical generalities about 'the human condition'. We are spared no detail of Polonius's attitude to his son's taste of *la dolce vita* in Paris or of Claudius's complex political manoeuvres at home and abroad. The predatory Norwegian army crosses Denmark on its way to Poland before our eyes and we are left to choose between two comments, the cynical acceptance of the Norwegian captain who sees this as the way of the world (Claudius has already expressed his attitude succinctly with 'It likes us well') and Hamlet's immediate linking of the project with the rottenness in the state of Denmark:

> This is th' imposthume[1] of much wealth and peace,
> That inward breaks, and shows no cause without
> Why the man dies.   (IV. 4. 26-8.)

The pitiless humiliation of Ophelia is revealed in pitiful detail. In one of the most painful scenes in all literature the words of human dignity and rationality enter like daggers into the ears of the wretched Queen and cleave in twain her corrupt but human heart.

The state of Denmark that unfolds before our eyes is presented with extraordinary realism and at the same time against an almost continuous undercurrent of thoroughgoing criticism. The criticism comes, of course, largely from Hamlet himself, especially in the soliloquies and the graveyard scene, but in some form or other it impregnates every scene in which he appears. It is this deep, insistent strain of irreverent, daring and radical criticism that represents the essential change wrought by Shakespeare upon his sources – the Danish chronicle from which, via an earlier 'revenge' play, he took his plot.[2] In the earlier play Hamlet's problems had been purely physical – how,

---

[1] imposthume = boil or ulcer

[2] The chronicle was the *Historica Danica* of Saxo Grammaticus, a 12th-century Dane whose work was translated in the sixteenth century into French, German and possibly English. The old *Hamlet* revenge-play, which may have been by Kyd, has never come to light but we know it to have existed from contemporary references and a German play *Der Bestrafte Brudermord* based on it. Some critics, like J. M. Robertson, have tried to explain the difficulties of Shakespeare's *Hamlet* primarily in terms of the unsuitable plot Shakespeare was saddled with. There is, of course, something in this, but it does not touch the principal point – why Shakespeare made the changes he did in his original source material.

when and where to get a revenge, the implications of which were never questioned. Shakespeare's rejection of the old feudal concepts of revenge (based on the feudal lord's refusal to accept any justice other than his own) first in *Romeo and Juliet* and then in *Hamlet* shows how far he had come from the more primitive morality which Kyd, only a few years earlier, had accepted as the moral and dramatic driving-force of his plays.[1]

Not that there is anything abstract or schematic about the insistent note of social criticism that gives *Hamlet* its particular flavour. On the contrary, the solid and detailed realism of the presentation of the Danish court is such that it is not surprising that readers and audiences who take the ways and values of class-divided society for granted should have tended to take Claudius's Denmark at its face value as the human norm.[2] Yet if one examines, say, Polonius's speech of advice to the departing Laertes – a speech which generations of schoolboys have had to get by heart as one of the ultimates in human wisdom – it turns out to be (quite appropriately in the context) a compound of stuffy platitudes and unconscious ironies culminating in the words (which I remember a worthy uncle inscribing in my autograph book as a child)

> This above all – to thine own self be true,
> And it must follow, as the night the day,
> Thou canst not then be false to any man.
>
> (I. 3. 78-80.)

The glib simile should be warning enough. If it followed as inevitably as that there would be no problem, and it is not the only time in the play that Polonius uses this particular image to reinforce his quarter-truths.[3] The 'moral' of his speech simply enshrines the cheerful self-deception of the individualist who

---

[1] While there is still no central national state strong enough to enforce its law and order, revenge is the individual's only means of getting justice. The decline of the 'revenge-tragedy' and changes in the feudal concept of 'honour' run parallel to the strengthening of a centralized state apparatus in the later years of Elizabeth's reign.

[2] Alternatively, like Laurence Olivier in the film, they abstract the significance of the play by offering an Elsinore in the clouds, a *Hamlet* with plenty of Prince but no Denmark.

[3] See Polonius's sycophantic speech in Act II. Sc. 2. after the exit of the Ambassadors from Norway.

cannot face the fact that his individualism brings him to an
insoluble impasse.

Hamlet has seen through Polonius. His contempt for him is
so complete that he cannot even spare him a moment's pity when
he has run his sword through him by accident.[1] For Hamlet,
who knows that a tear is an intellectual thing, has come to see
the horror, in terms of human misery and betrayal, of what
Polonius stands for. That is why it is wrong for an actor to play
the Lord Chamberlain simply as a clown: he is a responsible
figure who, in the context within which he works, knows perfectly well what he is doing and boasts of how skilfully he can
'By indirections find directions out'.[2] Politically he is a
machiavel: morally, as Hamlet tells him to his face, a fish-
monger. Before he has 'loosed' his daughter to Hamlet (a
good stock-breeder's term) he has expatiated at length to her
on her value on the marriage-market, fearing she has taken
Hamlet's 'tenders for true pay Which are not sterling' and
describing his vows as 'brokers, Not of that dye which their
investments show.'

It is not, of course, only Polonius that Hamlet has seen
through but the morality of a whole society which sees nothing
wrong with Polonius except his garrulousness. Hamlet has loved
Ophelia, but now, in the light of his new vision of the Danish
world, he sees her as, though personally innocent, a pawn in
the corrupt intrigues of the court. This is what lies behind his
contradictory and paradoxical shifts in his scene with her
(III. 1.). 'I did love you once' and then, immediately, 'I
loved you not'. He loved her, but now he sees her – and
women in general – differently, and what he sees he cannot
love. She were better in a nunnery. That is before he realizes
that Ophelia has been 'loosed' to him. After that he is pitiless
and in the play scene treats her with the utmost brutality as a
prostitute, humiliating both himself and her.

Hamlet's problem is the appallingly difficult one of finding

---

[1] He does say, a little later, "For this same lord I do repent", but adds immediately
"but heaven hath pleased it so" (III. 4.). For the death of Rosencrantz and
Guildenstern he feels even less remorse:
    Why, man, they did make love to this employment;
    They are not near my conscience; . . . (v. 2.57.8.)

[2] Act II. Sc. 1. Professor Harry Levin in his *The Question of Hamlet* (1959) is
good on Polonius and the court's political morality.

actions commensurate with his new vision of what 'is', what the world he lives in is actually like. He is not afraid of action as such. He has been, we are told more than once, a capable and popular prince. All through the play he acts boldly and decisively whenever he needs to – in following the ghost, in organizing the play, in facing his mother with the brutal facts, in killing the old man behind the arras, in coping effectively with the situation on the ship bound for England: and about none of these actions does his conscience bother him particularly, though his enigmatic display immediately after the death of Polonius shows his awareness of the moral complexities of that act. But it is really only over the killing of the King that he hesitates and that is certainly not because he dare not do it or looks on the killing as in some absolute way 'wrong'. The 'Now might I do it pat' speech (III. 3. 73.) expresses as clearly as any of his utterances his sense of the inadequacy of *merely* killing the King, of achieving nothing but the minimal formalities of revenge.

It is not good enough to describe Hamlet as a man who cannot make up his mind. More adequately one might say that he is faced with a situation which it is almost impossible for him to resolve satisfactorily in action. For, to put it crudely, what adequate actions could a young man take who, in the year 1600, could no longer look at society from the point of view of the ruling class? He might kill the king (as was, within fifty years, to happen in Britain) recognizing him as the source not only of his personal ills but of the corrupt state, the prison that is Denmark. But what then? Especially if young Fortinbras, just back from a successful mopping-up operation in Poland, is to reign in his stead.

It seems to me essential to see Hamlet's problem historically. To do so helps resolve one of the issues that has always worried actors who tackle the part: how can Hamlet be at the same time – what almost everyone feels instinctively he must be – a hero, yet also ineffective? It is this problem that has led to the tendency to sympathize with Hamlet *because* he is ineffective. I think this tendency, though wrong, is a tribute to the significance of the situation Shakespeare has put his finger on, a situation of great general interest in the modern world and the one which makes everyone recognize the typicality as well as the uniqueness of Hamlet. Hamlet is not merely a Renaissance prince. Along with Marlowe's Faustus he is the first modern intellectual in our literature and he is, of course, far more modern as well as much more intelligent than Faustus. And his dilemma is essentially the dilemma of the modern European intellectual: his ideas and values are in a deep way at odds with his actions. Thinking and doing have got separated, basically because power is in the hands of a class whose values humane people feel they must repudiate. Power and effectiveness tend therefore to be suspected by the intelligentsia who retreat physically into a world removed from vital power-decisions and mentally into a realm of ideas and art which they value above the world of action and try to defend from the corrupting inroads of cynical expediency.

In Hamlet all these tendencies and temptations are to be found, though, being a sixteenth-century prince, the practical possibilities of an escape from the world of action are not, for him, very great. But the lost young man of the opening acts, acutely conscious of 'not belonging', contemptuous, sardonic, even a bit exhibitionist, talking a language different from those around him,[1] speaks directly to the experience of the modern intellectual who proceeds to idealize this unhappy young man into the supreme expression of the eternal human condition epitomized in being an intellectual.

Shakespeare does not permit this idealization. Hamlet, having stood on the brink of despair, comes back to the court of Denmark, refusing to continue to contemplate the possibility of a separation of thought from action. From the moment at which, recalled to actuality in the graveyard by the death of Ophelia, he leaps into the grave with a cry 'This is I, Hamlet the Dane!', he puts behind him the most desperate of his haunting doubts.[2] The atmosphere of the fifth act, with its tense, controlled, unemphatic prose statements, is one of sad, almost (but not quite) passive acceptance of the need to act.

[1] Literally as well as metaphorically, as his baiting of Osric (v.2.) shows.
[2] It is worth noticing that Shakespeare delays Hamlet's description of his adventures on the voyage to England (v. 2.) until *after* this moment, though the events occurred before and could quite plausibly have been related to Horatio in the graveyard (v. 1.) This is surely because Shakespeare wants Hamlet to emerge as a man of action only after the funeral of Ophelia, thus linking the two.

The readiness is all. Hamlet is not taken in, nor has he become cynical: in his heart there remains a kind of fighting that will not let him sleep. Although all's ill about his heart he will meet the challenges that come bravely, without cynicism and without humbug.

The fifth act does not involve, it seems to me, a dramatic resolution of Hamlet's dilemmas in any full sense of the word, but rather some kind of salvaging of human decency and a rejection of philosophic idealism. Hamlet, the prince who has tried to become a man, becomes a prince again and does what a sixteenth-century prince ought to do – killing the murderer of his father, forgiving the stupid, clean-limbed Laertes, expressing (for the first time) direct concern about his own claims to the throne but giving his dying voice to young Fortinbras, the kind of delicate and tender prince that Hamlet himself could never again have been. Horatio, it is true, lives on, pledged to tell the truth and bearing the aspirations of the humanist cause; but Horatio without Hamlet will not be, we feel, a decisive force. The end then, is, in one sense, almost total defeat for everything Hamlet has stood for. But it is an acceptance of the need to act in the real world, and that is a great human triumph.

A twentieth-century spectator may well recall, at this point, another humanist hero, born in the same year as Shakespeare, confronted with problems more like those of Hamlet than at first seems obvious, and interpreted to our own time by the only twentieth-century dramatist whose name can be mentioned in the same breath as Shakespeare's. Galileo would have known what Hamlet was talking about when he says

> Thus conscience does make cowards of us all;
> And thus the native hue of resolution
> Is sicklied o'er with the pale cast of thought,
> And enterprises of great pith and moment,
> With this regard, their currents turn awry,
> And lose the name of action. (III. 1. 83-8.)

Neither Hamlet nor Shakespeare, in the year 1600, could resolve in action, even tragically, the dilemma of a young man from whose eyes the veils which shrouded so many truths about class-divided society had been torn. Shakespeare could do nothing about Hamlet's dilemma except express it with profound realism. But the 'except' is a tremendous one, pointing to the way art works and helps.

We begin to see the link between *Lear* and *Hamlet* when we recognize that Lear, unlike Hamlet in so much, is, like him, a hero.

A hero is a figure to whom, irrespective of faults and weaknesses, we feel a deeply sympathetic commitment. We do not, in the day-dream sense of the word, identify ourselves with him; but we do in a decisive way identify our hopes and fears with his career. It is not his more purely individual characteristics – his personality or his charm – that make a man a hero, nor his actions as such – he can (like Coriolanus) be strong or even brave without being heroic. What makes the hero, or heroine, heroic, is that he bears on his shoulders, sometimes without realizing it, something of the actual aspirations of humanity in its struggles to advance its condition. Prometheus is the greatest of heroes in that he embodies human aspiration itself. Most of his successors have a more limited burden and, because human aspiration is not something absolute and abstract but real and changing, the hero cannot as a rule be fruitfully taken out of his actual historical situation. The heroes of Renaissance drama are the men and women whose lives and struggles express the actual attempts of people at that time to extend the frontiers of human possibility. We commit ourselves to the career of Romeo and Juliet, though we know their love is in the pejorative as well as the sympathetic sense 'romantic', because we recognize the need of advancing men and women to choose their own lovers rather than subscribe to marriages arranged by their parents for dynastic or family purposes. In our attitude to a hero we are always *partisan*; to be indifferent to his fate would be to be indifferent to the outcome of our own lives. But our partisanship, even when it seems intuitive, is based on an assessment of the forces and values involved in his situation which has to bear the scrutiny of *objective* analysis. This, I think, is what Brecht was getting at in his insistence that a revolutionary drama must at the same time be 'committed' (i.e. committed to the solving of actual problems, to the changing of the world) and, in his sense of the word, 'epic' (i.e. involving the conscious realization by the spectator that he is watching actions that are outside himself, so that in one sense he must remain cool and uninvolved). Scientific humanism is the basis on which we can come both to *feel* our commitment (our identity as human beings with other human beings and our impulse to take the right side in human choices) and *understand* it (submit it to the tests of argument and experience).

Lear's story begins where most stories end. The old man seems to be at the finish of his reign and time. But in fact his journey has not yet begun. The opening scene is a statement – the statement of where we and Lear start from – and Shakespeare has neither the time nor the concern to make it naturalistically convincing in its every detail. Lear is there, every inch a king, disposing of his kingdom. Essentially one has to see him as a feudal king, but in saying this I refer less to the social and economic relations of feudalism than to its characteristic ideology. The point, and also its significance, becomes clear, when we remember that within Lear's kingdom there are, inside the ruling class, two tendencies or camps, which are not simply or primarily a matter of conflicting generations or social status. On the one hand are those who accept the old order (Lear, Gloucester, Kent, Albany) which has to be seen as, broadly speaking, the feudal order; on the other hand are the new people, the individualists (Goneril, Regan, Edmund, Cornwall) who have the characteristic outlook of the bourgeoisie.

These correspondences are underlined – as Professor Danby has very suggestively pointed out[1] – by the differing ways in which the people of the two camps use the word Nature, a key-word which crops up nearly fifty times in the course of the play. To Lear and those associated with him Nature is essentially a benignant traditional order, like the 'Natural Law' of the Middle Ages, in which human and divine society are at one. In Lear's language the 'offices of nature' are always linked with such concepts as

> bond of childhood,
> Effects of courtesy, dues of gratitude.   (II. 4. 177-8.)

Goneril and Regan become, to him, 'unnatural hags', and

[1] John F. Danby, *Shakespeare's Doctrine of Nature* (1949).

Gloucester, from his side, talks of 'the King falling from the bias of Nature, there's father against child'.

Such uses of the word are in direct contrast to Edmund's forthright

> Thou, Nature, art my Goddess; to thy law
> My services are bound. Wherefore should I
> Stand in the plague of custom . . .?   (I. 2. 1-3.)

Here Nature is seen as the opposite of custom, tradition, hierarchy, established order. And Professor Danby shrewdly points out that Edmund's use of Nature is precisely the use which, within half a century, the most remarkable and most consistently materialist of the early bourgeois philosophers, Thomas Hobbes, was to give the word. Hobbes, as is well known, saw the state of Nature as a state of war. Man was to him not *naturally* a social animal but had to be made one. The author of the *Leviathan* would not, of course, have approved of Edmund's worship of the Natural man; but he would have understood it and, in a wry way, appreciated its 'realism'.

In *King Lear* Shakespeare reveals, from the very start, a society in turmoil in which (in contrast to *Hamlet*) it is the representatives of the old order who feel that everything is out of joint.

> . . . love cools, friendship falls off, brothers divide; in cities, mutinies; in countries, discord; in palaces, treason; and the bond crack'd 'twixt son and father. . . . We have seen the best of our time: machinations, hollowness, treachery, and all ruinous disorders, follow us disquietly to our graves.   (I. 2. 102-10.)

It is Gloucester speaking and the particular speech is not a deep one (Gloucester himself being a conventional and – as he comes appallingly to realize – blind old man); but it is, from his point of view and, indeed, objectively, a quite true description of the state of affairs in Lear's kingdom. And it cannot but remind us of such a poem as Donne's *First Anniversarie*, written in 1611, in which the state of the contemporary world is strikingly expressed.

> 'Tis all in peeces, all cohaerence gone;
> All just supply, and all Relation:
> Prince, Subject, Father, Sonne, are things forgot,

For every man alone thinkes he hath got
To be a Phoenix. . . .[1]

Gloucester, in the speech I have just quoted, superstitiously
links the social crack-up with the eclipse of the sun and moon.
It is all, he insists, thoroughly unnatural. And he wanders off,
scratching his head, leaving his bastard son Edmund to pour
scorn in a brilliant soliloquy on his superstitious unscientific
outlook: 'An admirable evasion of whoremaster man, to lay his
goatish disposition on the charge of a star'. Edmund has none
of his father's amiable, conservative illusions. He is intelligent,
active and ruthless. His immediate personal motive is simple –
'Legitimate Edgar, I must have your land'. No beating about
the bush. Edmund is emancipated. The ancient sanctities of
law (he is in every sense illegitimate) and order (kingship,
the property rights of fathers, primogeniture, the identity of
the man-made hierarchy with a God-made one), these mean
nothing to him. He is the new man of the incipient bourgeois
revolution, the private enterprise man, the man who thinks
he has got to be a phoenix, the individualist go-getter, the
machiavel, Marlowe's aspiring hero taken to his extreme
conclusion: man with the lid off.

Edgar of course is Edmund's opposite. The brothers are
contrasted at every point, and it is not the crude static-moral
contrast of the good and the bad, even though something of
this – the structure of the old Morality plays – remains in
Lear. Edgar is the loyal son of the feudal father, pious, resource-
ful, kind, and above all legitimate, and when in the last act
he steps forward at the third trump to defend the right, he carries
on his shoulders all the glamour and the chivalry of a
formalized feudal past.

Edgar defeats Edmund. Gloucester, though hideously
punished for his moral laxity and political blindness, is avenged,
even redeemed, gaining in his suffering, through his contact

[1] Nonesuch *Donne* (1932), 202. I have drawn attention elsewhere (*Zeitschrift
für Anglistik und Amerikanistik*, Vol. IX No. 3, Berlin 1961) to the number of
phrases in this poem which are directly reminiscent of some of the key phrases of
Hamlet, e.g.:
> Then, as mankinde so is the worlds whole frame
> Quite out of joynt, almost created lame
and Donne's vision of
> Corruptions in our braines, or in our hearts,
> Poysoning the fountaines, whence our actions spring . . .

with Poor Tom, an insight which, seeing, he had lacked. His
profoundest moment is when he gives Tom his purse:

> Here, take this purse, thou whom the heavens' plagues
> Have humbled to all strokes. That I am wretched
> Makes thee the happier. Heavens, deal so still!
> Let the superfluous and lust-dieted man
> That slaves your ordinance, that will not see
> Because he does not feel, feel your power quickly;
> So distribution should undo excess,
> And each man have enough.   (IV. I. 65-72.)

It is a wonderful moment, the full significance of which lies
in its echoing of some of Lear's own words which I will refer
to in a moment. The power Gloucester has not seen because
he has not felt it can only, in the context, be that of common
humanity, embodied in Poor Tom. Yet in the Gloucester story,
even though Tom does save Gloucester and help him onwards,
this outburst, moving as it is, is not really developed. It is not
developed because the relation between Tom and Edgar
remains ill-defined or, rather, too well-defined. Edgar simply
pretends to be Tom and then becomes Edgar again. Tom is a
richer character than Edgar because he includes Edgar,
whereas Edgar doesn't include Tom. Edgar is not really changed
by being Tom, though the play is, through the experiences of
Lear and Gloucester. But the Edgar of the last act is essentially
St George, the feudal hero, and he has to be, for he will become
king. Only in the four final lines of the play does a doubt
creep in and we are allowed to wonder whether Edgar perhaps
remembers Tom.

The Lear story is deeper, more complex and more variously
moving than the Gloucester story, for Lear, unlike Gloucester,
is a hero.

At the beginning of the play he is not a hero at all, but a
king to whom the forms of kingship and hierarchy are the
basis and reality of the world. It is Cordelia who, at this stage
of the story, is the heroic one, for it is she who speaks the words
of aspiring humanity. When she has to define her feelings about
her father she can only say

> I love your Majesty
> According to my bond; no more nor less.
>
>   (I. I. 91-2.)

The words bear close scrutiny. Obviously they are not the words of a twentieth-century daughter, royal or common. Their form is essentially feudal, as the word 'bond' emphasises. Yet it becomes clear that by 'according to my bond' Cordelia is not thinking in formal feudal terms but defining as realistically and truthfully as she can a human relationship between two people, of whom one happens to be her father and a king and therefore has special claims on her. I think Cordelia's view of love is very much akin to that expressed two hundred years later in another poem about an innocent child faced with angry authority. In Blake's 'A Little Boy Lost' the child says to the inquisitor Priest:

> "And Father, how can I love you
> Or any of my brothers more?
> I love you like the little bird
> That picks up crumbs around the door". [1]

Such heresy, the expression of a relationship honourable and *natural* in senses which neither party in the *Lear* world can accept, leads the child to the stake as it leads Cordelia to the gallows. And it is interesting that, near the end of the play, in a beautiful scene which shows us a Lear and a Cordelia who have come through to 'a better way', the old man uses the very Blakean image

> We two alone will sing like birds i' th' cage.
>
> (v. 3. 9.)

It is also interesting that Cordelia's phrase 'no more nor less' is echoed by Lear when, the great rage dead, he comes to describe himself in the terms of his new understanding:

> I am a very foolish fond old man,
> Fourscore and upward, not an hour more nor less;
> And, to deal plainly,
> I fear I am not in my perfect mind.   (iv. 7. 60-4.)

He is now, like Cordelia, dealing plainly, describing the situation realistically. He has reached the view of Nature implicit in her first statement. I can find no better way of describing it than as the humanist view of nature. And in the course of

[1] Nonesuch *Blake* (1939), 77.

discovering it Lear has become a hero. His story, put in its simplest terms, is the story of his progress from being a king to being a man, neither more nor less. It is a story so fearful and yet so wonderful that all human society is shaken by the terrible beauty of it and at its supreme moments man and the universe are seen in relationships which it is scarcely possible for words other than Shakespeare's own to describe.

When I say that *Lear* is the story of how a king becomes a man I do not mean at all that it is an allegory or that we should use a word like 'symbolic' to describe it. For Shakespeare does not work in abstractions. He is a supremely realistic writer who presents us all the time with actual situations, actual relationships, and what general conclusions he offers are always based on particular observations and insights. He is not, of course, a *naturalistic* dramatist, attempting a 'slice of life' kind of realism, and he uses every resource of his teeming imagination to create means of penetrating, through words and fantasy, to the inner processes of the situations and people he presents. The storm in *Lear* 'works' artistically on a number of levels: the elemental storm, the social storm which shakes the divided kingdom, the inner storm that drives Lear mad, all are interconnected and reinforce one another to achieve what is, I suppose, the most extraordinary and harrowing representation of crisis in the whole of art. But every device of art is used to produce, not some effect above or beyond reality, but the deepest, most complex exploration of the actual nature of reality, its texture and its implications, its movement and its interconnectedness.

In the first three acts of *Lear* we have almost unrelieved horror and pessimism, broken only by isolated gleams of human decency and hope. It is one of Shakespeare's triumphs that, without compromising for a moment on their hideousness, he does not make the opponents of Lear crude villains. Edmund, with his gusto and energy, is in many respects a more vital creature than the rather colourless Edgar. Goneril and Regan have a terrible common-sense effectiveness, almost a normality, about them. Their very baiting of their father by the reduction of the numbers of his retainers is not mere insolence: they have a strong case and argue at least partly in the terms of a modern-

sounding contempt for the hierarchical principle.[1] They are
at once shrewd, able, shallow and morally impervious, and
they are rivals because they are alike.

It is the new people with their heartless rationalization –
'the younger rises, when the old doth fall' – who bring down
Lear. And his friends, the ineffectual unseeing Gloucester and
the loyal but too simple Kent, are unable to save him from the
new ruthlessness. Kent's role in the play is interesting because
he is of all the 'feudal' characters the most courageous and least
corrupt. And he is able to shield Lear to some extent. But his
ultimate failure to cope with the situation – he is unable to
hold Lear within the bounds of sanity and is in fact of far less
use to him than either the Fool or Poor Tom – is echoed by his
own prognostications of his death in the final scene. The ultimate
inadequacy of Kent despite his decent, old world virtues, is
one of the expressions in the play of the impossibility of a return
to the feudal past.

What we have, then, in the first three acts of *Lear* is a world
in which the old order is decadent and the new people un-
principled and both, as the treatment of Cordelia shows,
inhuman. Horror dominates. The terrible curse on Goneril –
made by Lear in the name of Nature –

> Into her womb convey sterility;
> Dry up in her the organs of increase;
> And from her derogate body never spring
> A babe to honour her! If she must teem,
> Create her child of spleen, that it may live
> And be a thwart disnatur'd torment to her
>
> (1. 4. 278-83.)

– this curse, whose imagery overflows into the verse of scene
after scene, is a measure of the depth of the horror; but not its
ultimate expression. For the equal horror is Lear's own im-
potence. When Goneril rejects him he still can threaten
vainly to 'resume the shape' of the past – to be king again.
When Regan's cruelty is added to her sister's, and personal
ingratitude is, so to speak, turned into a system, he is literally

---

[1] When Goneril and Lear argue about the question of Lear's retainers they use
the word 'need' in different senses. Goneril uses the word to mean something
like 'efficiency'; Lear's use of the word is very different.

unable to express his emotion, though he still mutters of
revenge.

> No, you unnatural hags,
> I will have such revenges on you both
> That all the world shall – I will do such things
> What they are yet I know not; but they shall be
> The terrors of the earth.   (II. 4. 277-81.)

Lear has, literally, no resources of action, language or even
emotion to be able to cope, within the bounds of the consciousness he has so far achieved, with the situation which
faces him. From here to madness is but a short step. And the
very word madness needs our thought. It can no more be
taken for granted in *Lear* than in *Hamlet*. The more one examines
the play the more one comes to feel that Lear's madness is not
so much a breakdown as a breakthrough. It is necessary.

In the storm scene comes the first hint of resolution, the
first turning-point of the play, the first breakthrough of
humanity, coincident with the words 'My wits begin to turn'.
For the phrase is followed by some words to the Fool:

> Come on, my boy. How dost, my boy? Art cold?
> I am cold myself. Where is this straw, my fellow?
> The art of our necessities is strange
> That can make vile things precious. Come, your hovel.
> Poor fool and knave, I have one part in my heart
> That's sorry yet for thee.   (III. 2. 68-73.)

The words represent a change in direction: away from self-
pity, pride, revenge and kingliness, towards fellow-feeling and
co-operation, the minimum qualities of humanity. I do not
want to present Shakespeare as some kind of 'unconscious'
precursor of Engels; but I think it is very interesting that at
this crisis of the play, when Lear is first beginning to feel his
way towards a new freedom, Shakespeare should use the
word 'necessities' and use it in a context which forbids any but a
materialist significance.

It is through his madness – his incapacity to deal with
reality any longer within the framework of his accepted standards of sanity – that Lear comes to a new outlook on life. The
moving prayer just before his meeting with Tom is now fairly
generally recognized as a crux of the whole play.

Poor naked wretches, wheresoe'er you are,
That bide the pelting of this pitiless storm,
How shall your houseless heads and unfed sides,
Your loop'd and window'd raggedness, defend you
From seasons such as these? O, I have ta'en
Too little care of this! Take physic, pomp;
Expose thyself to feel what wretches feel,
That thou mayst shake the superflux to them,
And show the heavens more just.   (III. 4. 28-36.)

This speech, echoed so soon by Gloucester's words to Tom, in which precisely the same ideas are expressed and the word 'superflux' returned to, is absolutely central to the structure and meaning of the play. Lear's incapacity to deal with the inhumanity of the new people is what drives him into a solidarity, and, later, an identification, with the poor. For in his powerlessness he is forced to recognize the pervasive helplessness of the poor in the face of the power of the rich, those who have property. Thus his direct personal contact with ruling-class inhumanity leads him to question the validity of property itself and the authority and exemption from elementary human moral values it confers. In this, Lear's development is not at all unlike that of later seventeenth-century radicals like Winstanley.

There is method, Polonius discovers, in Hamlet's madness; and Edgar, listening to Lear's mad wanderings, remarks to the audience 'Reason in madness!' The speech he is referring to contains some of the deepest and acutest social criticism in all Shakespeare, or indeed anywhere.

> . . . A man may see how this world goes with no eyes. Look with thine ears. See how yond justice rails upon yond simple thief. Hark, in thine ear: change places and, handy-dandy, which is the justice, which is the thief? Thou hast seen a farmer's dog bark at a beggar?
> *Gloucester.* Ay, sir.
> *Lear.*   And the creature run from the cur? There thou mightst behold the great image of authority: a dog's obey'd in office.
> Thou rascal beadle, hold thy bloody hand.
> Why dost thou lash that whore? Strip thy own back;
> Thou hotly lusts to use her in that kind

For which thou whip'st her. The usurer hangs the
[cozener.
Through tatter'd clothes small vices do appear;
Robes and furr'd gowns hide all. Plate sin with gold,
And the strong lance of justice hurtless breaks;
Arm it in rags, a pigmy's straw does pierce it.
None does offend, none, – I say none; I'll able 'em.
Take that of me, my friend, who have the power
To seal th' accuser's lips. Get thee glass eyes,
And, like a scurvy politician, seem
To see the things thou dost not. Now, now, now, now!
Pull off my boots. Harder, harder – so.

(IV. 6. 150-73.)

When that speech has the currency of Polonius's advice to
Laertes it will be seem less strange to British readers to refer to
the democratic content of the bourgeois-democratic revolution
and to link Shakespeare's greatness with his humanism.

If we describe Lear's, or Gloucester's, experiences as
'spiritual', that is to say, involving a change not just in fortune
and circumstance but in values and quality of being, it is
essential to recognize that Shakespeare links this change at
every step with actual actions and social attitudes. The social
emphases are not more or less casual sidethoughts but are
absolutely basic to the whole conception of the play. You
cannot understand it without them. The new humanity which
Lear achieves is not simply a self-knowledge acquired by
introspection or any kind of mystical or religious experience;
it is an outlook gained through experience and action, through
the necessity that has been forced upon him of exposing himself to feel that wretches feel, of facing reality in all its horror
and splendour, of judging men and women by their simplest,
most essential actions, and of learning who his friends are. The
experience results in a turning upside-down, handy-dandy, of
accepted social assumptions. The pulling off of the boots at the
end of the speech I have just quoted is, everyone realises,
significant. Already in the hovel in the storm Lear has insistently
taken off his clothes, feeling them an impediment, a mark of
rank, preventing complete identification with Poor Tom. 'Off,
off you lendings' he cries. The phrase is almost a summary of
the play. Lear, the king, reduced by the new people of the
bourgeois world to the depth of human humiliation, falls only

to rise, and becomes a man. And the people who help him to
achieve humanity are by no means the wise or great or powerful, but a Fool and a beggar who has gone mad.

The turning point of the play is Lear's losing of his wits to
find them; and it is followed by a decisive moment of action –
the first instant in the play when the evil characters are checked
in their deeds. Up to the moment of the blinding of Gloucester
the decent people have seemed impotent. And then of a sudden
a blow is struck – and again it is not by the great or the wise,
but by the servant who, his humanity outraged by the torturing
of Gloucester, kills the Duke of Cornwall. Regan's horrified
comment is more eloquent than a long speech:

> A peasant stand up thus? (III. 7. 79.)

And from now on a fight is put up.

I have said nothing so far of the role of the Fool. We should
not sentimentalize him or exaggerate his importance. He is
less significant to Lear's progress than Poor Tom. But his
comments – the shrewd and cynical paradoxes, the irreverent
thrusts at Lear's dignity – form a kind of choric counterpoint
to the main themes of the play which not only adds a depth
and complexity but helps define the essential 'popular' element
within this play of kings and nobles. It is not easy to get a
consistent pattern from the Fool's remarks. His Blakean
prophecy (at the end of Act III scene 2) is puzzling and
apparently inconsistent, yet it expresses with an exciting vivid-
ness the historical tensions and contradictions which lie
behind the whole play. Perhaps it is the cynical realism of his
comments which is most striking. He has been ground down too
long to have much hope of salvation, so that his resilience is
spasmodic, his pessimism deep-rooted. He reminds one a little
of the old soldier whose hatred and contempt of the army has
been fed on a lifetime of chastening experience and who
cannot – for all his irreverence – shake off the habits of servi-
tude he despises. One might describe him as the opposite of
the eternal butler, an eternal batman, a sort of Elizabethan
Schweik.[1]

[1] The most effective Fool I have seen on the stage was that of a German actor,
Edwin Marian, in a production at the Deutsches Theater in East Berlin in
1957. This Fool was a plain, down-to-earth, somewhat Brechtian peasant,
neither fey nor eccentric, like most British interpretations.

When Lear awakes from his madness the Fool is no longer with him, but Cordelia. The realm of Albion has indeed come to great confusion and Lear has come through to a new state of mind. He has not merely been purged of pride and learned a proper humility, as Christian critics point out, he has changed his whole attitude to people and society and there is, most significantly, no desire in him to get his throne back. On the contrary, the court is mentioned only with contempt, not at all unlike the contempt of Hamlet: Lear and Cordelia will

> hear poor rogues
> Talk of court news; and we'll talk with them too –
> Who loses and who wins; who's in, who's out –
> And take upon's the mystery of things
> As if we were God's spies; and we'll wear out
> In a wall'd prison packs and sects of great ones
> That ebb and flow by th' moon.   (v. 3. 13-19.)

The whole emergent world of bourgeois politics is somehow evoked and placed in that single sentence and a modern reader can scarcely fail to hear in *Lear* constant pre-echoes of Swift and Blake.

Towards the end of the play Cordelia, with whom Lear now unequivocally associates himself, is seen explicitly as the alternative to the old order (which by her honesty she has exposed) and to the new people who hate and fear her.

> Patience and sorrow strove
> Who should express her goodliest. You have seen
> Sunshine and rain at once: her smiles and tears
> Were like a better way.   (IV. 3. 16-19.)

'Sunshine and rain at once', the image of the rainbow, the pledge of future harmony arising out of contradiction, is associated with Cordelia. She seems to express in her very person the 'better way' to which Lear has come through. If there is a kind of utopian promise here – the sort of thing Shakespeare comes back to in his final plays – the suggestion is achieved without a removal of the play into the realms of abstraction or metaphysics. For it is because of what she does and thinks, not what in some safe way she 'is', that the new people cannot let Cordelia live. And Lear, too, in this ineffably beautiful yet most terrible play, must die. He cannot be set back – an even older but a wiser man – upon his throne. Shakespeare has revealed a struggle more desperate than such a resolution could encompass.

It is worth comparing the end of *Lear* with that of *Hamlet*. In both plays the protagonist has been defeated, not by his enemies or by his weaknesses but by history. Both plays end with the implied accession of a new king, a promise of continuity as opposed to death; but in neither case does the new king in any serious sense fill the bill. The point about Fortinbras, as we have seen, is that he is incapable of understanding what Hamlet has understood; so that there is, despite the survival of Horatio, a distinctly hollow sound in the closing commonplaces of the play. The most that can be said for Edgar is that he is something to be going on with. But he is, nevertheless, a considerable advance on Fortinbras. The final words of *King Lear* are moving and curiously profound.

> The weight of this sad time we must obey;
> Speak what we feel, not what we ought to say.
> The oldest hath borne most; we that are young
> Shall never see so much nor live so long.

That the experience and meaning of the play cannot be confined within the limits of seventeenth-century social thinking is implicit in these lines. Conventional assessment (what we *ought* to say) is quite inadequate. What raises Edgar so far above Fortinbras is that he recognizes his own inferiority; he has not seen what Lear has seen, but he has seen and felt enough to recognize the quality of Lear's experience, to know that he does not know. Perhaps, after all, he has not quite forgotten Poor Tom.

THE REALISM OF *ANTONY AND CLEOPATRA*

Dipak Nandy

Antony and Cleopatra is an astonishing play: *feliciter audax* was Coleridge's description of its style. The quality of the writing is indeed audacious, and when one finds lines like:

> I am so lated in the world that I
> Have lost my way for ever

one realizes where John Webster got *his* explosive style from. Along with the richness of its poetry, and the seeming inexhaustibility of its detail, there is about this play a certain air of finality. Composed about 1607-8, it gathers together a number of different strands in Shakespeare's plays up to that point. It continues the discussion – and critique – of 'romantic love' of *Romeo and Juliet* and *Troilus and Cressida*. It deals with the tension between the demands of public and private life explored in the History plays, in *Hamlet* and *Othello*. It is, of course, a Roman play. And it is also Shakespeare's final settling of scores with the Faithless Woman, the 'dark lady' of the Sonnets.

The title of the play tells us quite adequately what it is about. The theme of the play is not Antony's tragedy, nor the political conflict between Antony and Octavius Caesar.[1] These are parts of the setting for the theme, which is Antony *and* Cleopatra, the relationship between them. The play explores the nature and value of that relationship.

The construction of the play indicates the focus of its interest. It is episodic. The struggle between Antony and Octavius is related without dramatic suspense; the struggle *within* Antony between the conflicting claims of love and imperial duties

---

[1] Cf. Lord David Cecil's view that 'a large part of the play is concerned with [the rivalry between Octavius and Antony], and not with the love-story at all . . . its interest is largely political.' *Antony and Cleopatra* (Glasgow University Publications, LVIII, 1944), 13.

might not exist at all, so total is the lack of any psychological tension. Indeed, one is never in any uncertainty as to the outcome of either struggle. Both are predetermined, and this predetermination constitutes our *datum* for considering something else. The scene shifts from Alexandria to Rome and back in a quick scanning movement, probing all the while the two worlds within the context of whose collision the relationship between Antony and Cleopatra is set and scrutinized. The play attempts to define the terms of the choice (so that we may judge of its validity or otherwise) : what is it that Antony rejects, and what is it that he chooses? Or, to put it another way: what are these worlds, the Roman and the Egyptian, which struggle for Antony? For the clash at the heart of this play is more than a clash of incompatible personalities: it is a clash of values, of different ways of looking at the world. And there is, as Professor Danby rightly suggests, a perilously even balance held throughout the play between the two sides.[1] Out of the collision of contraries there emerges an understanding of the nature of a human relationship.

The contrast is between the condition of Egypt, whose heart and core is Cleopatra, and the condition of Rome, embodied and personified in Octavius Caesar. These are the twin poles between which the action works out. Antony's career is a discovery, I want to suggest, of his true bearings in relation to these poles. Enobarbus's career is a *confirmation* of this discovery. Cleopatra's career, especially the events of the last act, is a revelation of the full implications of her relationship with Antony.

The first scene sounds the major theme whose working out constitutes the play, and it does this by presenting simultaneously two different and mutually exclusive interpretations of a single situation: Antony's relationship with Cleopatra. The contemptuous opening remarks of Philo to Demetrius give us one side of it; the first words of Antony and Cleopatra give us the other. The effect is startling, and indeed this is perhaps the finest example in Shakespeare of his amazing faculty of what Blake

---

[1] See 'The Shakespearean Dialectic: An Aspect of *Antony and Cleopatra*' in *Scrutiny* Vol. XVI (1949) 196-213, reprinted in *Poets on Fortune's Hill* (1952), the best analysis of this play.

called 'double vision',[1] a faculty which he shares only with the
great metaphysicals, Donne and Marvell, and Blake. I ought to
call it, for precision, Shakespeare's *dialectical vision*, since the
accommodation of two incompatible views results, not in a
paralysis of judgment, but in a sharpening of our awareness of
the situation. Thus, 'lust' is totally inadequate as an evaluative
category in this context; on the other hand, there is no idealization of the lovers, no blindness to the political implications of
their attachment. Again, Rome is corrupt, but Antony's rejection of his Roman responsibilities and obligations is not therefore held up for easy admiration. Here, in the very first scene,
we have the clash of two ways of looking at the world. One
way of seeing (which corresponds to the romantic school of
Antony and Cleopatra criticism) accepts the validity of the
generous, even extravagant, magnanimity of 'There's beggary
in the love that can be reckon'd', of the limitless claims involved in 'Let Rome in Tiber melt, and the wide arch / Of
the rang'd empire fall'. The other is the view of 'realism', of
hard-headed common sense.

What would the whole story look like seen in terms solely of
this kind of 'realism'? Here is one account of it:

> '. . . a spendthrift, smitten with a courtesan whom he
> lavishly supports, decides, in order to repair his fortune,
> to marry a woman whom he does not love; hardly has
> the ceremony been concluded before he returns to his
> mistress, to consume with her the dower of his wife.
> The deserted wife seeks the protection of her brother,
> who, in a rage, challenges the husband. A duel follows:
> the spendthrift falls, and the courtesan in despair
> commits suicide.'[2]

Such is J. F.-V. Hugo's reduction of the action 'to its lowest
terms', and it is interesting to note that in transcribing the
play for a 'realistic' setting ('the narrow circle of bourgeois
life') it becomes impossible to describe Cleopatra's end in
terms other than 'despair', or some such, or even to talk about
the extraordinary mixture of sorrow and exaltation, of aware-

---

[1]   For double the vision my Eyes do see,
       And a double vision is always with me.
  Letter to Thomas Butts, 22 November 1802, *Nonesuch Blake* (1956), 860.
[2] François-Victor Hugo, Introduction to *Oeuvres Complètes de Shakespeare* (1868),
  Vol. VII, 9, quoted in *Variorum Antony and Cleopatra*, 496-7.

ness with self-deception, that characterises her end. It is the achievement of Shakespeare's play that it provides us at its close with terms more adequate to comprehend its conclusion.

It is necessary to define more closely at this point the terms of the conflict – what the Roman and Egyptian poles stand for, what qualities they exemplify, remembering though that Shakespeare's presentation is nothing like so abstract as these words might suggest. To start with simplifications: the milieu of Rome is the public world, the world of politics and action, where concepts like 'honour' and 'glory' are invoked, often to cover motives and methods which are considerably less exalted; Egypt, in the person of Cleopatra, and her court, is the private world of love and (by Roman standards, as Philo, Caesar and Pompey make clear) of irresponsibility. Thus, Philo and Deme-trius, although they are listed as 'friends to Antony', speak in fact from the point of view of Rome. When Cleopatra comments on Antony's decision to return to Rome, we are presented directly with Egypt's view of Rome:

> Good now, play one scene
> Of excellent *dissembling*, and let it look
> Like perfect *honour*.   (I. 3. 78-80; my italics.)

Cleopatra's first jibe at Antony is that he has been pushed out in the manoeuvring for power in the world of imperial power politics:

> . . . who knows
> If the scarce-bearded Caesar have not sent
> His pow'rful mandate to you: 'Do this, or this;
> Take in that kingdom and enfranchise that;
> Perform't, or else we damn thee.'   (I. I. 20-24.)

In Octavius Caesar the essence of this whole way of life is captured and expressed in individual terms. He is 'typical' of Rome. There is about him the same cold inhumanity and mechanical efficiency that, in a powerful image in *Coriolanus*, Shakespeare attributes to:

> . . . the Roman State, whose course will on
> The way it takes, cracking ten thousand curbs
> Of more strong link asunder than can ever
> Appear in your impediment.   (I. I. 67-70.)

He is the epitome of the Renaissance 'politique': note his patrician indignation at Antony who conducts high affairs of state 'I' the market-place . . .I' the common show-place' (III. 6.), who 'reel(s) the streets at noon, and stand(s) the buffet / With knaves that smell of sweat' (I. 4.). So completely is he identified with his public function that the consideration of political advantage enters even into his personal relationships. He chides Octavia when she returns from Athens for not sending advance notice of her arrival, so that a suitable public display could have been arranged of their meeting, no doubt to impress 'the common body', the people. 'You have prevented', he complains,

> The ostentation of our love, which left unshown,
> Is often left unlov'd.   (III. 6. 51-3.)[1]

Personal ties are important in his world only to the extent that they contribute to political advantage. Like the Lear of Act I scene 1, what he seeks is not the relationship, but its appropriate and ritual display.

The picture of Rome here is substantially that of *Coriolanus* and, even more strikingly, of Hamlet's Scandinavia: it is a basically corrupt society with a small entrenched ruling class, in which various groups jockey for position in a deadly struggle for survival, based on a large, ignorant and unstable populace. It is a society caught in a vicious circle of peace and prosperity, which breeds factions, leading to periodic wars, civil or imperialist, which in turn lead to a strong government and a corrupting peace, and so endlessly.[2] There is neither progress nor development.

---

[1] The Arden editor, in a charitable mood, construes this to mean: 'love which is unshown is often *thought to be* unfelt' (New Arden *Antony and Cleopatra*, ed. M. R. Ridley, 116; my italics), taking *left unlov'd* as 'written off as unfelt'. The clear parallelism between 'left unshown' and 'left unlov'd' indicates, however, that the latter phrase is to be taken in the same straightforward sense as the former. Caesar means exactly what he says: 'love which is not displayed might as well not exist, be felt'.

[2] Cf. the contemporary analysis of Thomas Fenne: 'Warre bringeth ruine, ruine bringeth povertie, povertie procureth peace, and peace in time increaseth riches, riches causeth statelinesse, statelinesse increaseth envie, envie in the end procureth deadly mallice, mortall mallice proclaimeth open warre and battaile: and from warre againe as before is rehearsed.' *Fennes Frutes* (1590) f. 53ᵛ.

Our Italy
Shines o'er with civil swords: Sextus Pompeius
Makes his approaches to the port of Rome;
Equality of two domestic powers
Breed scrupulous faction; the hated, grown to strength,
Are newly grown to love. The condemn'd Pompey,
Rich in his father's honour, creeps apace
Into the hearts of such as have not thriv'd
Upon the present state, whose numbers threaten;
And quietness, grown sick of rest, would purge
By any desperate change.   (I. 3. 44-54.)

Shakespeare is appealing here to a commonplace of Renaissance
political theory. A long period of rest and peace fills the body
politic, like the human body, with an excess of humours, with
bad, infected blood. If this is not periodically purged, the
body is racked with fevers. The purging, blood-letting, corresponds to foreign wars; the fever to a civil war. Shakespeare
uses the idea here to 'place' the Roman world.[1]

Rome is fever-wracked, corrupt, and in this corrupt society
the 'outs' join forces against the 'ins'. But allegiances are
shifting and unreliable, and the populace, the pawn in these
elaborate moves and counter-moves, is at best apathetic, at
worst fickle:

It hath been taught us from the primal state
That he which is was wish'd until he were;
And the ebb'd man, ne'er lov'd till ne'er worth love,
Comes dear'd by being lack'd. This common body,
Like to a vagabond flag upon the stream,
Goes to, and back, lackeying the varying tide,
To rot itself with motion.   (I. 4. 41-7.)

---

[1] The two principal effects of a protracted peace were overpopulation and the
corruption of manners through excessive wealth. Periodic foreign wars are
advocated throughout the later decades of Elizabeth's reign to reduce the first
and cure the second, in opposition to Elizabeth's cautious foreign policy. The
whole question is discussed in terms of the theory of humours, one of the clearest
applications being in Giovanni Botero: 'Just as a doctor can relieve the dis-
ordered humours of the human body by diverting them elsewhere with cauteriz-
ing and blood-letting, so a wise prince can placate an enraged people by
leading it to war against an external enemy, or by some other means which
will turn it from its original evil intention.' *Della Ragion di Stato* (1589) Bk. V.
Chap. 9 (Eng. tr., 1956, 112). See G. R. Waggoner 'An Elizabethan Attitude
toward Peace and War', *Philological Quarterly* Vol. 34, 1954, 20-33.

The image is extraordinarily potent, and it is not fanciful, I think, to see it as representative in some way of Rome itself, or even of the political condition. (Though one should be careful of the word 'politics' here, for the 'politics' that Shakespeare is concerned with is what we should perhaps call court politics or diplomatic intrigue, a purely ruling-class affair; anything in which the lower classes participated came dangerously near to rebellion and hence was liable to become cosmic in scope.) What is being referred to here is essentially non-progressive, static and decadent, and nothing could be more striking than the contrast between this image of Rome, and the set of images – of another type of cyclical motion, dynamic and health-giving – that are used to characterize the Antony–Cleopatra relationship and Egypt.

Rome is the world of utilitarian realism ruled by the principle of political self-interest, where values are arrived at by calculation (even the 'factions' are 'scrupulous'), as opposed to the Egyptian world where 'there's beggary in the love that can be *reckon'd*.' Now it is not enough, if one wants to make clear that these qualities characterize a whole *society* and not merely an individual, to show only Caesar as their exemplar. It is necessary to have someone sharing the same values and assumptions about ends as Caesar, but *opposed* to him, someone who is a rebel but who nevertheless *abides by the 'rules of the game'*. This is the function of the scene between Pompey and Menas in Act II scene 7, and the thirty lines or so between them is enough for Shakespeare to show unambiguously how the Roman world ticks. It is governed by elaborate rules and conventions which conceal appalling depths of moral cynicism. The moral of the exchange between Pompey and Menas, who offers to cut the throats of the three pillars of the world, is that you can accept a piece of treacherous assassination so long as you are not told in advance of it; if you are, you must invoke 'honour' and, alas, repudiate it. It is in scenes like this, and the Reynaldo scene (II. I.) in *Hamlet*, even more than in explicit speeches such as Falstaff's on 'honour', that the emptiness and worse of conventional moral clichés are ripped open to our view. That brief scene in Act II, like the Reynaldo scene, exists for the purpose, one might say, of *moral definition*. It defines for us, unmistakably, what Rome is like. It enables us to decide how much weight to put on the ideals of 'duty' and 'honour' which that world constantly invokes.

Rome, then, is the political world, the sphere of public administration and government with its lofty ideals and its barely concealed duplicity and corruption.

The court of Egypt is unique, and that because its presiding genius is *sui generis*, a very nonpareil. She is meant to be so – at least to Antony. 'Cunning past man's thought', she is something new to the man of action, and Cleopatra's method of keeping Antony's affection is to remain this way, perpetually new, calculatingly wayward and unpredictable.

It is easy to be romantic about Cleopatra and hedge at this point. But Shakespeare's Cleopatra (to the perplexity of her romantic admirers) is in fact just as 'politic' in the Machiavellian sense in the pursuit of her personal ends as Caesar is in the pursuit of his political objectives. This is, indeed, the profound realism of Shakespeare's portrait, for in this way he manages to enrich the contrast between the two worlds, which might otherwise appear too schematic, with the entirely realistic perception that ideologically opposed groups may nevertheless employ identical means, that there may be a plausible similarity between the tactical methods by which such conflicting groups seek to encompass their strategically opposed and mutually exclusive objectives. Cleopatra's unpredictability and waywardness may reasonably be construed as dissimulation of exactly the kind that she attributes to Rome, and if Shakespeare has been at pains to stress the hypocrisy and corruption involved in the public sphere, he can hardly be said to have understressed the capacity for deception that Cleopatra possesses. This is the function of the Seleucus scene (v. 2.), so clear and unequivocal in Plutarch ('Cleopatra finely deceiveth Octavius Caesar, as though she desired to live'), and so deeply and, one must assume, *intentionally* ambiguous in import in Shakespeare's play.[1]

[1] Prof. Kenneth Muir's argument (*Shakespeare's Sources*, 1957, Vol. I, 205) that because Cleopatra's motives are explicit and unambiguous in Plutarch we are not meant to be puzzled by Shakespeare's version seems to me mistaken. Shakespeare does manage to invest the scene with an extraordinary ambiguity, and this is not by any means inevitable. Shakespeare, after all, is quite capable of following his source when he wants to, and it would have been perfectly easy for him to resolve the real uncertainty of our response, had he wanted to do so.

Antony is, in a sense, deceived to the very end, and the occasion of his death is Cleopatra's message that she has taken her own life. But the important thing about Antony's death is not the immediate cause or occasion, but the realization to which he attains by the time we have reached this point in the play. Antony was first seen hesitating between the rival claims of Cleopatra and his Roman responsibilities. 'These strong Egyptian fetters I must break / Or lose myself in dotage', he says in Act I. 2, echoing Philo's words, and revealing thereby how far he has succumbed, for the moment at least, to the Roman point of view. But the overmastering force of his attachment to Cleopatra asserts itself, and Cleopatra wins in the end.

Her influence over Antony is presented by the 'realists' in the play as a triumph of irrational desire over reason and judgment. For Caesar, he is 'to be chid':

> As we rate boys who, being mature in knowledge,
> Pawn their experience to their present pleasure,
> And so rebel to judgment.   (I. 4. 30-3.)

And, after the defeat, Enobarbus says bitterly to Cleopatra:

> Antony only [is at fault], that would make his will
> Lord of his reason. What though you fled
> From that great face of war, . . .
>   why should he follow?
> The itch of his affection should not then
> Have nick'd his captainship, at such a point.
>   (III. 13. 3-8.)

It is certainly inviting to see the matter in these terms, but, again, Antony's throwing away 'the greater cantle of the world' *cannot* be described in terms of reasoned and calculated decisions, for it is in precisely this respect that the Roman world is contrasted with the Egyptian: the habit of calculation of the Romans is set against the impulsive spontaneity of the Egyptians. Antony's attachment to Cleopatra is seen in terms of the imagery of food and taste: 'He will to his Egyptian dish again', says Enobarbus, commenting on Antony's marriage of pure political expediency with Octavia, 'Antony will use his affection where it is; he married but his occasion here' (II. 6. 123 ff), the suggestion being that his passion for Cleopatra has the same compulsive force as the hungry appetite. However, more needs to be said on the matter.

To understand the nature of Antony's attachment is to understand Antony, and vice versa. Antony belongs to the old guard of Roman leaders, and he faces Octavius, the 'new man', without any defences. A gulf of mutual incomprehension separates them. 'Honour', the key concept of the Roman world, is invoked by both Caesar and Antony, but the content of the concept is different for each of them. Antony's 'honour' is primarily the soldier's honour, a reputation for military prowess, and it is in keeping with his martial qualities and his sensitivity to his reputation (as well as his Essex-like impetuosity), that he should choose to fight Caesar on sea rather than on land 'Because he dares us to't', that he should challenge Caesar to a personal duel to settle the issue. Antony cannot understand why Caesar refuses to accept the challenge (an evident sign of lack of 'honour'), but in Caesar's world there is no special advantage accruing from this sort of display:

> . . . Let the old ruffian know,
> I have many other ways to die, meantime
> Laugh at his challenge. (IV. I. 4-6.)

Caesar's world is a utilitarian and impersonal one, Antony's a personal and (to borrow a term) 'face-to-face' world – one which emerges in its full human appeal in the moving scene (IV. 2.) of Antony's 'last supper' with his servants and followers:

> Well, my good fellows, wait on me tonight.
> Scant not my cups, and make as much of me
> As when mine empire was your fellow too,
> And suffer'd my command.

> . . . Mine honest friends,
> I turn you not away; but, like a master
> Married to your good service, stay till death.
> (IV. 2. 20-3, 29-31.)

Antony's relationship with his friends has a misleadingly 'democratic' character. They belong, however, to the 'face-to-face' society of the feudal order, where relationships are those of personal dependence, both intimate and hierarchical

('master' and 'servant').[1] Antony treats his friends, not as
means to his ends, but as *people*, in a spirit of rough *camaraderie*.
His relationships are not politic (like Caesar's with, for example,
Lepidus), but constant ('till death'). The quality of Antony's
relationships is presented in Cleopatra's daring 'metaphysical'
image:

> For his bounty,
> There was no winter in't; an autumn 'twas
> That grew the more by reaping.   (v. 2. 86-8.)

It expresses the nature of a genuine human relationship, self-
enriching in its generosity, as contrasted with false, predatory
ones (as in Blake's *The Mental Traveller*, where 'she grows young
as he grows old'). It is this aspect of Antony that Shakespeare
stresses, and it enables him to add a dimension to his presentation of the central relationship. It helps us to understand the
nature of the affinity Antony feels with Cleopatra, and his
complementary alienation from Rome.

For the moral of Antony's career is not the simple one of
the passions overpowering reason, or lust judgment (just as, on
the other side, it is not that of 'the world well lost'). There is a
quality of depth in the Antony of his last scene, Act IV. 14, and
especially in the profound speech beginning 'Sometimes we see
a cloud that's dragonish . . .', whose point is to convey to us
the indeterminacy, even the nothingness, of Antony without
Cleopatra, to express the quest of Antony for his identity in a
world in which their relationship no longer holds:

> . . . Here I am Antony;
> Yet cannot hold this visible shape, my knave.
> I made these wars for Egypt; and the Queen –
> Whose heart I thought I had, . . . she, Eros, has
> Pack'd cards with Caesar, and false-play'd my glory
> Unto an enemy's triumph,   (IV. 14. 13-20.)

there is a depth here, and in lines like 'Unarm Eros, the long
day's task is done / And we are for the dark', that marks a
growth in maturity from the opening scenes. The rhetoric of
'Let Rome in Tiber melt . . .' has changed into the spare,
intensely felt movement of:

---

[1] Compare the similar feel of the relation between master and journeymen in
that idyllic picture of social harmony, *The Shoemaker's Holiday* (1599).

I will o'ertake thee Cleopatra, and
Weep for my pardon. So it must be, for now
All length is torture. Since the torch is out,
Lie down, and stray no farther. Now all labour
Mars what it does; yea, very force entangles
Itself with strength.   (IV. 14. 44-9.)

What is the essence of this change? In the very first scene,
Cleopatra utters four enigmatic words: 'Antony will be himself.'
Editors are undecided about the meaning: Either, 'Antony
will once more be his noble self', or, 'Antony will yet play the
lover, his true role'.[1] Which is the correct meaning? We do
not know, and we are not meant to know – yet. The point,
I think, is that we find out the meaning *in the course of the play*.
Only at the end can we say – can *Antony himself* say – what
Antony's 'self' consists in. 'If I lose mine honour / I lose myself',
he had said to Octavia. Defeated in battle and dishonoured, he
sends his ambassador to make an ignominious peace. Caesar's
rude rebuff shows him finally that it is impossible for him any
longer to 'send humble treaties, dodge / And palter in the
shifts of lowness' again. The 'Egyptian fetters' now reveal themselves to him as the true condition of his existence, for it
becomes impossible for him to retreat again to the Roman
world. With the news of Cleopatra's 'death' the realization
dawns on him that he has his very being in her. With her
death all action loses its point: 'all length is torture' and 'now
all labour / Mars what it does'. The infatuation, the irrational
compulsive power of his attachment to Cleopatra, which is
seen by others as 'dotage' and 'lust' (a view to which he himself
lends sanction: 'Or lose myself in dotage'; 'I' th' East my
pleasure lies') is revealed to him as the very ground of his being.
Without her he is nothing. It is a revelation echoed by Cleopatra:

            . . . Shall I abide
     In this dull world, which in thy absence is
     No better than a sty?   (IV. 15. 60-2.)

And because of this it is possible to say that Antony is not
merely deceived. He makes no comment when it is broken to him
that Cleopatra is still alive, for, in a way, that hardly matters

[1] Cf. Arden edition (M. R. Ridley), 7, and New Cambridge edition (Dover
Wilson), 143.

to him. The spiritual affinity with Cleopatra that he has discovered, an affinity from which his own being grows (so that any other mode of being, e.g. of the man of action, becomes impossible for him), which now gives substance to his defiant gesture of 'Kingdoms are clay', all this makes her paltry shifts things of no consequence. Antony has found himself.

This would be at best one man's dying fantasy, were it not backed up in the play by a similar shift and evolution in another character, a growth that has the effect of *confirming* the validity of Antony's discovery. Enobarbus, the source, in the play, of scepticism and irony, is finally drawn into and overwhelmed by Antony.

The character of Enobarbus is one of Shakespeare's important deviations from Plutarch.[1] His career is crucial to understanding how we are to take Antony and Cleopatra and their relationship, and the contrast between Shakespeare and Plutarch is startling. Plutarch's Domitius Enobarbus is a shadowy, even marginal, figure: he is mentioned only three times and appears principally as a deserter:

> '. . . he being sick of an ague when he went and took a little boat to go to Caesar's camp, Antonius was very sorry for it, but yet he sent after him all his carriage, train, and men, and the same Domitius, as though he gave him to understand that he repented his open treason, he died immediately after.'

In Plutarch Enobarbus's desertion takes place *before* the Battle of Actium (Act III. 7 in the play). Shakespeare thus draws out the process of Enobarbus's deliberation, for it is not until six scenes later that he makes his decision, and it takes another two scenes before we hear of the actual desertion.[2] Shakespeare's Enobarbus, then, is an entirely original character, and his importance in the play is not to be underestimated or taken for granted. It must matter to the effect that Shakespeare wants to convey in *Antony and Cleopatra* that Enobarbus, the realist, the choric commentator on the ambiguous action of the play,

---

[1] See the excellent analysis of Elkin C. Wilkinson, 'Shakespeare's Enobarbus', in *J. Q. Adams Memorial Studies*, Washington 1948, 391-408.

[2] See Kenneth Muir, *Shakespeare's Sources*, Vol. I, 204-5.

hesitates for so long in his choice between Antony and Caesar and dies, not of an ague, but of a broken heart.[1]

There is a conflict in Enobarbus between his loyalty and his common sense, his reason. In Act III. 10 he has become aware of the irrationality of his loyalty:

> I'll yet follow
> The wounded chance of Antony, though my reason
> Sits in the wind against me.   (III. 10. 35-7.)

When Cleopatra entertains Caesar's messenger he begins to see the absurdity of such loyalty:

> Mine honesty and I begin to square.
> The loyalty well held to fools, does make
> Our faith mere folly.   (III. 13. 41-3.)

When Antony is won over once again by Cleopatra at the end of the scene, Enobarbus decides to leave the sinking ship; and Antony recognizes the validity of the decision: 'Oh my fortunes have / Corrupted honest men'. Enobarbus changes masters, and clearly expects some gain from it. Yet this is where he is most deeply disillusioned. Enobarbus has been throughout the play the source of what one might call *critical realism*: he is that in person. But he is not attuned to the amoral *cynical realism* of the Roman world. He has forgotten the proverb about turncoats. In Caesar's world, turncoat once, turncoat always, and Caesar has no use for him, as he has no use for Alexas, Canidius, and the rest of the time-servers. And what awakens Enobarbus to a realization of this fatal lapse in his 'reasoning' is the treasure that Antony sends after him. That generosity cannot really be justified in terms of 'reason'; it is nearer allied to the spontaneous and extravagant bounty that characterises the Egyptian pole. Critical realism must still be humane, and it is nearer to the human, if illogical, generosity of Antony,

---

[1] The important speech in Act II. 2. which ushers us into the world of Cleopatra's magic is given, interestingly, to Enobarbus. He is the one genuine realist, the one detached observer, the only figure in the play, in fact, who can be at all *objective* about Cleopatra, neither extravagant nor undervaluing (he himself has told us earlier on about Cleopatra's technique: 'I have seen her die twenty times upon far poorer moment . . . she hath such a celerity in dying', 1. 2.). Dryden in *All for Love* transfers this speech to Antony.

than to the cold, calculating policy of Caesar.[1] There is more essential *humane value* in Antony's spendthrift (if irresponsible) generosity than in that approach to life, hardboiled, cynical and calculating, that Caesar exemplifies. There is in the latter no logical stopping-point short of a total attachment to self-interest, glorified, as occasion may require, as dispassionate *staaträson*. Enobarbus's final compliment to Antony in Act IV. 5, his dying recognition of the value of the 'irrationality' that he had himself previously condemned, is therefore in the context more than merely personal. It is artistically decisive. It brings the weight down on the side of Antony, and thus of Egypt, and what it implies is a recognition of Antony's *humanity*.

The effect of Enobarbus's awakening to the humanity of Antony tilts the balance towards the Egyptian pole and makes certain that whatever our doubts, our common-sense hesitations about accepting so unearthly an experience as the last act, they will occur within the context of a dominating attitude of acceptance of the validity of Antony and Cleopatra's relationship and their way of life. This does not in the least simplify the play. It provides, on the contrary, a stable framework in these last scenes against which Shakespeare can play off as many ironic insights as he pleases (of which the Seleucus scene is the best example). The case provides, if nothing else, a beautiful exercise in the nice calculation of the tension thus generated between conviction and suspicion. But it is of course much more than this. It makes it possible for us to feel that Cleopatra's 'ascension' is, given the history, inevitable, without making us feel that it is *automatic* (which is what a fully romantic view would have it be). She is Cleopatra still, and she *might* not have chosen to do what she does. The result is that rich complexity, density almost, of Cleopatra's character that resists analysis into generalized and abstract formulae. Who will say why she does what she does?

There is nothing romantic about Shakespeare's Cleopatra. Against her he concentrates the full intensity of that loathing and disgust with sexual infidelity that had bulked so large in

<hr>

[1] Professor L. C. Knights, the most consistently unromantic of *Antony and Cleopatra* critics, sees Antony's generosity as 'a vain and arrogant pomp' in dispensing mere *material wealth*, and his betrayal by his followers as its inevitable result. (*Some Shakespearean Themes*, 1960, 148, n.3). One asks: how else could his 'bounty' have been *shown*?

Troilus, Hamlet, Lear and *Timon*. She is also the Dark Lady of the Sonnets. Antony himself might have said: 'My love is as a fever longing still / For that which longer nurseth the disease', or 'When my love says that she is made of truth / I do believe her though I know she lies'. But she is more than that, and the merely negative attitude of Troilus and Hamlet is transcended here in Shakespeare's final portrait of the lady.

He spares us nothing. For three acts of the play there is little to distinguish her from Hugo's 'courtesan': glorified, no doubt, but still, a professional. No longer in her prime, the imagery invoked to describe her is predominantly that of over-ripeness and decay:

> See my women,
> Against the blown rose may they stop their nose
> That kneel'd unto the buds. (III. 13. 38-40.)

The curious thing is how this is transformed into a suggestion of *fertility*. The Nile is the symbol of the indissoluble unity of the processes of growth and decay, and twice (III. 13; V. 2.) Cleopatra links the Nile with herself. It is almost as if Shakespeare were hinting at a distinction between the corruption that characterizes Rome and the over-ripeness that he attributes to Cleopatra-Egypt. Rome and its 'common body' rotting itself with motion is, in human terms, an arid waste land: there is a kind of death at its core. Cleopatra's kind of corruption, linked through the imagery with the river, seems to suggest an undercurrent of dynamic processes continuing beneath and through decay.[1]

What concerns us here, however, is the change that comes over the whole scene from the moment Antony is carried to Cleopatra's monument. The change is marked by Cleopatra's startling words:

> O sun,
> Burn the great sphere thou mov'st in! Darkling stand
> The varying shore o' th' world. O Antony,
> Antony, Antony! (IV. 15. 9-12.)

[1] See Derek Traversi's excellent account in *An Approach to Shakespeare* (1956), 249-53. For this reason (as well as for others) I cannot accept L. C. Knight's view that the relationship is 'in [Shakespeare's] final judgment, discarded and condemned'.

They establish the level of this last scene. In those unparalleled passages, she successively projects their relationship in terms of the vast natural rhythms of the sun and moon, of the tides, the continuing cycle of the seasons, which she invokes in the very act of wishing them to cease. Their relationship shares in the corruption of their world, but it also transcends it. It transcends it to the extent that the image of the stagnation of the Roman world is transcended by these images of natural cycles of flux, in which there is place for both decay and growth. These images assimilate their relationship to the profound rhythmic alternations that characterize the universe, themselves a guarantee that the processes of life are ceaselessly at work. In these moments, Cleopatra achieves an awareness of the nature of their relationship that lies beyond the reach of Hugo's 'realism'.

It is a vision beside which anything else life has to offer pales into obscurity:

> My desolation does begin to make
> A better life. 'Tis paltry to be Caesar:
> Not being Fortune, he's but Fortune's knave,
> A minister of her will; and it is great
> To do that thing that ends all other deeds,
> Which shackles accidents and bolts up change,
> Which sleeps, and never palates more the dung,
> The beggar's nurse and Caesar's.   (v. 2. 1-8.)

Through their love they have achieved a level of humanity beside which what Fortune has to offer – wealth, status, power – cannot but seem qualitatively inferior and transient. The 'dung' that nourishes both man and beast (I. I.), beggar and Caesar, is a symbol at once of fertility and of lowliness. By the world's criteria (of respectability and dignity) their relationship has been mean and degrading. But it contains that principle of life which is shared alike by human beings in any condition, low or elevated. So, in her moment of mingled despair and exaltation, Cleopatra sees herself not, as Iras suggests, as 'Royal Egypt: Empress', but:

> No more but e'en a woman, and commanded
> By such poor passion, as the maid that milks
> And does the meanest chares.   (IV. 15. 73-5.)

Like Lear in the storm, she has broken through the bondage of convention and status to an essential humanity that belongs equally to the privileged and to the naked wretches. She has gone beyond the convention that makes Octavia Antony's 'wife' and Cleopatra his 'whore':

> Husband, I come.
> Now to that name my courage prove my title.
> (v. 2. 285-6.)

Her affinity with Antony, an affinity and relationship in which they, great princes of the world, approach nearest to common humanity, entitles her to the use of that word, 'husband'.

Hence she refuses to resign herself to Caesar's plan. She refuses not merely because it involves a degradation of her *status* (though this will clearly figure in an account of her motives), but because Caesar's intentions involve a degradation, an intolerable cheapening, of the transforming experience she has known. To calculating, pragmatical Rome, their story will at best 'point a moral or adorn a tale'; at the worst, it will be scorned and laughed at by people with no conception of the moving power of their mutual love. The force of that eventuality is dramatically visualized in an astonishing passage that 'shatters' (in Middleton Murry's words) 'the dramatic illusion':[1]

> Saucy lictors
> Will catch at us like strumpets, and scald rhymers
> Ballad us out o' tune; the quick comedians
> Extemporally will stage us, and present
> Our Alexandrian revels; Antony
> Shall be brought drunken forth, and I shall see
> Some squeaking Cleopatra boy my greatness
> I' th' posture of a whore. (v. 2. 213-20.)

This passage deserves to be considered at length, not only because of the superbly economic way in which it presents to us the inextricable tangle of Cleopatra's motivation (is she concerned with the degradation of her status, 'boy my *greatness*', or of her love, 'I' th' posture of a *whore*'?), but also because of the light it sheds on Cleopatra's transformation at the end,

---

[1] J. Middleton Murry, *Shakespeare* (1936), 379.

a point to which we shall have to return below. For Cleopatra at this stage there can be no drawing back. Her end is inevitable: after what she has known, there is no way but one. Any other life would be an anticlimax and, by implication, an undervaluation of their entire experience. Neither the Roman nor (since its triumph) the Egyptian world can comprehend (in both senses, contain as well as understand) her vision, and therefore she must 'again for Cydnus / To meet Mark Antony'.

What are we to make of this scene? We have to return to the passage in which Cleopatra envisages herself being led through Rome in Caesar's triumphal procession. The significance of that passage – shattering, as it does, the dramatic illusion – emerges, I think, when we consider it in the light of Brecht's use of what he called the 'alienation effect' (*Verfremdungseffekt*). The purpose of the alienation effect was to prevent any blurring of dramatic illusion with the reality of which it was a report. It was designed to remind the audience constantly that what they were witnessing was not life itself, but a representation of life. The spectator was to be discouraged from losing himself in, identifying himself with, the dramatic characters. What the alienation effect achieved was the 'estrangement', the *distancing*, necessary to adopt and maintain a *critical* attitude towards the 'events' on the stage.

This, I feel, is exactly the effect that Shakespeare achieves. For there *is* a kind of illusion in Cleopatra's moving day-dream of Antony, there is a real sense in which her final ascension, so to speak, is *play-acting*, and Shakespeare breaks the magic with incredible audacity at this point, just because we are in danger of being swept up in her dream and resigning ourselves uncritically to a romantic stupor. The full import of that passage is difficult to explain. What we are witnessing in this scene is the transformation of the 'courtesan' (defined in terms of a function) into a person, at once peerless and richly human, and what this passage reveals is a profound and acute perception of the sheer difficulty of any genuine human transformation. The Cleopatra of the last act *is* transformed, but to achieve it she has to *think herself into a new role*. And we are meant to feel simultaneously the reality and wonder of the transformation as well as the artificiality, the play-acting quality, of the means by which it is achieved.

It is a prelude to her death. Yet death is not in this play Time's last revenge on beauty and love (as in the Sonnets and *Troilus and Cressida*). Professor Wilson Knight points out that 'melting' is a key image in *Antony and Cleopatra*: 'We should observe especially the idea of "melting", "dissolving" – it is a crucial theme in the play. . . . Death is thus [seen as] a change of mode, a melting, a dissolving and, perhaps, a reforming in some newer fashion of this "visible shape", the body.'[1] The suggestion is, I think, that death is a release from the bondage of stagnation and makes possible a merging into the more inclusive rhythms of the universe. The Cleopatra of the last scene finds in death not a mere quietus, but release.

I want to say of this end that it is Shakespeare's mode of resolving the clash of values at the heart of this play. But it remains nevertheless a doubtful sort of resolution. Is it not merely escapist to 'vanquish' Caesar simply by committing suicide? I think not, on balance, for to say of an action or an attitude that it is 'escapist' is to imply a judgment that the agent should not even *want* to 'escape'. After what Shakespeare has shown us of the Roman world, it is a judgment that cannot wholly be sustained by the experience of the play (it certainly requires an abnormal degree of detachment from that experience). Given the almost supernatural inevitability of the triumph of Caesar (indicated by the prophecies of the Soothsayer and the music under the earth), it is impossible, within the terms dictated by the play, to conceive of a world in which these three characters and their mutually exclusive values may sustain even a precariously peaceful coexistence.

The significance of Cleopatra's end is not, then, to be dismissed as 'escapism'. If we are to characterize it, we must describe it as *utopian*, for the vision of death in *Antony and Cleopatra* as a merging into the universe and its processes of life seems to me ultimately to constitute a cosmic act of faith, a belief that in the long run the forces of life, humane values, will reassert themselves because they are a part of the universe and its mode of existence. This is utopian (though not, of course, for that reason false), for it is the sort of proposition that can neither be proved nor disproved this side of utopia.

Her end is noble: the word 'royal' echoes through the last

[1] *The Imperial Theme* (1931), 237, 239.

scene, the only conceivable epithet. Yet the nobility derives not from her regal status, but from the course she is embarked on, a point which Cleopatra herself clarifies: 'What poor an instrument / May do a noble deed'. Her true nobility lies not in the crown of Egypt nor in the kingdoms lavished on her by Antony, but in what her love has made of her. It is the point that Donne makes, in *The Sunne Rising*:

> She' is all States; and all Princes, I,
> Nothing else is.
> Princes doe but play us; compar'd to this,
> All honour's mimique; All wealth alchimie.

The royalty is a measure of the *value* of the relationship, not of the *status* of the participants. Status may (sometimes) reflect value, but cannot create it in any important or enduring sense.

With this immense assertion of the value of the love-relationship the play ends. But nothing in the conclusion negates the progressive clarification of the relationship effected by the dialectical vision. For *Antony and Cleopatra* is less an *expression* of the theme of romantic love, as the form in which the relationship between human beings is most intensely experienced, than Shakespeare's *assessment* of that theme.[1]

A work of art as profoundly realistic as this demands a commensurate degree of realism in its interpreters, and it has to be recognized that many features of the central relationship *are* romantic. There is, for instance, the curious echoing of each other's words through the play by Antony and Cleopatra – the verbal equivalent of that unique kinship and *rapport* between two personalities which, two hundred years later and borrowing a term from contemporary chemical theory, Goethe was to call 'elective affinities'. ('Whatever our souls are made of, his and mine are the same . . . Nelly, I *am* Heathcliff!' says Cathy in *Wuthering Heights*). There is the strong sense of such a relationship being set apart from and *ineluctably opposed to* a hostile society with its restrictive conventions and demands, aptly expressed in Max Weber's remark: 'The genius or demon of politics lives in an inner tension with the god of love. . . . This

---

[1] For the remarks which follow I am indebted to discussions with Dr. Arnold Kettle.

tension can at any time lead to an irreconcilable conflict.[1]
There is the conflict between love and the institution of marriage.
There is, finally, the welcoming of death, not only as a release
from the toils of the tragic conflict, but even, in a curious way,
as the *fulfilment* of the relationship (as in the *höchste Lust*,
'highest bliss', of Isolde's *Liebestod*):

> But I will be
> A bridegroom in my death, and run into't
> As to a lover's bed.   (IV. 14. 99-101.)

> The stroke of death is as a lover's pinch,
> Which hurts and is desir'd.   (V. 2. 293-4.)

To this extent, *Antony and Cleopatra* does express some of the
characteristic features of romantic love and invites discussion
on the same terms. In posing a personal relationship (the
kinship and deep need of two people for one another) as an
alternative to the problem of coming to grips with existing
society and establishing satisfactory social relationships,
romantic love asserts, on the positive side, the possibility of a
relationship more fully human than those which society at that
particular stage of development provides, and, more dubiously,
sponsors an attitude which is escapist or, at best, utopian
(inevitably, since society has not caught up with the possibilities
which individual human beings have come to recognise as
necessary). Both these aspects are vividly realized in *Antony and
Cleopatra*. The triumphant assertion of love at its close does not
blunt the perception of what is negative and unrealized about
it and makes it potentially vulnerable to the charge of romanticism in the pejorative sense.

Love stands as the model of genuine human relationships,
as opposed to the false relationships that society has to offer.
But lest love be idealized out of its human context, it is necessary to insist on the profound realism of the mature Shakespeare's
assessment of it. It is to be found, of course, in the operation
of the dialectical vision, but more specifically it is to be found
in Shakespeare's Cleopatra – in the splendid *awareness* she
achieves, not without struggle, at the end. Unlike the *Liebestod*

[1] 'Politics as a Vocation', in *From Max Weber*, ed. H. H. Gerth and C. Wright
Mills, 1948, 126.

of romantic love, Cleopatra's death involves a wonderfully realistic assessment of the objective features of the world around her. Shakespeare, unlike Wagner, is not enshrining Death for Love as valuable in itself. If the play suggests anything, it is that the values involved in Cleopatra's choice are indeed higher than those in any alternative solution open to her.

Elsewhere, in an important and difficult Sonnet (No. 124), Shakespeare dwells on the same theme:

> If my dear love were but the child of state,
> It might for Fortune's bastard be unfathered,
> As subject to Time's love, or to Time's hate,
> Weeds among weeds, or flowers with flowers gathered.
> No, it was builded far from accident,
> It suffers not in smiling pomp, nor falls
> Under the blow of thralled discontent,
> Where to th' inviting time our fashion calls:
> It fears not policy, that heretic,
> Which works on leases of short-number'd hours,
> But all alone stands hugely politic,
> That it nor grows with heat, nor drowns with showers.
> To this I witness call the fools of Time,
> Which die for goodness, who have liv'd for crime.

In its dissociation of genuine love from the accidents of rank and status ('state') and the transitory glories of the milieu of court politics, in its rejection of human relationships based on short-run expediency and calculation (implied in the image drawn from estate-management), in the assertion of the constancy of genuine relationships, it is in fact an epitome of the play. Especially is it relevant to the play in its view of love as being, not merely *opposed* to 'policy', but in truth *wiser* and more *aware* of its own long-term interest than the politic Machiavellian. In the metaphoric brilliance of the vision of the love that 'all alone stands hugely *politic*' is contained the audacious realism of *Antony and Cleopatra*.

LOVE AND SOCIETY: *MEASURE FOR MEASURE* AND OUR OWN TIME

David Craig

We are right, I believe, to distrust efforts to enlist Shakespeare by force as one of the moderns – whether by treating him as a kind of copy-writer for British jingoism or by playing Angelo or Hamlet as a full-blown study in neurosis out of a wish to spice jaded palates. Yet there is one case in which a 'modern' spirit does seem to belong quite integrally to the work as Shakespeare wrote it: *Measure for Measure* must surely impress us as approaching its theme-problems in a remarkably free and open spirit. To put the point as a comparison: I find I need make little adjustment in passing from *Measure for Measure* to many a tale of D. H. Lawrence's. Tales of his such as 'Daughters of the Vicar', 'The Captain's Doll', 'St Mawr', and 'The Virgin and the Gypsy' are, indeed, the pieces of later literature in English that I find most akin to this play of Shakespeare's.

These works are generally alike in that they analyse, by dramatic means, values that reach to the core of our lives – love and fulfilment, integrity, personal freedom; and they do so with a piercing or cleansing effect that comes from their remarkable freedom from the sort of loose ardour, uplift, overt sermonizing, or floundering in depths without surface that are the likely failings of such work. Both Shakespeare and Lawrence are masters at affirming 'humanity' and at sensing, and rising triumphant over, whatever is 'anti-life'. 'Humanity' and 'life', however, are by themselves such general (if indispensable) terms – so prone to do little more than boost or dignify the particular viewpoint of whoever uses them – that it will be best to consider right away the specific likenesses between these works that belong together.

Negatively speaking, the gap bound to exist between writers so separated in time is remarkably narrow in this case because

Shakespeare is here concerned so much with core-values, so little with surface manners: for example, the hero, Claudio, though nominally a gentleman of Vienna, has few particular foibles or turns of phrase to mark him as such – little of the courtliness that appears as burlesque in Sir Andrew Aguecheek and seriously in those superb compliments paid by Florizel to Perdita in the Pastoral scene from *The Winter's Tale*. Claudio is sheerly human, above all in his speech affirming life itself that opens, 'Ay, but to die, and go we know not where'. It might be said that Shakespeare's tragedies are concerned no less than *Measure for Measure* with such core-values as love and integrity. But the method of the tragedies is to expose humanity to the most terrifying and extraordinary forces conceivable, whereas *Measure for Measure* likens itself to the finest modern fiction by virtue of dealing directly with the kind of experience that comes to us all, exceptional or not, and with the kind of integration we must bring to such personal relations if we are to live them through happily.

The very personal nature of the play starts from its subject – the young man who has committed the crime and sin of having intercourse with his loved one before they are married, the temptation to similar behaviour on the part of the governor who sits in judgment over him. The treatment this subject demanded, the kind of truth to intimate experience, comes out in the many likenesses (quite unusual for a supreme Shakespeare play) to his own most personal work – his poems. When Claudio says, in helpless disgust at his own fall:

> So every scope by the immoderate use
> Turns to restraint. Our natures do pursue,
> Like rats that ravin down their proper bane,
> A thirsty evil; and when we drink, we die,
>
> (I. 2. 121-4.)

he is not far from the more extreme state of mind presented in the sonnet on lust (No. 129):

> Enjoyed no sooner but despised straight;
> Past reason hunted, and no sooner had,
> Past reason hated, as a swallowed bait,
> On purpose laid to make the taker mad.

The Duke's lofty pretended tribute to Angelo at the start of Act V,

> O, your desert speaks loud; and I should wrong it
> To lock it in the wards of covert bosom,
> When it deserves, with characters of brass,
> A forted residence 'gainst the tooth of time
> And razure of oblivion,   (v. 1. 9-13.

echoes thoughts common in the Sonnets, especially the middle group on time and transience ('brass eternal slave to mortal rage'; 'brass, nor stone, nor earth, nor boundless sea / But sad mortality o'er-sways their power'). Indeed the consonance between the Sonnets and the play is such that Sonnet 94 almost attaches itself to the play as a condensed characterization of the Angelo type – the man who pursues virtue by keeping himself rigidly intact from experience. As the sonnet puts it:

> They that have power to hurt and will do none,
> That do not do the thing they most do show,
> Who, moving others, are themselves as stone,
> Unmoved, cold, and to temptation slow –
> They rightly do inherit heaven's graces, . . .

The profound ironies to which the sonnet then moves are precisely those dramatized in *Measure for Measure*. The imagery the poet needs is very close to that regularly used by the other characters about Angelo:

> Lord Angelo is precise;
> Stands at a guard with envy; scarce confesses
> That his blood flows, or that his appetite
> Is more to bread than stone.   (I. 3. 50-3.)
> . . . he, a marble to her tears, is washed with them, but
> relents not. . . .   (III. 2. 238.)

Indeed the quite strong likelihood of a seventeenth-century date for the later, maturer sonnets[1] makes it possible that these poems belong to literally the same point in the development of his preoccupations as does the play, which was probably first produced on Boxing Day, 1604.

The Angelo imagery leads us to the heart of the play and

---

[1] The arguments for and against this dating are reviewed by Ivor Brown in his Introduction to the Nonesuch *Complete Works of Shakespeare* (1953), I, p. xxvi.

also of its kinship with the Lawrence tales. We shall see that
the freedom Claudio has enjoyed with his betrothed, Juliet, is
by no means approved by the dramatist in a spirit of moral
anarchism. Yet there is also an important sense in which Claudio
(who has followed his impulse) confronts Angelo (who has
begun by guarding against just that) as a champion of life
against whatever thwarts or deadens it. The speech in which
Claudio overflows into his affirmation of life must be quoted
in full, for there are few passages in English that express with
such deep-reaching power what it is to be a human being alive
in the world. Claudio is meant to be pleading with his sister
not to value her own chastity above his life, but the speech is
not an argument: it bursts out of him, without logical calculation, as an irresistible expression of that sheer adherence
to living, breathing consciousness without which we could
hardly carry on:

> *Claudio.*   Death is a fearful thing.
> *Isabella.* And shamed life a hateful.
> *Claudio.* Ay, but to die, and go we know not where;
> To lie in cold obstruction, and to rot;
> This sensible warm motion to become
> A kneaded clod; and the delighted spirit
> To bathe in fiery floods or to reside
> In thrilling regions of thick-ribbèd ice;
> To be imprison'd in the viewless winds,
> And blown with restless violence round about
> The pendent world; or to be worse than worst
> Of those that lawless and incertain thought
> Imagine howling – 'tis too horrible.
> The weariest and most loathed worldly life
> That age, ache, penury, and imprisonment
> Can lay on nature is a paradise
> To what we fear of death.   (III. 1. 117-33.)

One would not have believed that things literally beyond the
possibility of experience could be imagined with this physical
intensity that pierces right home to our senses. Thus a value is
created which must be a dominant one in any reading of the
play. It is not that Claudio is 'right' in what he has done. It
is that, as his imagery shows, he is, in his own being – in the
way he takes life and can express its most essential conditions –

the antithesis of Angelo, with his deathly wish to ignore and repress real feelings.

Before we consider how this conflict is resolved inside the quite strict morality of the play, some of the likenesses to Lawrence call to be mentioned. He too can show us what makes for fullness of experience and what ties it down to a narrow, deadening habit by contrasting pairs of people through the imagery that establishes the contrasting types. In 'Daughters of the Vicar'[1] there are the two girls, one of whom acts, thinks, and marries as is expected of one 'in her position', the other of whom breaks passionately out of the Victorian class taboos. Mary with her 'white brow and grey eyes' contrasts in every way with Louisa, 'short and plump and rather flushed'. Mary accepts the curate Massey who 'lacked the full range of human feelings, but had rather a strong, philosophical mind, from which he lived. . . . There was no spontaneous exclamation, no violent assertion or expression of personal conviction, but all cold, reasonable assertion.' 'Cold' is the Angelo word, 'warmth' is Claudio's; and Louisa is attracted by the young miner Alfred – 'she wanted to see his face more distinctly in her mind, ruddy with the sun' (he has been in the Navy), 'his golden-brown eyes, kind and careless, strained now with a natural fear, the fine nose tanned hard by the sun, the mouth that could not help smiling at her.' The perfectly lifelike fullness of the description at every point rules out any lapse into too glib or foregone a contrast; yet we cannot mistake the clear contrast between the lifeful and the deathly – the curate so worried about his child's health that he cannot enjoy his fatherhood, the vicar's family virtually disowning the young couple who have followed their impulses across the class barrier.

This basic contrast or 'polarity' (a key term of Lawrence's) figures in his fiction again and again. In *The Rainbow* it exists in the couple Skrebensky and Ursula, the girl warm-hearted, outspoken, the man a cavalry officer at the heyday of imperialism and the subjugation of Africa, so rigid in his adherence to the military code (' "It's about the most serious business there is, fighting. . . . It matters whether we settle the Mahdi or not" ') that Ursula comes up against him on every essential issue,

[1] *The Tales of D. H. Lawrence* (1948 ed.), pp. 53, 55, 59-60.

until their very love-making, to which finally they have to will themselves, reaches a stony dead-end, expressed in images of hardness and sterility that recall the Angelo language.[1]

In 'The Virgin and the Gypsy' a like polarity is created through imagery still closer to Shakespeare's poetry. The urbane rector, deserted by his wife for Another Man, defends his pride by shutting his imagination against this woman who must still exist somewhere. He takes refuge in an idealized image of the pure young bride that by itself suggests the shrinking from experience that will have driven her to leave him:

> For in the pure loftiness of the rector's heart still bloomed the pure white snow-flower of his young bride. This white snow-flower did not wither. That other creature, who had gone off with that despicable young man, was none of his affair. . . . Yes, the white snow-flower was forgiven. He even had made provision in his will for her, when that other scoundrel – but hush! Don't even *think* too near to that horrid nettle in the rank outer world! She-who-was-Cynthia. Let the white snow-flower bloom inaccessible on the heights of the past. The present is another story.[2]

The imagery here – and the passage is virtually poetic – is from that same vein repeatedly drawn on to characterize Angelo:

> A man whose blood
> Is very snow-broth, . . .   (I. 4. 57-8.)

or as the lowest gossip of the town puts it:

> Some report a sea-maid spawn'd him; some, that he was begot between two stock-fishes. But it is certain that when he makes water his urine is congealed ice; that I know to be true. . .   (III. 2. 100-3.)

This is also the vein of imagery that Lawrence uses in 'The Captain's Doll' when he wants to suggest the inner vitality of the inscrutable, seemingly indifferent Captain Hepburn. Hepburn, in Austria just after the Great War, rejects the nostalgic escapism (as he sees it) that makes a cult of bare

---

[1] *The Rainbow* (Penguin ed., 1949), pp. 313-4, 486.
[2] Lawrence, *Tales*, pp. 1026-7.

mountains. His trip to the glacier with Hannele, the woman he will marry, shows how he turns towards whatever makes for relationship and humanity. Here is his reaction to the fanatically open-air young people who so oddly helped pave the way for the triumph of Nazi racialism: ' "Their loftiness and their uplift," ' he says to Hannele. ' "I hate their uplift. I hate people prancing on mountain-tops and feeling exalted. I'd like to make them all stop up there, on their mountain-tops, and chew ice to fill their stomachs." ' And on the glacier itself, amongst veritable snow-flowers, we arrive at metaphors that directly recall those Claudio used to figure his sense of the deathly nullity of non-life beyond the grave, the 'thrilling regions of thick-ribbèd ice'. So Hepburn glimpses, and gladly turns his back on,

> A world, a terrible place of hills and valleys and slopes, all motionless, all of ice. Away above the grey mist-cloud was looming bigger. And near at hand were long huge cracks, side by side, like gills in the ice. It would seem as if the ice breathed through these great ridged gills. One could look down into the series of gulfs, fearful depths, and the colour burning that acid, intense blue, intenser as the crack went deeper. And the crests of the open gills ridged and grouped pale blue above the crevices. It seemed as if the ice breathed there.
>
> The wonder, the terror, and the bitterness of it. Never a warm leaf to unfold, never a gesture of life to give off. A world sufficient unto itself in lifelessness, all this ice.[1]

It is, however, 'The Virgin and the Gypsy' that shows most fully the Shakespearian quality of Lawrence's treatment of passion and restraint – or the Lawrentian quality of Shakespeare's. When we read in Lawrence's tale that the rector's ex-wife had been, as a mother, 'glamorous but not very dependable . . . a great glow, a flow of life, like a swift and dangerous sun in the home, forever coming and going', and that the rector's falsely hallowing memory of her 'like a porcelain wreath, froze on its grave', we are oddly reminded of the image that closes Shakespeare's 'Angelo' sonnet: it gives us another, related way of regarding the unnatural

[1] *Ibid.*, pp. 540, 545-6.

stagnancy that comes of repression, the denial of life:

> Lilies that fester smell far worse than weeds.

Here is Lawrence's image for the obsessive suspicions that the rector and his doting mother project onto his former wife: 'out of the squalid world sometimes would come a rank, evil smell of selfishness and degraded lust, the smell of the awful nettle, She-who-was-Cynthia.' This readiness to smell depravity, the potential of hidden nastiness that it suggests, comes out in the drama of the tale when Yvette is challenged by her father regarding her friendship with the 'immoral' Eastwoods – the Major living with a married woman until her divorce comes through and they can marry:

> When his conservatism and his abject sort of fear were uppermost, he always lifted his lip and bared his teeth a little, in a dog-like sneer.
>
> 'I hear your latest friends are the half-divorced Mrs. Fawcett and the *maquereau* Eastwood,' he said to Yvette.
>
> She didn't know what a *maquereau* was, but she felt the poison in the rector's fangs.
>
> 'I just know them,' she said. 'They're awfully nice, really. And they'll be married in about a month's time.'
>
> . . . He looked at her in hate, as if he could kill her. And he backed away from her, against the window-curtains of his study, like a rat at bay. Somewhere in his mind he was thinking unspeakable depravities about his daughter, as he had thought them of She-who-was-Cynthia. He was powerless against the lowest insinuations of his own mind. (pp. 1079-80.)

Angelo enjoys an absolute power not possessed by the rector, and will use it to the limit of blackmail, seduction, and execution. But there is little to choose between their inner selves. In *Measure for Measure*, too, the man is surprised and undermined by his own impulses (after his first interview with Isabella, come to plead for her brother's life):

> What's this, what's this? Is this her fault or mine?
> The tempter or the tempted, who sins most? Ha.
> Not she; nor doth she tempt; but it is I
> That, lying by the violet in the sun,
> Do as the carrion does, not as the flow'r,

Corrupt with virtuous season . . .
O, fie, fie, fie!
What dost thou, or what art thou, Angelo?
(II. 2. 162-73.)

(And a little later, on the verge of the second interview):

. . . O heavens!
Why does my blood thus muster to my heart,
Making both it unable for itself
And dispossessing all my other parts
Of necessary fitness?
(II. 4. 19-23.)

The rector and Angelo do not know themselves.[1] There is a gross discrepancy between their 'perfect' public exteriors and the inner suggestibility by the repression of which their dignified fronts (the law, the Church) have been maintained. These two master-writers are supreme in their ability to trace their way through this conflict of impulses that goes to make us what we are. This is what gives depth to their analyses of the more public values such as justice, righteousness, discipline, authority.

So far the account might have suggested a simple opposition, in the play and the tales, between the 'artificial' surface of social living and the 'real' life of personal feelings; or a too-easy satirical viewpoint that works by simply suggesting that every principle or public attitude is a sham that crumbles at the test. This would have been so if Shakespeare had set Claudio free without any ordeal of condemnation and imminent execution, or if Lawrence had made Yvette take the easy road into a fool's paradise of 'free love' with her gypsy. In fact there is no primitivist or anarchic opposition, in these works, between control and freedom. In both 'pure freedom' is radically tested. Lucio the libertine asks Claudio why he is in jail:

> *Lucio.*   Why, how now, Claudio, whence comes this
> [restraint?

---

[1] 'Knowing oneself' – an essential theme of *Measure for Measure*: in one of her strongest appeals to Angelo, Isabella speaks of
> . . . man, proud man,
> Dressed in a little brief authority,
> Most ignorant of what he's most assur'd,
> His glassy essence, . . .   (II. 2. 117-20.)

and Escalus' highest praise for the Duke is that he was
> One that above all other strifes, contended especially to know
> himself.   (III. 2. 219.)

Claudio. From too much liberty, my Lucio, liberty;
As surfeit is the father of much fast,
So every scope by the immoderate use
Turns to restraint.   (I. 2. 118-22.)

The reader of Lawrence is at once reminded of the opening of
'St Mawr': 'Lou Witt had had her own way so long, that by
the age of twenty-five she didn't know where she was. Having
one's own way landed one completely at sea.' The same idea, a
basic one of Lawrence's, is used in 'The Virgin and the Gypsy' to
define the rather aimless pleasure-seeking in which Yvette and
her sister have been virtually encouraged by the rector's falsely
easy-going, man-of-the-world 'broadmindedness'. Lawrence
says about the girls and their friends (Bright Young Things of
the Twenties), 'they had nothing really to rebel against, any of
them. They were left so very free in their movements. Their
parents let them do entirely as they liked. . . . The keys of their
lives were in their own hands. And there they dangled inert.'[1]

Some such critique of 'pure freedom' is, I should say,
indispensable for an understanding of social responsibility – a
theme basic to *Measure for Measure*. As Maxim Gorky once put
it: 'I'm against freedom beyond that line at which freedom
becomes abandon, and this conversion is known to begin where
man, no longer aware of his actual social-cultural value, gives
free rein to the ancient Philistine individualism concealed in
him' (the rector's 'conservative anarchism') 'and cries out,
"I'm so charming, original, unique, but I am not allowed to
live as I please." '[2] What is so difficult is the drawing of the
'line' in the right place. This is a problem of government in any
society, and particularly in the Vienna of *Measure for Measure*.
The play, it has been said, 'analyses the inherent difficulty of
practical government to a sensitive mind'. This critic, Wilson
Knight, goes on to say that the play unfolds 'a deeply Shakespearean sexual ethic, close alike to Gospel teaching and modern
psychology . . . pharisaic righteousness is shown as superficial
and natural instinct treated with sympathy.'[3] In practice it

---

[1] Lawrence, *Tales*, pp. 556; 1037.

[2] Quoted by L. F. Ilyichov at a meeting between Party and Government
Leaders and Writers and Artists, Moscow, December 17, 1962: see Supple-
ment to *Soviet Literature* (Moscow), 1963, No. 2, p. 12.

[3] G. Wilson Knight, 'The Shakespearean Integrity': *Shakespeare Criticism,
1935-1960*, ed. Anne Ridler (1963), p. 187.

is not so easy to see how Christian teaching and modern psychology are unified in the play. It is Isabella who has the agonizing dilemma of attempting such a reconciliation: shall she, the virgin, about to take a nun's vow of chastity, give herself to Angelo to win a reprieve for her brother who has behaved unchastely with his betrothed? The problem involved here might be put like this: does Shakespeare approve of Isabella's fiercely uncompromising chastity?

In the best-known single study of the play R. W. Chambers pushes the Christian answer to this problem as far as it could well go, and perhaps further: 'Isabel decides without hesitation [not to defile herself to save Claudio]. Now whatever we think of that instant decision, it is certainly not un-Christian. Christianity could never have lived through its first three hundred years of persecution, if its ranks had not been stiffened by men and women who never hesitated in the choice between righteousness and the ties to their kinsfolk.'[1] All we now have to do is to equate this with 'modern psychology'. The most modern psychologists I know who have raised this problem are the Professor of Mental Health in the University of Edinburgh, G. M. Carstairs, in his 1962 Reith Lectures called *This Island Now*, and some members of the committee who recently published *Towards a Quaker View of Sex*. In his third lecture Professor Carstairs suggested that the old, Pauline notion of chastity appears to have been left behind by the behaviour of young people, more and more of whom have intercourse before marriage and do not mind if their eventual marriage partner has done so too: 'It seems to me that our young people are rapidly turning our own society [like the Trobriand Islanders', the Samoans', etc.] into one in which sexual experience, with precautions against conception, is becoming accepted as a sensible preliminary to marriage; a preliminary which makes it more likely that marriage, when it comes, will be a mutually considerate and mutually satisfying partnership.'[2] The Christian ministers who commented on this lecture were opposed, in a proportion of two to one, to Professor Carstairs's recommendation of permissiveness, and so were

[1] See Ridler (*op. cit.*), p. 9.

[2] *The Listener*, 29.11.62, pp. 892-3; *Towards a Quaker View of Sex* (Friends Home Service Committee, 1963), pp. 6, 15, 17-18.

the responsible Church bodies, for example the Temperance and Morals Committee of the Church of Scotland. The present-day Christian view appears to be, in the words of the Moderator of the Church of Scotland's General Assembly, that 'the Christian emphasis on chastity is absolutely essential.'[1]

Here something of the distance inevitable between seventeenth and twentieth-century outlooks begins to appear. For I think it is true, as F. R. Leavis says, that 'A Claudio who took an advanced twentieth-century line in these matters might have made a more interesting "character"; but such an emancipated Claudio was no part of Shakespeare's conception of his theme. Nor . . . are there any grounds for supposing that Shakespeare himself tended to feel that the prescription of pre-marital chastity might well be dispensed with.'[2] This is useful because it makes clear the definite view of conduct that the play involves. But the hint of a sneer in the words 'advanced' and 'emancipated' is not so acceptable. For it seems to me that Shakespeare achieves that necessary, and difficult, compromise between principle and our real behaviour by showing how chastity can be maintained only *at a cost*. In that second interview with Angelo, Isabella says, in one of her most vehement protestations,

> . . . were I under the terms of death,
> Th' impression of keen whips I'd wear as rubies,
> And strip myself to death as to a bed
> That longing have been sick for, ere I'd yield
> My body up to shame.   (II. 4. 100-4.)

The impression this makes is erotic – this sense cannot be shaken off. And the effect is to move Isabella a little nearer to Angelo as one of those whose rigorous principles serve unconsciously as a defence against the unacknowledged strength of her own passions. As Professor Carstairs put it in his third lecture: 'It has always been those whose sexual impulses have been precariously repressed who have raised the loudest cries of alarm over other people's immorality.' In Isabella's speech, it seems, some unfulfilled sensuality is seizing the chance offered

---

[1] See Professor Carstairs's article in *The Scotsman*, 24.12.62; also *The Observer*, 9 12.62.

[2] F. R. Leavis, 'The Greatness of *Measure for Measure*': *The Common Pursuit* (1952), p. 162.

by the threat of violation to flow out and satisfy itself by imaginary indulgence in the pangs of martyrdom.

R. W. Chambers handles this issue by a simple appeal to history:

> We may call this fanaticism: but it was well understood in Shakespeare's day. Foxe's *Martyrs* was read by all; old people could still remember seeing the Smithfield fires; year after year saw the martyrdoms of Catholic men (and sometimes of Catholic women like the Ven. Margaret Clitherow). It was a stern age – an age such as the founder of Christianity had foreseen when he uttered his stern warnings. . . . 'If any man come to me, and hate not his father, and mother, and brethren and sisters, he cannot be my disciple'.

But merely to state facts of history surely evades just those issues of real feelings, real moral dilemmas, that *Measure for Measure* was framed to explore. Martyrdom will have been familiar to Shakespeare's fellow-citizens, yes – but why must we conclude from this that Shakespeare will have uncritically taken over the familiar unthinking and accepting attitudes to it? Chambers has to say later that 'For all her silence and modesty, Isabel has the ferocity of the martyr.' No analyst of human complexities as profound as we have seen Shakespeare to be could have missed the peculiar strain or flaw of integration expressed in such a tension between modesty and ferocity. It is this kind of tension that the old master-writers could depict by sheer insight and the modern psychologist has been able to account for by his theories of how personality develops.

Beside such insights a literal adherence to certain Church tenets appears naïve. Chambers is as naïve when he argues that Claudio is subdued into accepting death by the sheer goodness and rightness of Isabella's Christian arguments. 'We find,' he says, 'that Claudio, who before Isabella's outburst ['Wilt thou be made a man out of my vice?'] had been gripped by the mortal fear of death, is now again master of his soul:

> Let me ask my sister pardon. I am so out of love with life that I will sue to be rid of it.'   (III. I. 170-1.)

In fact Claudio's turn into submission follows on the disguised Duke's pretence that Angelo had only been testing Isabella's virtue: Claudio must die anyway, according to the original sentence. It is crucial for the drift of the whole play to realize that it is this, not Isabella's appeal, that has made Claudio submit, for this is the scene (III. I.) in which the great speech for life is uttered. After this speech comes Isabella's outburst:

Is't not a kind of incest to take life
From thine own sister's shame? What should I think?
Heaven shield my mother play'd my father fair!
For such a warped slip of wilderness
Ne'er issu'd from his blood.   (III. I. 140-4.)

Even after all this Claudio still reacts by broken-off, agonized pleading: 'Nay, hear me, Isabel. . . . Oh hear me, Isabella. . . .' The force of living impulse in him is not, and could not be, damped down by his sister's invoking of sacred chastity. If it had been, the play would have been a far less vital thing than it is; for that speech of Claudio's, clinging to the 'warm motion' of the 'delighted spirit', is one of the play's deep centres, and to suppose it negated or outweighed by lofty 'principles' would be to suppose Shakespeare setting his face against what we must call *life*.

So neither the free-living Claudio nor the sternly chaste Isabella emerges from the play with unqualified value. Lawrence's qualification of the Isabella type is actually much more drastic than Shakespeare's – he is that much further from the pure doctrine of the Church. The authors of *Towards a Quaker View of Sex* quote and approve John MacMurray's suggestion that nowadays we must think of 'chastity' not as abstinence but as 'emotional sincerity'.[1] This idea is perfectly Lawrentian: it might almost have come from, say, the passage on what a critic must be from his essay on John Galsworthy: 'A critic must be emotionally alive in every fibre, intellectually capable and skilful in essential logic, and then morally very honest.'[2] As one who led the reaction against the long Victorian régime of strict taboo on the discussion of intimate experience, Lawrence was bitterly against the *cults* of innocence, 'purity', and self-sacrifice at the expense of passional fulfilment. His attitude to love outside marriage is given in his brief, unanswerable com-

[1] The phrase is from MacMurray's *Reason and Emotion*; see *Quaker View of Sex*, p. 47.
[2] 'John Galsworthy': *Phoenix*, ed. Edward D. MacDonald (1936), p. 539.

ment on the adultery in *Anna Karénina*: 'Nobody in the world is anything but delighted when Vronsky gets Anna Karénina.'[1]

This insistence on passional realities belongs closely with Lawrence's many criticisms of the 'purity' that the so-spiritual Victorian tradition had exalted: together these two views form one of his main touchstones for sincerity in literature. In that same essay, for example, he says of Tolstoy's *Resurrection*: 'The convict train is quick and alive. But that would-be-expiatory Prince is as dead as lumber.' And the following passage, inspired by Hawthorne's *The Scarlet Letter*, could almost be a gloss on aspects of *Measure for Measure* (as well as his own tales):

> Oh, Hester, you are a demon. A man *must* be pure, just that you can seduce him to a fall. . . .
> His [Arthur Dimmesdale's] spiritual love was a lie. And prostituting the woman to his spiritual love, as popular clergymen do, in his preachings and loftiness, was a tall white lie. Which came flop.
> We are so pure in spirit. Hi-tiddly-i-ty!
> Till she tickled him in the right place, and he fell.
> Flop.
> Flop goes spiritual love.
> But keep up the game. Keep up appearances. Pure are the pure. To the pure all things, etc.

In *The Scarlet Letter*, Dimmesdale, who *has* 'fallen', does what Isabella's words have only hinted at ('The impressions of keen whips I'd wear as rubies') – he flogs himself, punishing himself for his illicit love for Hester Prynne:

> Previously, he had governed his body, ruling it, in the interests of his spirit. Now he has a good time all by himself torturing his body. . . . He wants to get a mental grip on his body. And since he can't quite manage it with the mind, witness his fall – he will give it what for, with whips. His will shall *lash* his body. And he enjoys his pains. Wallows in them. To the pure all things are pure.[2]

---

[1] 'The Novel': *Reflections on the Death of a Porcupine* (1934 ed.), p. 104. On the whole subject of the 'Victorian' moral tradition in literature, its causes, and Lawrence's reaction to it, see David Craig, Introd. to J. G. Lockhart, *Adam Blair* (Edinburgh, 1963), pp. xv-xix.

[2] *Studies in Classic American Literature* (New York ed., 1953), pp. 99-100.

The points at which this applies to Angelo will have been plain.
Lawrence is criticizing what he calls 'spirituality', the false
saintliness that can preserve itself pure only by escape from life.
Isabella is not quite this, though she is nearer it than Chambers
allows. Lucio, the rake, who yet speaks for fertility and naturalness, is allowed to say to Isabella:

> . . . though 'tis my familiar sin
> With maids to seem the lapwing, and to jest,
> Tongue far from heart – play with all virgins so:
> I hold you as a thing enskied and sainted,
> By your renouncement an immortal spirit,
> And to be talk'd with in sincerity,
> As with a saint.   (I. 4. 31-7.)

It matters considerably for the interpretation of the play
whether Lucio says (and the dramatist means) this straight.
Isabella replies at once, 'You do blaspheme the good in mocking
me.' So Lucio's tone has seemed cynically bantering. Is this
because he, the rake, can't speak otherwise? Or because her
inexperienced modesty is quick to suspect such a man of
insincerity? Once again, I feel, the truth is mixed: Lucio does
mean that she is 'out of this world' in the perfection of her
virtue, yet he is himself so eloquent a spokesman for full life
(his next speech marvellously evokes fertility – in tribute to
Juliet's pregnancy) that his tribute to Isabella turns double-
edged: there is so much richness in this world that to be 'above
it' is an impoverishment as well as a setting-free.

Words such as 'saint' or 'righteousness' or 'purity' thus cannot be used simply in the context of works such as these. Yet
again it must be said that the other extreme to piety – a
fleering at religion or an automatic overturning of all hallowed
values, is not to be found in them either. Both writers hold a
difficult balance. In Lawrence, who spoke out so directly on
problems of modern living, the difficulty sometimes led to
real uncertainty and self-contradiction – now he is for free behaviour when it strikes a blow at the straitlaced, now he jibs
at it when he sees young people taking gladly to the freedom in
lovemaking which he himself had helped to release and create
acceptance for.[1] Undoubtedly the weight of that moral

---

[1] E.g. compare 'Pornography and Obscenity' (*Phoenix*, p. 174) with 'The Novel'
(*Death of a Porcupine*, p. 122).

authority which he won for himself by the deep sensitivity of his writing about sex went to the support of 'emotional sincerity', whether or not this clashed with the respectable code. He is rather typical of the 'romantic love' tradition, however, in tending to present his couples as living out their experiences together on a kind of super-social plane of their own, mercifully freed from the necessities (child-bearing and rearing, earning, home-making) which are in fact inseparable from stable love-relations as we know them and have thus helped to build up the norms of sexual behaviour that we need.

Here we reach the point beyond which the likeness between the Elizabethan writer and the modern cannot be taken. The two could arrive at insights so akin because of the continuity, through changing social epochs, of the human organism with its characteristic feelings. But successive epochs do put the stress on rather different fibres in the organism. The historically typical thing about *Measure for Measure* is that it could figure *a necessary relationship between the most intimate experiences and a social code*. It analyses 'the inherent difficulty of practical government to a sensitive mind', and the specific thing to be governed is our most intimate kind of experience. Not that Shakespeare is writing a dramatic tract meant to influence a government in its marriage legislation. The form of the play is rather, as Leavis puts it, 'a controlled experiment' – an acting-out of a situation as though to test what degree of personal freedom is tolerable in a society. But the society, though not historical, is very realistically there, with its state apparatus of ruler and deputy, constable, prison, and executioner, laws and penalties.

I think that point has only to be stated for us to feel how unthinkable it is for a modern writer to make intimate experience the subject of a presentation so dependent on the public and the organized. Shakespeare seems to have been able to feel status, role, function, the whole of the more communal side of life, as continuous with the most private experience. In the 'Angelo' sonnet he can use imagery from business to convey the deeper levels of character:

> They rightly do inherit Heavens' graces,
> And husband nature's riches from expense;

> They are the lords and owners of their faces,
> Others, but stewards of their excellence. . . .

This is also the style of Shakespeare's contemporary, Donne.
Donne doesn't at all detract from the passionate quality of a
love-poem such as 'The Anniversarie' or 'The Canonization' by
drawing his imagery from public life – indeed he strengthens
and universalizes it:

> And then wee shall be throughly blest,
>   But wee no more, than all the rest;
> Here upon earth, we'are Kings, and none but wee
> Can be such Kings, nor of such subjects bee.
> Who is so safe as wee? where none can doe
> Treason to us, except one of us two? . . .
> . . . And thus invoke us; You whom reverend love
>   Made one anothers hermitage;
> You, to whom love was peace, that now is rage;
>   Who did the whole worlds soule contract, and drove
>   Into the glasses of your eyes
>   (So made such mirrors, and such spies,
> That they did all to you epitomize,)
>   Countries, Townes, Courts: Beg from above
>   A patterne of your love!

I think I am right in saying (though the generalization is
so large as to be almost unverifiable) that public imagery would
have been felt as an intruder in almost all poetry of personal
experience from the middle seventeenth century down to our
own times. Until the Restoration, personal poetry was over-
whelmingly that of an aristocracy, accustomed to warfare,
statecraft, a cultivated life, and the ceremonies of the Court.
The social supremacy and unified outlook of so exclusive a
class made possible a very well-accepted and confident habit
of expression that could draw on their whole way of life when
materials were needed for the idioms, metaphors, allusions that
are the stuff of language. To mention a single example: this
nobility was skilled in arms, and there is almost nothing in the
lyric poetry of the later Tudor and early Stuart period for
which the military life cannot supply an image – think of the
love-poems of Wyatt, Donne, and the Irishman Pierce Ferriter;
the wedding-hymn from Chapman's *Hero and Leander*; Bishop
King's grave, tender 'Exequy' for his young wife; Marvell's

most graceful poetry on the splendours of the country-house and, even, his metaphysical dialogues that balance against each other the abstractions of philosophers and theologians.

These poets of the nobility and higher gentry could say anything, without worrying about being thought 'low' or censured by polite opinion for failing to *keep up appearances*. No later school of writers enjoyed quite this immunity. One or another bourgeois taboo (or the opposite – the deliberately scandalous or free) has affected our literature ever since. It is not only that the more passionate poetry of the generations after the Commonwealth was chary of allowing public references into the more intimate sorts of writing; for a long time there was very little passionate expression at all. What remarkable literature of tenderness or desire can we remember from after the Cavaliers until the close of the eighteenth century? Only Rochester's fearlessly frank lyrics; and the only thing at all like them (apart from folk-songs) is the love-poetry of Burns, who came from another culture. The squalid manoeuvres of the Restoration drama hardly deserve to count; and the great Augustans (Dryden, Pope, Johnson) were more interested in politics, business, the literary life, and abstract morals than in what touches us most intimately.

The age that preceded the Victorian saw the Romantic Revival, which is generally thought of for its rediscovery of individual passion. But it is remarkable how rarely the passions expressed are those dealt with in *Measure for Measure*. Byron – again the exception is an aristocrat – can describe a love-affair with uninhibited fullness (in *Don Juan*); but the other Romantics tended to think of love as a kind of specialized experience, to cultivate it in a hot-house artifically isolated from the host of links it has with the rest of our lives. In Keats's last sonnet, saturated though it is with passion in a way the eighteenth century had found impossible, we yet feel that the poet is enclosed in his *own* emotions, in what his own imagination is making of his love:

> Pillow'd upon my fair love's ripening breast,
> To feel for ever its soft fall and swell,
>   Awake for ever in a sweet unrest,
> Still, still to hear her tender-taken breath,
> And so live ever – or else swoon to death.

This typically Romantic way with passion has little of Donne's lively sense of his sweetheart as a distinct other person, so close to him yet existing in her own right with a reality as intense as his own feelings for her:

> Then since that I may know;
> As liberally, as to a Midwife, shew
> Thy self: cast all, yea, this white lynnen hence,
> There is no pennance due to innocence.
> To teach thee, I am naked first; why then
> What needst thou have more covering than a man. [1]

In Shelley, as in Keats, the loved one tends to disappear into the overwhelming glamour of the poet's own imaginings:

> Rose leaves, when the rose is dead,
> Are heaped for the beloved's bed;
> And so thy thoughts, when thou art gone,
> Love itself shall slumber on.

The watery poetry of the Victorians could not recover for literature the full image of love; and the Victorian novel, great in almost every sphere it touched, is wanting precisely in a candid treatment of passion – although it deals in every sort of substitute or sublimation, particularly that rather hectic spirituality which is common to the best writers (George Eliot, Hawthorne, the Brontës) and the feeblest (Florence Barclay, Gene Stratton Porter). [2]

The deepest kind of encounter between men and women, after dawning again in Hardy's last novels, re-emerged into the light of a full artistic presentation in Lawrence – above all, I would say, in the passages on young love in *The Rainbow* and in those superb love-scenes in *Lady Chatterley's Lover*, both beautiful and intensely real, that have been blown upon lately with every kind of smoking-room horse-laugh and literary sneer. Lawrence, however, hardly recovered the wholeness of a Donne or Shakespeare, for he could not re-unite the public and the intimate at the level of *Measure for Measure* or Donne's *Songs and Sonets*. Although Lawrence was a profound student of societies and adept at seizing on the essential qualities of a

---

[1] Donne, Elegie XIX, 'To his Mistris Going to Bed'.
[2] See Q. D. Leavis, *Fiction and the Reading Public* (1932), pp. 245, 326; and the *Adam Blair* Introd. cited above.

community or an age, yet *organized society* is usually felt in his work to jeopardize rather than support or order the personal life. There are exceptions. In 'The Captain's Doll' it is notable that when, towards the end, Hepburn wants to put into words his fundamental idea of relations between a man and a woman, he turns to an accepted formula – the words of the marriage ceremony: ' "I tried marriage once on a basis of love, and I must say it was a ghastly affair in the long run. . . . And yet I want marriage. I want marriage. I want a woman to honour and obey me". ' Yet when Lawrence writes a novel large enough to present a whole society with its collective habits and traditions, for example *Women in Love*, the essential trend is away, away from the communally organized, out onto a limb where at least the unique individual can 'be himself'. In *Women in Love*, the home life of the working class is seen as barbaric, aboriginal; the organized workers are seen as selfish, destructive, anarchic; and domestic middle-class life is seen as a dreary dead-end – ' "the world all in couples, each couple in its own little house, watching its own little interests, and stewing in its own little privacy – it's the most repulsive thing on earth . . ." '.[1] This is the gist of every passage on homes and the common habits of people; it is what the hero, Birkin, says at the points where he is most plainly carrying the author's message;[2] and towards the end, in the chapter 'Flitting', we are left with the two main women, Ursula and Gudrun, explicitly repudiating as 'unthinkable' the ordinary life with a man 'in the social world'. Although Lawrence did with another part of himself greatly value the societal impulse in man, in practice his attitude was more often the contemptuous one expressed in 'The Novel' – 'Men clotting together into social masses in order to limit their individual liabilities: this is humanity'. And he regarded social organization as something only minimally relevant to our deeper experience – his long essay 'Democracy' is at one on this point with the letter already cited: 'I think the state is a vulgar institution. But life itself is an affair of aristocrats. In my soul, I'd be as proud as hell. . . . The state is an arrangement for

---

[1] *Women in Love*, chap. 25 (Pocket ed., 1950), p. 372.
[2] E.g. compare Birkin on 'liberty, equality, fraternity' – chap. 8 (pp. 106-7) – with Lawrence's letter of 3.1.1915 to Lady Ottoline Morrell: *Letters*, ed. Aldous Huxley (1932), p. 213.

myriads of peoples' living together. And one doesn't have brothers by arrangement.'[1]

Something like this view is so fashionable at present that one very rarely reads an acknowledgement of how many of the means of life, and even the values, which we literally live by depend on just such 'arrangements for myriads of peoples' living together'.

This side of life was so impatiently discounted in Lawrence's thinking that one cannot feel he was sufficiently wise when it came to practical-social issues. Without such wisdom, what Gorky called our 'actual social-cultural value' is liable to get distorted by an extreme individualism that cannot help retreating into more and more despairing isolation. It is no good blaming Lawrence's peculiar temperament for the extremity of his position. At a time when the very surroundings in which we have our community – i.e. the pattern of our towns – are shaped almost exclusively by convenience for the making of profits, it is indeed hard for a sensitive man to feel social organization as a source of values or as part of ourselves.

No doubt this could not be taken for granted by Shakespeare either. It has been suggested that *Measure for Measure* itself comes at a point when Shakespeare was increasingly concerned 'with the shortcomings of authority' (Angelo embodies this). 'Shakespeare was still fully conscious of the dangers of disorder, but he was now more concerned with the evils of power,' and less inclined to rest in 'order' as an indubitable value.[2] Yet the very fact that he could conceive of a problem of passionate love as able to be presented inside a very definite framework of social organization shows how it still came much more naturally for him to acknowledge our fundamental dependence on community than it does for Western writers at the present time.

---

[1] *Letters*, p. 213; for his developed views on democracy, see the essay 'Democracy': *Phoenix*, pp. 701-4.

[2] Kenneth Muir, '*Timon of Athens* and the Cash Nexus': *Modern Quarterly Miscellany*, No. 1 (1947), pp. 62-6.

TROILUS AND CRESSIDA AND THE SPIRIT OF CAPITALISM

Raymond Southall

A great deal of speculation and research has been stimulated during the past half-century by Max Weber's contention that the process of social change during the sixteenth and seventeenth centuries was determined by the character of prevailing religious belief.[1] Weber's thesis, very briefly, was that without the presence of a Protestant ethic the development of capitalism would have been greatly retarded, as it was in the case of those countries which maintained the institutions of Catholicism, such as France, Spain and Italy. The weakness of Weber's argument is that it overlooks the fact that the manumission of feudal relationships promoted a strong and persuasive bourgeois ethic that was fundamentally anti-Christian. Weber's error, a typically academic one, was that he concentrated attention upon the consciously formulated systems of ethics (Catholic, Protestant) which existed in the period and ignored the ethics that inspired actual social life. What these were was suggested by John Wheeler, Secretary of the Merchant Adventurers, when, writing in 1601, he caustically observed that:

> there is nothing in the world so ordinarie, and naturall vnto men, as to contract, truck, merchandise, and trafficke one with an other, so that it is almost vn-possible for three persons to conuerse together two houres, but they wil fal into talk of one bargaine or another, chopping, changing, or some other kinde of contract. Children, assoone as euer their tongues are at libertie, doe season their sportes with some merchandise, or other: and when they goe to schoole, nothing is so common among them as to change, and rechange, buy and sell of that, which they bring from home with

[1] Max Weber, *The Protestant Ethic and The Spirit of Capitalism* (tr. Talcott Parsons), 1930.

them. The Prince with his subiects, the Maister with his seruants, one friend and acquaintance with another, the Captaine with his souldiers, the Husband with his wife, Women with and among themselues, and in a word, all the world choppeth and changeth, runneth & raueth after Marts, Markets and Merchandising, so that all thinges come into Commerce, and passe into traffique (in a maner) in all times, and in all places: not onely that, which nature bringeth forth, as the fruits of the earth, the beasts, and liuing creatures, with their spoiles, skinnes and cases, the metals, minerals, and such like things, but further also, this man maketh merchandise of the workes of his owne handes, this man of another mans labour, one selleth words, another maketh traffike of the skins & bloud of other men, yea there are some found so subtill and cunning merchants, that they perswade and induce men to suffer themselues to bee bought and sold, and we haue seene in our time enow, and too many which haue made merchandise of mens soules.[1]

Here, through the eyes of an acute contemporary, we see what actually determined the character of an Elizabethan's relations to his fellows; the ethic of 'ordinary' life was 'naturally' that of the market place and not that of the pulpit; indeed, it was an ethic which justified making '*merchandise* of mens soules'. Thomas Nashe's Pierce Penilesse was informed, 'that a certain blind retailer, called the devil, used to lend money upon pawns or anything and would let one for a need have a thousand pounds upon a statute merchant of his soul'. But contemporary recognition of the fact that social life was essentially bourgeois and anti-christian in spirit is commonplace: Dekker remarked that 'the thrifty citizen . . . seeing the golden age returned into the world again, resolves to worship no saint but money' and Pierce Penilesse is advised to look for the Devil 'amongst the rich merchants of the exchange.'[2]

The point is that the manumission of feudal relations brought about a change in social behaviour and that the new forms of

[1] John Wheeler, *A Treatise of Commerce* (1601), pp. 6, 7.
[2] Thomas Nashe, *Pierce Penilesse His Supplication to the Devil*, in *Three Elizabethan Pamphlets* (ed. G. R. Hibbard), 1961, p. 78. Nashe, *ibid.*
Thomas Dekker, *The Wonderful Year* in *Three Elizabethan Pamphlets* (ed. G. R. Hibbard), 1951, p. 176.

behaviour expressed a new ethic, an ethic in which all human
relationships, the most public (as that of prince and subjects),
the most private (as that of husband and wife) and even the
most other-worldly (as that of worship), are mediated by a
common bourgeois concern. In the matter of religious obser-
vance, for instance, what Dekker said of worship – 'the thrifty
citizen . . . resolves to worship no saint but money' – is ampli-
fied by Shakespeare in *The Merchant of Venice*; notice how the
bourgeois concern mediates between the Christian merchant
and 'the holy' in the following lines:

> Should I go to church
> And see the holy edifice of stone,
> And not bethink me straight of dangerous rocks,
> Which touching but my gentle vessel's side,
> Would scatter all her spices on the stream,
> Enrobe the roaring waters with my silks,
> And, in a word, but even now worth this,
> And now worth nothing?   (I. I. 29-36.)

The same mediation transforms intimate secular relationships,
as that between lovers. Previously this had found its apparently
natural expression in terms of service and feudal obligation:

> The lover devoted himself to the service of his mistress,
> who became his liege lady. He was her *baillie*, and had to
> render her the submission of a vassal.[1]

Shakespeare, casting the lover as a thrall or vassal offering
service to his lady, still reflects the feudal love ethic in his
sonnets and early comedies. But even before Elizabeth assumed
the throne this had become *recherché* and the language in which
the ethic was couched had ceased to express anything more
vital than old fashioned gallantry. In its place the new bourgeois
ethic, emerging spontaneously from changed relations in every-
day life, made its appearance, as in Sir Philip Sidney's:

> My true love hath my heart and I have his,
> By just exchange one for another given:
> I hold his dear, and mine he cannot miss,
> There never was a better bargain driven.

Love, in Spenser and Shakespeare as well as in Sidney, frequently finds its apparently natural expression in mercenary

[1] G. C. Brook (ed.) *The Harley Lyrics*, Manchester, (2nd. ed.), 1956, p. 9.

terms. And in view of the changing value of love even such an event as the appearance of Ovid, translated into English during the late sixteenth century, becomes something more than an instance of the Renaissance interest in classical literature:

> Ovid's lusty young men who pursue and his coy young women who resist with reluctance reflect the bargaining and haggling that always goes on over a purchasable commodity.[1]

The undermining of the old feudal relations and the emergence of a potent bourgeois ethic, therefore, is pertinent to any truly sociological consideration of Elizabethan literature, but it is particularly so, as I hope to show, in the case of Shakespeare's *Troilus and Cressida*.

The Trojan story came to Shakespeare already imbued with feudal notions of chivalry and courtly love. This is obvious in several passages of the play: in the procession of knights returning from the field, watched by Lady Cressida, and including as the main item of interest, 'Brave Troilus! the prince of chivalry' (I. 2.); in the argument of the Trojan council scene (II. 2.); in Hector's challenge to the Greeks (I. 3.) and in his preparation to meet Ajax, when:

> The glory of our Troy doth this day lie
> On his fair worth and single chivalry   (IV. 4. 146-7.)

as also in his dismissal of attempts to dissuade him from the day's fighting with the bland assurance:

> I am today i' th' vein of chivalry;   (V. 3. 32.)

in Diomed's decision to wear Cressida's favour and in his order:

> Go, go, my servant, take thou Troilus' horse;
> Present the fair steed to my Lady Cressid.
> Fellow, commend my service to her beauty;
> Tell her I have chastis'd the amorous Troyan,
> And am her Knight by proof.   (V. 5. 1-5.)

The Trojan story also had a kind of contemporary, local relevance arising out of the fact that London was, at the time,

[1] David Lloyd Stevenson, *The Love Game Comedy*, New York, 1946, pp. 11, 12.

commonly and proudly eulogized as Troynovant, the New Troy.

Leaving aside the inherent character of the story, the distinctively Shakespearian activity in the play is to be found in the emphatic coarsening of that kind of life represented by romance and chivalry. This is most remarkable in the so-called love poetry of the play. Critics have reached such a unanimity of opinion concerning what J. C. Maxwell has called 'the genuine intensity of the love poetry' that Mr. Maxwell himself did not feel it necessary to consider the matter:

> because it has never gone unrecognised, whereas the degree to which Shakespeare qualifies our response to it has often been underestimated. That the love of Troilus, for all the youthful ardour which sometimes tempts us to think of Shakespeare as entirely carried away by it, essentially belongs to the shallow and corrupt world of Troy, is shown also by the arrangement of the scenes.

But after this slight heresy Mr. Maxwell is quick to return to received opinion and to point out that 'In its intensity Troilus's love is very different' from that of Paris and Helen, 'who must surely represent the norm of sophisticated love-intrigue at Troy'.[1] Apart from the logical oddness of this assertion (the only Trojan love-intrigues are those of Paris and Helen and Troilus and Cressida) it is to be noted that Mr. Maxwell, along with many other critics, implicitly accepts the love ethic of Troilus and all that it entails. Bearing in mind how easy it is for all of us to accept current ethical attitudes without appreciating their actual social implications,[2] this is not perhaps surprising; nonetheless, a certain obtuseness on the part of Shakespearian critics is significant in that it serves as a forcible reminder that we are still in and of a world in which it is natural to view love as a commercial transaction.

In the play itself instances of the coarsening of sensibility which such a view of love involves are so numerous that, unless the above explanation is accepted, it is extremely difficult to

---

[1] J. C. Maxwell, 'Shakespeare: The Middle Plays', in *The Age of Shakespeare* (ed. Boris Ford), 1955, p. 218.

[2] Note, for instance, how easily the bourgeois ethic of Freud passes unnoticed. 'The field of human relations in Freud's sense is similar to the market': Erich Fromm; *The Fear of Freedom*, (1942), pp. 8, 9.

understand why they should not have been generally recognized. In the first scene of the play Troilus defines his evaluation of the love relationship for us in the oft-quoted lines:

> Tell me, Apollo, for thy Daphne's love,
> What Cressid is, what Pandar, and what we?
> Her bed is India; there she lies, a pearl;
> Between our Ilium and where she resides
> Let it be call'd the wild and wand'ring flood;
> Ourself the merchant, and this sailing Pandar
> Our doubtful hope, our convoy and our bark.
>
> (I. 1. 97-103.)

Thus Troilus remarks his transformation into a merchant for whom Cressida is a desirable commodity and Pandar a trading vessel – elsewhere he describes Pandar as a broker. Later he refers to the more general transformation that has been effected when he seeks to justify the retention of Helen by arguing that she too is a pearl, but one:

> Whose price hath launch'd above a thousand ships,
> And turn'd crown'd kings to merchants.
>
> (II. 2. 82-3.)

Talk about the manumission of feudal relations, therefore, is not an impertinence foisted upon the play, but something to which the text itself draws attention.

It might be thought, nonetheless, that this particular element in the play has some kind of unresolved religious significance, that Troilus is paraphrasing *Matthew* XIII, 45, 46:

> Again, the kingdom of heaven is like unto a man that is a merchant seeking goodly pearls: and having found one pearl of great price, he went and sold all that he had, and bought it.

But in the context of the play as a whole this biblical echo is lost.

Troilus is a 'prince of chivalry', a feudal prince, who has been spiritually transformed and who, when eventually he must part with Cressida, is reduced to the commerically-minded lament:

> We two, that with so many thousand sighs
> Did buy each other, must poorly sell ourselves
>
> (IV. 4. 38-9.)

But the corrupted judgment that weighs men and women in the scales of the market place is not monopolised by Troilus. When Hector has issued his chivalrous challenge to the Greeks, for instance, Ulysses takes Nestor aside and suggests:

> Let us, like merchants, show our foulest wares
> And think perchance they'll sell. (I. 3. 359-60.)

their 'foulest wares' being Ajax, who is, according to the much maligned Thersites, 'bought and sold among those of any wit, like a barbarian slave' (II. I.). After the brief encounter with Ajax, Hector is entertained by the Greeks and Achilles desires the opportunity to look him over, 'As I would buy thee' (IV. 5.). In the meantime, Calchas, Cressida's father, pleads with the Greeks that Cressida be procured from Troy as ransom for the captive Trojan Antenor, 'he shall buy my daughter' (III. 3.). Agreeing to the exchange the Greeks dispatch Diomed to effect it. It is whilst this Grecian broker is waiting in Troy for Cressida that Paris asks him who really deserves Helen and Diomed proceeds to strip the war of its chivalrous trappings:

> He merits well to have her that doth seek her,
> Not making any scruple of her soilure,
> With such a hell of pain and world of charge;
> And you as well to keep her that defend her,
> Not palating the taste of her dishonour,
> With such a costly loss of wealth and friends.
> He, like a puling cuckold would drink up
> The lees and dregs of a flat tamed piece;
> You, like a lecher, out of whorish loins
> Are pleas'd to breed out your inheritors.
> Both merits pois'd, each weighs nor less nor more;
> But he as he, the heavier for a whore. (IV. I. 57-68.)

Paris, however, is inspired by the same mercenary spirit as Troilus and waves Diomed's biting comments aside with a glib:

> Fair Diomed, you do as chapmen do,
> Dispraise the thing that you desire to buy;
> But we in silence hold this virtue well:
> We'll but commend what we intend to sell.
>
> (IV. I. 77-80.)

Plainly, and to avoid labouring the obvious, summarily, such expressions of the nature of love and war reveal a spirit that is neither ancient (Greek or Trojan) nor medieval (romantic or chivalrous) but Elizabethan-Jacobean as portrayed by Wheeler, in short, the spirit of capitalism.

The coarsening of life associated with this spirit is made explicit by Shakespeare, then, in the use of the language of commerce to define, amongst other things, the nature and dignity of love. That this is what Shakespeare is doing in the play requires no external evidence. The coarseness that finds its natural expression in the vocabulary of trade is evident in the character of the 'love' poetry. In the opening and, according to Shakespearian practice, the directive scene of the play Troilus is impatient with the delay in procuring a meeting with Cressida and protests to Pandar:

> I tell thee I am mad
> In Cressid's love. Thou answer'st 'She is fair' –
> Pour'st in the open ulcer of my heart –
> Her eyes, her hair, her cheek, her gait, her voice,
> Handlest in thy discourse. O, that her hand,
> In whose comparison all whites are ink
> Writing their own reproach; to whose soft seizure
> The cygnet's down is harsh, and spirit of sense
> Hard as the palm of ploughman!   (I. I. 50-8.)

It takes Shakespeare just over fifty lines to reach this point, a point at which we already notice the predicament in which Troilus is involved; he is torn between what he is capable of imagining and what he feels capable of enacting. We are made especially aware of this gap by the disjunction of feeling marked by the expression 'soft seizure'. This disjunction serves to create a gulf between what can be handled in 'discourse' or imagination and what Troilus later refers to as 'the capacity of [his] ruder powers.' But it is the *character* of Troilus's imagination that defines the quality of his 'love' poetry: the sensual anticipation of 'handlest' becomes an anticipated rape in 'soft seizure' and a recognition that the 'spirit of sense' will prove incapable of distilling the fullest enjoyment out of the imagined situation.

Troilus returns to his predicament when left alone to soliloquize in Act III, scene 2:

I am giddy; expectation whirls me round.
Th' imaginary relish is so sweet
That it enchants my sense; what will it be
When that the wat'ry palate tastes indeed
Love's thrice-repured nectar? – Death, I fear me;
Swooning distraction; or some joy too fine,
Too subtle – potent, tun'd too sharp in sweetness,
For the capacity of my ruder powers.   (III. 2. 17-24.)

Here he is again thrown completely off balance ('I am giddy; expectation whirls me round' cf. 'I tell thee I am mad') by the realization that the capacity of his 'ruder powers', his senses, sets a limit to the enjoyment he can hope to get out of the physical possession of Cressida and it is characteristic that such a natural limitation should appear to him to be, as he tells Cressida, monstrous:

> This is the monstruosity in love, lady, that the will is
> infinite, and the execution confin'd; that the desire is
> boundless, and the act a slave to limit.   (III. 2. 78-80.)

The act, it will be noticed, is invariably one of touch and taste, an act of handling, seizing, of relishing with the palate, a motion firmly circumscribed by the 'spirit of sense' and the capacity of the 'ruder powers'. Thus, in the opening scene of the play, Troilus and Pandar discuss the wooing of Cressida in terms of the preparation of a cake and when, towards the end of the play, she passes to Diomed, Troilus remarks that only:

> The fractions of her faith, orts of her love,
> The fragments, scraps, the bits and greasy relics
> Of her o'er-eaten faith, are bound to Diomed.
>
> (V. 2. 156-8.)

He almost invariably thinks of Cressida with his belly; beginning as a tasty titbit yet to be enjoyed she ends as a piece of left-over meat. The sentiment of these last lines is inherent in the characterization of Troilus. Already in the council scene (II. 2.) he has found it apposite to liken Helen to left-over meat; he argues there that she should not be returned to the Greeks because:

> the remainder viands
> We do not throw in unrespective sieve,
> Because we now are full.   (II. 2. 70-2.)

In the reply of Diomed to Paris, which has already been quoted, we are offered an appraisal of Helen remarkably similar to those of Helen and Cressida made by Troilus. According to Diomed, Agamemnon is prepared to 'drink up The lees and dregs of a flat taméd piece', Helen, whom Diomed later describes as 'carrion'. The point of this observation is that the spirit which emerges in the characterization of Troilus is not simply a piece of characterization. The figure of Troilus, as has been seen in his use of the vocabulary of trade, expresses the central preoccupations of the play. The Greeks in the figure of Achilles share the debility of Troilus:

> Imagin'd worth
> Holds in his blood such swol'n and hot discourse
> That 'twixt his mental and his active parts
> Kingdom'd Achilles in commotion rages,
> And batters down himself.   (II. 3. 167-71.)

However, where the disjunction of imagination and action in Troilus arises from the fact that he looks on Cressida to lust after her, in Achilles it arises from self-love, or pride. And as Troilus's passion is defined as the grossest of belly-appetites, so too is the pride of the Greeks, Achilles and Ajax; Ulysses remarks of them:

> How one man eats into another's pride,
> While pride is fasting in his wantonness!
>
>   (III. 3. 136-7.)

But the whole of the play is busily reducing life to the demands of the belly:

> He that is proud eats up himself.   (II. 3. 150.)
>
> . . . lechery eats itself.   (V. 4. 34.)
>
> . . . the Troyans taste our dear'st repute
> With their fin'st palate   (I. 3. 337-8.)
>
> Now . . . I begin to relish thy advice;
> And I will give a taste thereof forthwith
> To Agamemnon.   (I. 3. 388-90.)
>
> The grief is fine, full, perfect, that I taste,
>
> . . . .
> If I could temporize with my affections
> Or brew it to a weak and colder palate,
> The like allayment could I give my grief. (IV. 4. 3-8.)

He eats nothing but doves, love; and that breeds hot
blood, and hot blood begets hot thoughts, and hot
thoughts beget hot deeds, and hot deeds is love.

(III. I. 122-4.)

And Diomed, it will be remembered, scorns Paris for 'Not
palating the taste' of Helen's dishonour. Space forbids ex-
haustive quotation, but these few examples serve to make the
point that Ulysses's contention that 'appetite' is 'a universal
wolf' (I. 3.) touches the very quick of Shakespeare's conception
of the spirit of capitalism as a force which reduces life to the
mere satisfaction of the appetites.

> For it was of the essence of trade to drag into a position
> of solitary prominence the acquisitive appetites; and
> towards these appetites, which to most modern thinkers
> have seemed the one sure social dynamic, the attitude
> of the medieval theorist was that of one who holds a
> wolf by the ears.[1]

The extent of this concern can be seen when Troilus, chaffing
against the natural limitations of his appetites, his senses,
touches upon the subject of Time. Critics have made it abun-
dantly clear that Time has a special significance in the play;
that this is superficial is apparent when Troilus, on parting with
Cressida, expands upon the theme of *tempus fugit*:

> Injurious time now with a robber's haste
> Crams his rich thievery up, he knows not how.
> As many farewells as be stars in heaven,
> With distinct breath and consign'd kisses to them,
> He fumbles up into a loose adieu,
> And scants us with a single famish'd kiss,
> Distasted with the salt of broken tears.   (IV. 4. 41-7.)

The thematic function of Time here is simply to define the
sensibility of Troilus and, consequently, that of the play:
Time is appetitive, sensual and limiting – Time with 'haste
Crams his rich thievery up. . . . And scants us with a single
famish'd kiss, Distasted . . .'; more especially, Time is lecherous
– 'He fumbles up into a loose adieu'; there can be little doubt as
to the dominant sense of the ambiguous word 'loose' (cf.
'loose woman'). The association between Time and Troilus is

[1] R. H. Tawney, *Religion and the Rise of Capitalism*, 1938, p.47.

not circumstantial; the lines above bring together the gluttonous anticipation of the passage from Act III, scene 2, 'I am giddy; expectation whirls me round,' and the implicit lecherousness of the passage from the opening scene, 'I tell thee I am mad' (compare, for instance, 'Handlest in thy discourse' with 'He fumbles up into a loose adieu').

Something like the full enormity of accepting naïve romantic accounts of Troilus, such as that of Professor Wilson Knight in *The Wheel of Fire* or that of Dr. Tillyard who saw him as 'a romantic and unfortunate lover',[1] should now be apparent. It is inordinately difficult, at least when reading the play, to understand where Mr. Maxwell finds any intensity in the love of Troilus, or rather any love in the intensity of Troilus. Of course, Troilus is in contact with the remnants of a chivalrous world, but he is in contact with them as an agent of corruption. It is as such, and certainly not as a chivalrous lover, that Troilus desires access to Cressida, as must be obvious to the most biased reader when Troilus begs Pandar:

> O, be thou my Charon,
> And give me swift transportation to these fields
> *Where I may wallow in the lily beds*
> Propos'd for the deserver!   (III. 2. 10-13; my italics)

The real nature of the disjunction between action and imagination in Troilus is, in the lines just quoted, made explicit in his conception of the love relationship. Love to Troilus is the relationship between his own inherent capacity for pig-like (to 'wallow') defilement – his 'ruder powers', his 'spirit of sense' – and what he imagines to be the delicate purity ('the lily beds') of Cressida – 'love's thrice repured nectar', 'In whose comparison all whites are ink' and 'The cygnet's down is harsh'. And Troilus, with his mercenary-mindedness and appetitiveness, is but an abstract of the corruptive spirit which the play as a whole is 'about'.

Naturally, the corruption of Elizabethan life did not escape the attention of Elizabethans; there is a considerable literature in which they expound the relation between the growing predominance of the middle class and the deterioration of social relationships. The growth in wealth and power of the

[1] E. M. W. Tillyard, *Shakespeare's Problem Plays*, 1951, p. 63.

middle class is one of the principal distresses of the Common-weal cited by Armigail Waad in a memorandum (probably intended for Cecil) which he introduces with the explanation, 'I do here grossly fashion our commonweal, sick or diseased'.[1] In the same manner Shakespeare fashions the corruption of life in *Troilus and Cressida*. Troilus refers to his desire as 'the open ulcer' of his heart in the opening scene and, in the council scene, Hector puts down the persuasions of Troilus and Paris to 'the hot passion of distempered blood' and warns Troilus that:

> . . . the will dotes that is attributive
> To what infectiously itself affects   (II. 2. 58-9.)

Although Troilus does not accept this diagnosis, the symptoms he reveals a little later demonstrate its veracity:

> My heart beats thicker than a feverous pulse;
> And all my powers do their bestowing lose
>   (III. 2. 35-6.)

And the sickened quality of his passion – sickness is a prominent strain in Troilus's 'love' poetry – assumes almost Hamletesque proportions in lines such as those which commend the keeping of Helen:

> We turn not back the silks upon the merchant
> When we have soil'd them; nor the remainder viands
> We do not throw in unrespective sieve
> Because we now are full.   (II. 2. 69-72.)

Actual vomiting is strongly suggested in the last two and a half lines. Troilus is thrusting forth his own sick view of Helen as good reason. His nausea surges up again when confronted with Cressida's defection:

> The fractions of her faith, orts of her love,
> The fragments, scraps, the bits, and greasy relics
> Of her o'er-eaten faith are bound to Diomed.

It is, of course, Troilus who has played the glutton throughout, Troilus who has 'o'er-eaten', and, clinging to the belief that lily beds can be wallowed in without defiling their purity, he regurgitates the truth for which he has no stomach.

[1] 'The Distresses of The Commonwealth, With The Means To Remedy Them', reprinted in Henry Gee, *The Elizabethan Prayer-Book and Ornaments*, 1902, Appendix III, pp. 206-15.

According to the diagnosis of their complaint, offered to the Greeks by Ulysses, each Greek:

> . . . sick
> Of his superior, grows to an envious fever
> Of pale and bloodless emulation.
> And 'tis this fever that keeps Troy on foot
>
> (I. 3. 132-5.)

The metaphor upon which Shakespeare is relying is not immediately obvious. The plague is mentioned frequently, but this is not very precise. Thersites is always at hand to damn Greeks and Trojans alike with the plague and to speculate upon its effect:

> Agamemnon – how if he had boils full, all over, generally? . . . And those boils did run – say so. Did not the general run then? Were not that a botchy core? . . . Then there would come some matter from him . . .
>
> (II. 1. 2-9.)

But the disease is closely associated with the appetites and infects the blood and only gradually makes its presence felt. And it is only gradually, as one approaches the end of the play, that the nature of the disease is made a little more specific. The suppressed metaphor comes to the surface in Thersites' reference to the Neapolitan bone ache, a reference that is taken up, by Pandar in the epilogue when he begs 'A goodly medicine for my aching bones' and bequeathes his diseases to 'Brethren and sisters of the hold-door trade'. The play, in fact, draws to n end on an almost apocalyptic note with Troilus invoking he gods:

> Sit, gods, upon your thrones, and smite at Troy.
> I say at once let your brief plagues be mercy,
> And linger not our sure destructions on!
>
> (v. 10. 7-9.)

A vision of disease and destruction which Pandar expands in his epilogue.

The epilogue is addressed to members of Pandar's company, those that are 'of Pandar's hall', namely, 'traders' and 'bawds', 'Good traders in the flesh', 'Brethren and sisters of the hold-door trade' – within the play, to those who have been revealed to us as 'Good traders in the flesh', Troilus, Paris, Diomed, Ulysses, Calchas, Nestor, etc. He acknowledges and bemoans their lot:

> O traders and bawds, how earnestly are you set a
> work, and how ill requited!   (v. 10. 37.)

Their only reward is incurable disease – encroaching blindness ('Your eyes, half out') and 'aching bones' – and final destruction:

> Some two months hence my will shall here be made.
> . . . .
> Till then I'll sweat and seek about for eases,
> And at that time bequeath you my diseases.
>   (v. 10. 51-5.)

The dramatic irony of the epilogue's complaint hardly requires comment. The epilogue fitly concludes the play's exploration and definition of that manumission of life, specifically of romantic love and chivalrous war, that was being effected by the spirit, or the ethic, of emergent capitalism.

The distinctively Shakespearian activity in the play, then, assesses the weakening of feudal relations that had taken place during the sixteenth century by bringing to bear upon a world of romance and chivalry (the world of the Trojan War as traditionally presented by medieval and Elizabethan writers) the powers of personal and social corruption inherent in the appetitive spirit of capitalism. Shakespeare's definition of this spirit in terms of the appetites is a traditional one and belongs to that medieval conception of social life which viewed the appetitive forces as necessary but subservient to what was distinctively human in life, expressing as they did man's animal as opposed to his human nature. Shakespeare, therefore, implicitly condemns the reduction of life to the pursuit of appetitive satisfaction because it is a reduction; it is life depressed to a level at which gluttony and lechery become its dominant qualities and man is devoted to the pursuit of the demands of his appetites and the means to satisfy them, as Troilus is devoted to Cressida and Dekker's 'thrifty citizen' is devoted to gold.

In the play, Shakespeare's implicit conception of society is that of medieval humanism. Society is a super-individual, it is the body politic with a head, members, and all the other components, with their various functions, analogous to the constitution of a person. So it is that in a society such as that observed by Wheeler, where human activity is directed by the demands of the appetites, terms such as 'gluttony' and 'lechery', which we would use in judgment of an individual, serve as terms of political appraisal, applying to the state of that super-individual, the body politic. Social analysis, therefore, such as that of Armigail Waad and Shakespeare, is often in the form of a medical diagnosis, which a twentieth century reader may understand in a metaphoric fashion. For Shakespeare and Waad, however, the use of such apparently personal terms as 'disease', 'gluttony' and 'lechery' whilst ambiguous was not metaphoric – society *was* (to them) a gigantic individual with all of an individual's characteristics. It is in the ambiguity of this essentially medieval cast of mind that Shakespeare's political humanism lies and in *Troilus and Cressida* we can appreciate its power and integrity not in spite of but because of its limitations.

In the play, the body politic of medieval social theory has become a creature of appetite, 'a universal wolf' to use Ulysses's phrase, and has become afflicted with the incurable diseases that follow in the wake of over-indulgence, it is, therefore, doomed to eventual death. The integrity of this use of medieval social theory can be appreciated if it is borne in mind that the theory reflects medieval social life, feudalism; that form of living had been corrupted and was doomed. The limitation, on the other hand, is that such a view of society, being rigidly feudal, does not allow of any perception of new forms of social growth. Today we can see that out of a coarse and vulgar appetitiveness arose a new respect for man's material well-being and out of sensual curiosity arose modern science. But such an awareness of the limitations within which *Troilus and Cressida* operates is very largely rendered irrelevant by the direction of Shakespeare's interest. Shakespeare concentrates our attention upon an area of life, and that the most intimately human, in which the spirit of capitalism works without hope of redemption. 'Love', as D. H. Lawrence observed, 'is no deal, nor merchant's bargaining'.[1]

[1] D. H. Lawrence, 'The Overtone', in *The Lovely Lady*, New York, 1946, p.154.

THE WINTER'S TALE AND JACOBEAN SOCIETY

Charles Barber

The Winter's Tale looks unpromising material for a volume like the present one. In critical writings about it in the present century, as in those about Shakespeare's final plays in general, there are perhaps two main kinds of attitude: (1) that it is essentially a fairy-tale, dream-like and remote from reality; (2) that it is to be read as a myth, and that essentially it is religious or metaphysical in meaning.[1] While I do not wish to deny the presence in the play of elements that support either of these views, I should like to suggest that the play is more directly concerned with the problems of Jacobean society than is usually recognized.

The first type of view now looks rather old-fashioned. It can be found for example in Sir Arthur Quiller-Couch's *Shakespeare's Workmanship* (1918). In the chapter on *The Winter's Tale*, he talks about various anachronisms in Shakespeare's later plays, and then goes on:

> 'Faery – deliberate faery' is the answer – 'the light that never was on sea and land' – but do we not *wish* it was? Faery – deliberate faery: the nursery tale of Snowdrop translated into *Cymbeline*; Danae and the floating cradle translated into *Pericles*: the princess turned goose-girl, the disguised prince, the clownish foster-father and foster-brother, translated into this play.
>
> (p. 297.)

The tone here is slightly wistful, indulgent: he *wants* the make-believe ('do we not *wish* it was?'). Most people today distrust an addiction to 'deliberate faery' and would not rate the play as highly as Quiller-Couch does if they accepted his account of it.

[1] For a detailed survey of twentieth-century criticism on the play, see Philip Edwards, 'Shakespeare's Romances: 1900-1957', in *Shakespeare Survey* 11, ed. Allardyce Nicoll (Cambridge 1958).

All the same, I think he has pointed to some things that really are there in the play – the folk-tale themes and characters, the affinity in atmosphere to the late Greek romances.

A more sophisticated version of this approach is found in Lytton Strachey's article 'Shakespeare's Final Period', reprinted in his *Books and Characters* (1922). He argues that, until *Coriolanus*, Shakespeare's plays are essentially realistic, dealing with real men and women, but that in the last plays we move to a world of enchantment, of shifting visions, in which the pretences of reality are preserved, but only the pretences. Like Quiller-Couch, he singles out the fairy-tale and folk-tale elements in the plays, but insists that they include unpleasant things: in the world of faery there are nightmares and goblins, as well as fairies and dreams. But they are all unreal, and he finds the plays rather dull, their personages boring:

> It is difficult to resist the conclusion that (Shakespeare) was getting bored himself. Bored with people, bored with real life, bored with drama, bored in fact with everything except poetry and poetical dreams.   (p. 60.)

It would be a mistake to underestimate the extent to which an attack of this kind could be pressed home; but, in the form in which Strachey presents it, the case seems to rest on misconceptions. For one thing, he seems to confuse *reality* with *naturalism*: some of his complaints amount to saying that the late plays are not naturalistic, which is by no means the same as saying that they are remote from reality. And for another thing, when he says that Shakespeare's interest in the late plays is not in drama or people or real life, but 'merely' in poetry, he surely underestimates the way in which Shakespeare used poetry (even in the late plays) precisely for the ends of drama and for presenting real people and real life. Indeed, the best refutation of Strachey's view of these plays is simply to examine their texture, their poetry. Consider for example the way Leontes talks in the first half of *The Winter's Tale*:

> Nor night, nor day, no rest: It is but weakness
> To bear the matter thus: mere weakness, if
> The cause were not in being: part o' th' cause,
> She, th' adultress: for the harlot-king
> Is quite beyond mine arm, out of the blank

And level of my brain: plot-proof: but she,
I can hook to me: say that she were gone,
Given to the fire, a moiety of my rest
Might come to me again. Who's there?

(II. 3. [*First Folio punctuation*] 1-9.)

This is a *dramatic* use of verse. It gives us directly Leontes'
neurasthenic state, his pathological self-torture. It is given,
for example, by the restless tortured movement of the first
sentence; and the restlessness is reinforced by the repetition
('weakness . . . mere weakness') which is the obsessed mind
coming back in a circle to the same idea. The *If*, isolated and
drawn out at the end of the line, gives an agonized tone. And
the involved syntax, with its two parentheses ('part of the cause
. . .' and the one about the harlot-king) and its switch of construction in mid-career (at 'but she'), gives a sense of the twistings and
turnings of Leontes' mind, and of the essential irrationality of
his thought-processes. The feeling that he is not getting anywhere, that he is just going round obsessively in a circle, is
confirmed by the way the end of the speech comes back to the
beginning ('no rest . . . my rest'). The imagery is of violent
destruction: artillery ('blank And level') and ships grappling in
battle ('hook to me'); this embodies the violent destructive
impulses within Leontes himself, just as the word 'fire' really
tells us about his own condition: it is plainly just a delusion for
him to think that he can cure himself of his own feverous state
by burning someone else. This is writing that is rooted in
reality, in a concrete grasp of human nature; and it is by no
means an exceptional passage: there are much more striking
examples in some of Leontes' earlier speeches.

But, granted a texture of this kind, we are still left with the
problem of the shape and meaning of the play as a whole. It is
plain that it is a good deal further than Shakespeare's earlier
plays from the conventions of naturalism. We cannot approach
Leontes as we do Othello: Shakespeare is concerned with the
process of becoming jealous in Othello, but not in Leontes. In
the latter case, the jealousy is a datum, one of the postulates
of the play, and Shakespeare is only concerned to convince us
that Leontes in fact *is* jealous, not to show us how he became so.
Similarly, the restoration of Hermione at the end of the play is
not conceived in naturalistic terms: an explanation in such

terms is given for those who need it, but is given very perfunctorily, indeed is very much thrown away. And there are other pretty obvious difficulties for an audience with naturalistic preconceptions: the oracle and its fulfilment, the death of Mamillius, the bear, the survival of Perdita, the coincidence of Florizel's meeting her, and so on. We need not assume, like Strachey, that a play can deal with reality only if it is naturalistic; but we are entitled to ask *why* the play presents a world different from the familiar one, what it is all about.

The play in fact seems to invite explication in terms of myth or of symbolism, and since the 1930s there have been quite a number of analyses of the late plays in these terms. On the whole, there has been a tendency to see the myth or the symbolism as *religious*, and the meaning of the play has been taken to be metaphysical or transcendental. An example of this is the account of the play given by D. G. James.[1] In his last plays, James says, Shakespeare turns to myth, and is no longer primarily concerned to show forth a human situation. The essential myths concern the finding of what is lost (Perdita), the bringing to life what is dead (Hermione), and the recovery of a lost royalty. Royalty is a symbol for a spiritual beauty and love, and for the divine destiny of the soul. That which is lost is man's most treasured possession, 'the jewel of his soul', and James cites parallel themes from the Gospels. The dead returning to life (the restoration of Hermione) stands for the Resurrection. James sees Shakespeare as trying to express his sense of the supernatural without using overtly religious beliefs and language; but he thinks he fails, partly because of a confusion in the symbolism (royalty, for example, stands both for the divine destiny of the soul *and* for all the worldly values which the royalty of the free spirit discounts); and the use of purely human symbols causes the characters often to behave with extreme silliness.

It would be foolish to deny that the play has strong religious tonings. The account of Apollo's oracle (III. 1.) is clustered round with imagery evoking both reverence and the sense of a life-giving power; Leontes' rejection of the oracle in the trial-scene is presented as blasphemous, and is immediately followed by divine thunder and the news of Mamillius's death; the

[1] *Scepticism and Poetry* (London 1937), 205-41.

account of Leontes' penance (v. 1.) is given in Christian terms; Hermione is constantly associated with the idea of Grace, and the scene of her final restoration to Leontes is charged with Christian phraseology. Moreover, in the matter of Hermione's supposed death Shakespeare goes against his normal practice by concealing the truth from the audience until the very end. Normally, he takes the audience into his confidence, preferring dramatic irony to the shock of surprise that can be gained by concealment. The effect of concealment in the case of Hermione is certainly to make the statue-scene into a kind of miracle, a return from the dead.

However, even when this is granted, it is difficult to make out a convincing reading of the play as a *consistent* myth with some kind of metaphysical meaning; and critics who try to make it into this may well conclude, like James, that it is a failure. In fact there are many things in the play, some of them very mundane things, that will not fit into a neat symbolic scheme; and the recent critics who have written most appreciatively and most illuminatingly about it (G. Wilson Knight,[1] for example, and D. A. Traversi[2]) have found a good deal of rich and immediate human experience in it, however much they may emphasize the elements of moral or metaphysical myth.

I should like to argue that *The Winter's Tale* not only contains a good deal besides religious symbolism, but also has themes that are more closely related to the problems of early seventeenth-century society than most accounts of the play would suggest. As my starting point I take what seems to me to be the key theme of the play: the contrast and conflict between court and country.[3] Central to the play is the contrast between the artificiality and sophistication of the court, and the 'natural' qualities of the cottage. The whole structure of the play is contained within a movement from court to countryside, and then back to court again, the transitions occurring at Act III scene 3 and Act V scene 1. There is a kind of thesis-antithesis-synthesis pattern. In the first movement, we see evil passion and destructive tyranny arise at the court. Characters move from the court to

---

[1] *The Crown of Life* (London 1947), Chapter III.

[2] *Shakespeare: the Final Phase* (London 1954); *An Approach to Shakespeare* (2nd ed. London 1957).

[3] This theme has been discussed by S. L. Bethell in *The Winter's Tale: A Study* (London 1948), but he gives it a less central place in the play than I should.

the cottage (Perdita, Florizel), and the second movement depicts
the virtues of rural life. The characters who move from court to
cottage are rejected by the court (Perdita by Leontes before
moving there, Florizel by Polixenes after); but regeneration is
achieved when these characters move back to the court in the
final movement, and the cottage-bred girl Perdita brings to
the court the virtues of another class, yeoman farmers or cottage
peasantry, to bring moral renewal to the courtly life.

Of course it is insisted, in line with contemporary views on
inherited nobility, that the royalty of Perdita's blood shines
through, and makes her different from her supposed relatives.
Her refined and delicate behaviour towards Florizel is contrasted with the behaviour of the comic rustic girls, Mopsa and
Dorcas, towards the Clown her 'brother'. And Polixenes says
of her:

> nothing she does, or seems
> But smacks of something greater than herself,
> Too noble for this place.   (IV. 4. 157-9.)

This is a typical bit of Jacobean having-it-both-ways: having
the rustic virtues without forfeiting the qualities thought to
come from high birth. But it is really quite appropriate here,
since Perdita has the function in the play of representing the
combination of both virtues: she has royal blood and rustic
upbringing. Moreover, when she goes to court she does not go
alone: she takes her rustic relatives with her, where they prepare
to be absorbed into the gentry, and make a good deal of shrewd
comment on the qualities of the court and on social mobility.

The court is represented as the source of passion which
leads to tyranny. Paulina practically calls Leontes a tyrant to
his face:

> I'll not call you tyrant;
> But this most cruel usage of your Queen –
> Not able to produce more accusation
> Than your own weak-hing'd fancy – something savours
> Of tyranny, and will ignoble make you,
> Yea, scandalous to the world.   (II. 3. 115-20.)

Leontes angrily rejects the charge of tyranny, but it is clear that
at this point Paulina is canalizing the feelings of indignation in
the audience (rather as Emilia does in the last scene of *Othello*).

And by contemporary definitions of a tyrant (for example, one who rules for himself or for his faction, disregarding the law and the common good),[1] Leontes is certainly close to being one. He is touchy about the charge of tyranny, and goes out of his way to deny it at the beginning of the trial-scene (III. 2.), asserting that he is giving Hermione a just trial by due order of law; but the way he then goes on to conduct the trial hardly bears out his assertion. The passion that leads to this tyrannical behaviour is irrational: Leontes has no evidence, and is impervious to argument. He is trapped in an obsession, and this leads him to suborn the murder of a guest, to accuse Camillo of treason, to order the murder of his daugher, and to place his wife on trial for adultery. This would not strike the Jacobean audience as mere fairy-tale: for example, the trial and execution of Anne Boleyn for adultery were still near enough in time for behaviour of this kind to be reckoned practical politics.

The irrationality of Leontes' jealousy is underlined by its sudden eruption, without the process of development seen in Othello. This treatment of the theme is sometimes given a metaphysical interpretation: it shows that evil simply is a state that fallen man is subject to. However, it can equally well be given a political interpretation: irrespective of the psychology of the individual king, the tenure of the crown tends to produce passion and tyranny. There is no such eruption of evil in the cottage; but the other king in the play, Polixenes, also becomes irrational and tyrannical. This is when he denounces the proposed marriage of Florizel and Perdita. The language he uses in threatening the Shepherd and Perdita is intemperate and cruel, full of images of physical violence:

> Thou, old traitor,
> I am sorry that by hanging thee I can but
> Shorten thy life one week. And thou, fresh piece
> Of excellent witchcraft, . . .
> I'll have thy beauty scratch'd with briers and made
> More homely than thy state.   (IV. 4. 412-18.)

The element of irrational passion in this is nicely pointed up

---

[1] See for example the criteria for tyranny given by Sir Thomas Smith in his *De Republica Anglorum* (ed. L. Alston, Cambridge 1906, 14-16). Smith's phraseology is echoed by Milton when, in 1649, he defends the execution of Charles I in his *Tenure of Kings and Magistrates*.

by the fact that, earlier in the same scene, he has argued to Perdita the importance of mixed marriages for the renewal of the nobility. This is in the famous gillyvor passage, in which Polixenes argues that Perdita need not reject gillyvors from her garden on the grounds that they are hybrids, the product of man's interference with nature:

> You see, sweet maid, we marry
> A gentler scion to the wildest stock,
> And make conceive a bark of baser kind
> By bud of nobler race. This is an art
> Which does mend nature – change it rather: but
> The art itself, is nature.   (IV. 4. 92-7.)

Polixenes is justifying horticultural techniques, and his reference is specifically to the technique of budding, in which a slit is made in the bark of one variety (e.g. of apple-tree) and a bud from another variety is grafted in; the *scion* is grafted on to the *stock*. But the phrases are so chosen as to make it clear that this is an image for human marriage, and moreover for marriage between different classes: *noble, gentle,* and *base* were all quite specific class-terms in Shakespeare's day. This is, in fact, an eloquent justification of intermarriage between the nobility and gentry on the one hand and the non-gentry (the 'baser kind') on the other. But this, we soon discover, is mere theory in Polixenes: when his own son wants to contract such a marriage he bursts out into a violent denunciation which, in the hints it contains of the irrational and pathological, reminds us of the earlier anger of Leontes.

Polixenes' violent pride in birth is nicely put in its place immediately afterwards by Perdita:

> I was not much afear'd; for once or twice
> I was about to speak and tell him plainly
> The self-same sun, that shines upon his court,
> Hides not his visage from our cottage, but
> Looks on alike.   (IV. 4. 434-8.)

The sun image suggests the equality of souls before God; so it asserts the essential brotherhood of man, the dignity of our common humanity transcending the dignity of class (a central feeling throughout Shakespeare's work). And Florizel, who of course believes that Perdita really is of low birth, asserts that his failure to keep his faith and marry her would be a violation of the order of nature:

> It cannot fail but by
> The violation of my faith; and then
> Let Nature crush the sides o' th' earth together
> And mar the seeds within! (IV. 4. 468-71.)

In *Macbeth* and *King Lear* very similar images had been used for the universal disorder that follows from the violation of Degree: but Florizel says that disorder will follow if he *fails* to violate Degree (by disobeying his father, and by marrying out of his class). At the end of the same scene, the violence of Polixenes is nicely parodied by Autolycus, in the scarifying account that he gives to the Old Shepherd and the Clown of the punishments in store from them for presuming to 'draw our throne into a sheep-cote'.

Besides being the source of passion and tyranny, the court is shown as being in danger of spinelessness and of over-artificiality. The spinelessness is seen in the failure of Leontes' courtiers to resist his tyrannous whims. It is left to a woman, Paulina, to tell the king a few home-truths (II. 3.), and the role of Leontes' courtiers (after an ineffectual attempt to keep her out) is almost limited to assuring the king that Antigonus is quite innocent of setting her on to do this. There is no Kent (as in *King Lear*) to tell the king he does evil.

The over-artificiality is seen in the prose speeches of the courtiers, which tend to be just a little bit too stilted, too mannered. The note is struck immediately at the opening of the play:

> *Archidamus* If you shall chance, Camillo, to visit Bohemia, on the like occasion whereon my services are now on foot, you shall see, as I have said, great difference betwixt our Bohemia and your Sicilia.
> *Camillo*   I think this coming summer the King of Sicilia means to pay Bohemia the visitation which he justly owes him.
> *Archidamus* Wherein our entertainment shall shame us we will be justified in our loves; for indeed –
> *Camillo*   Beseech you –
> *Archidamus* Verily, I speak it in the freedom of my knowledge: we cannot with such magnificence, in so

> rare – I know not what to say. We will give you sleepy
> drinks, that your senses, unintelligent of our insufficiency,
> may, though they cannot praise us, as little accuse us.
>
> (I. I. I-15.)

That is courtly and elegant, but a trifle self-conscious in its
balanced structure, its rounded periods. The opening speech,
for example, is a single complex sentence in which the main
verb is held back a long time – which gives a sense of contrivance, not of spontaneity; and is neatly rounded off with the
balance of 'our Bohemia, and your Sicilia'. Even when Archi-
damus cannot find words to express his sense of inadequacy
('we cannot with such magnificence . . .', etc.), and breaks off a
sentence unfinished, we do not feel that he is *really* groping for
words, but that the very sense of incoherence is contrived by
the speaker, is a deliberate rhetorical device. And the end of
his speech ('though they cannot praise us, as little accuse us')
has a neatness that reminds us of Euphuistic prose.

This elegant but slightly contrived style is typical of the
prose used at court in this play. But there is one scene where the
mannered quality is more exaggerated, and we are given
something very near parody. This is the scene where a courtier
describes Perdita's recognition. It is supposed to be an account
of a very moving event, but there is a constant contrast between
the sense of overflowing emotion and the rather contrived
prose in which it is related. For example:

> One of the prettiest touches of all, and that which angl'd
> for mine eyes – caught the water, though not the fish –
> was, when at the relation of the Queen's death, with the
> manner how she came to't bravely confess'd, and
> lamented by the King, how attentiveness wounded his
> daughter; till, from one sign of dolour to another, she
> did with an 'Alas!' – I would fain say – bleed tears;
> for I am sure my heart wept blood.   (v. 2. 90-99.)

Here again we see the same elaborateness of clause-structure, the
same neatness and balance; and the would-be artless parentheses give even more strongly the sense of contrivance. Above
all, the conceits ('caught the water, though not the fish',
'attentiveness wounded his daughter') are contrived to the
point of preciosity.

In contrast to the tyranny and artificiality of the court, the cottage is the source of humanity and of naturalness. The humane virtue of the cottage is seen in the Old Shepherd, who, when he finds Perdita, says 'I'll take it up for pity' (III. 3.); this is quite disinterested, for the gold that Antigonus left with Perdita has not yet been discovered. The same basic humanity is seen in his son, the Clown, in the comic scene where Autolycus picks his pocket (IV. 3.), a parody of the story of the Good Samaritan. And the cottage is a centre of neighbourliness and hospitality, as seen in the sheep-shearing feast, and in the account of the Old Shepherd's wife as hostess.

The naturalness of the prose spoken by the rustics, in contrast to the artificiality of court prose, hardly needs illustration. Moreover, the inhabitants of the cottage are constantly associated with nature, both by image and by event: for example, Perdita is 'the Queen of curds and cream'; her eyes are water and Florizel the moon that gazes into it; she is constantly linked in the poetry with flowers; her guests are given flowers; and her supposed brother and father are, unlike poor Antigonus, on easy terms with the bear. In the gillyvor passage, Perdita and Polixenes are slightly at cross purposes. She is asserting the cottage virtue of naturalness against courtly artificiality, an implication which is well brought out by her rejection of cosmetics:

> No more than were I painted I would wish
> This youth should say 'twere well, and only therefore
> Desire to breed by me.   (IV. 3. 101-3.)

Polixenes, on the other hand, is concerned with the relationship between art and nature; he asserts that man is a part of nature, and that in manipulating nature he is only using the means that nature herself provides. And he generalizes so powerfully that he includes in his vision of the relationship between man and nature the idea of the necessary intermarriage of court and country: he has gone beyond Perdita, and here adumbrates the outcome of the play (however little he may be able to accept it in practice).

For the England of 1610 or 1611, when *The Winter's Tale* was written, the theme of court and country has a clear topical reference: for at that time the division between the court and the country, both politically and culturally, was becoming increasingly obvious. Shakespeare, indeed, does not make the theme *pointedly* topical, and this is hardly surprising, in view of the increasingly courtly patronage of his theatre at this period; but the theme is clear enough. Shakespeare envisages, plainly, a reconciliation between court and country, in which renewal will be brought to the court from below, while the inhabitants of the cottage will be refined by the influence of the court. In contemporary social and political terms, this involves social mobility, and the rejection of the demands of Degree insofar as they imply a fixed hierarchy; though a kind of escape-hole is left, for the courtiers in the audience who need it, by Perdita's actual royalty of blood. The character who insists on Degree is Polixenes, when he denounces the proposed marriage:

> Mark your divorce, young sir,
> Whom son I dare not call; thou art too base
> To be acknowledg'd – thou a sceptre's heir,
> That thus affects a sheep-hook!   (IV. 4. 430-43.)

Florizel has behaved in a way that Polixenes finds unfitting his gentle birth, and the word *base* combines moral and class connotations. Polixenes goes on to underline further the social inferiority of the cottage: the Old Shepherd is a *churl* (another word that combines class-feeling with moral judgment), and when Perdita's beauty is scratched with briars she will be made more homely than her state, i.e. her looks will be made inferior even to her social class. This, as Camillo recognizes, is 'fury': the insistence on Degree is associated with intemperate anger and tyrannical behaviour. We have already looked at Perdita's comment, on the sun shining alike on court and cottage, and at Florizel's assertion that it would be *unnatural* of him to abandon Perdita: there is never any suggestion, even from Polixenes, that it would be *unnatural* for a prince to marry a shepherdess.

Social mobility is discussed explicitly when the Old Shepherd and his son come to court, and we have the comedy of the parvenu:

> *Autolycus* I know you are now, sir, a gentleman born.
> *Clown*   Ay, and have been so any time these four hours.

Shepherd   And so have I, boy.

Clown   So you have; but I was a gentleman born
before my father; for the King's son took me by the
hand, and call'd me brother; and then the two kings
call'd my father brother; and then the Prince, my
brother, and the Princess, my sister, call'd my father
father. And so we wept; and there was the first gentle-
man-like tears that ever we shed.   (v. 2. 130-39.)

This of course is farce, but all the same it presents a situation
which the play accepts with good humour and equanimity –
the yeoman rising to be a gentleman; and the comically reiter-
ated terms of relationship underline the brotherhood of
humanity already suggested by Perdita's sun shining on court
and cottage alike. The tone of the passage is markedly different
from some earlier ones in Shakespeare on the same subject:
for example the reference in *King Lear* (III. 6.) to the yeoman
that sees his son a gentleman before him, and the one in
Hamlet (v. 1.) to the toe of the peasant coming so near the heel
of the courtier that he galls his kibe. The passage in *The
Winter's Tale* lacks the caustic overtones of these earlier references; the situation is comic, but no subject for satirical bitterness. The Clown's sons and daughters (as the Old Shepherd
says) 'will be all gentlemen born'; and that's how things
go. Moreover, it is hinted that the court in its turn will have a
refining influence on these shrewd but clumsy peasants: they
agree to do Autolycus a good turn, because, as the Shepherd
says

we must be gentle, now we are gentlemen.

(v. 2. 146.)

Here the double meaning of *gentle* is used to suggest that the
achieving of the social status will lead to the achieving of the
appropriate moral qualities.

This central theme of the relationship of court and country
has various subsidiary themes grouped round it. One of these
is man's control of nature. Many critics (and notably Wilson
Knight) have discussed the theme of Art and Nature in the
play. But it is important to see that in Shakespeare's time the
word *Art* had a wider sense than it has today: it included what
were called the *useful arts*, which today we call technology; and

when Polixenes talks about Art in the gillyvor speech he is in
fact talking about horticultural techniques, man's manipulation
of nature. Many critics have pointed to the abundant nature-
imagery in the play; but most of the nature-images are in
fact concerned with *domesticated* nature, nature brought under
man's control: cows and calves, eggs, fishponds, hens, garden
flowers and herbs, and so on. Incidental references to domesticated nature crop up constantly in the imagery of the play, at
court as well as in the cottage – as for example in the following
speech of Hermione's:

> What! Have I twice said well? When was't before?
> I prithee tell me; cram's with praise, and make's
> As fat as tame things. One good deed dying tongueless
> Slaughters a thousand waiting upon that.
> Our praises are our wages; you may ride's
> With one soft kiss a thousand furlongs ere
> With spur we heat an acre.   (I. 2. 90-6.)

The words *cram* and *fat as tame things* refer to the fattening of
domestic animals or birds; and then the imagery shifts to
another domesticated animal, the horse. It does not seem that
the imagery here is meant to reflect badly on Hermione's
relationship with Leontes, to suggest that for him she is merely
a hen in a coop; rather the images of domesticated nature are
felt as rich and satisfying, suitable vehicles for discussion of the
closest human relationships.

Throughout the play, the imagery constantly reminds us in
this way that man lives in nature, and lives by manipulating
nature with his arts. Undomesticated nature also occurs: the
storm, the wolf that threatens the sheep, the bear that kills
Antigonus: but these are exceptional in the play, representing
the area of experience that man has not yet brought under his
control. And it is noticeable that the rustic characters are
not much perturbed by these things: the Clown, for example,
knows all about bears ('they are never curst but when they are
hungry') and so can cope with the situation: the bear is not
domesticated, but human knowledge of its ways can keep man
out of danger from it. The jealous Leontes, by contrast, is 'a
feather for each wind that blows' (II. 3.).

The theme of man's control of nature through his arts is

linked (in a way not obvious to the modern reader) with another theme in the play: that of maturity, and the growth to maturity. This theme has been especially discussed by Traversi, who sees it as a central motif of the play, and traces it through the imagery of the seasons, of age and youth, and of nature. But it is important to realize that, in Shakespeare's day, maturation was one of the basic *scientific* ideas.[1] For the Renaissance, the basic sciences, the ones that were used as models for the others, were the *biological* ones. Today, we tend rather to use the structural concepts of physics and chemistry as the basic ones, and try to explain the biological sciences in their terms: we begin from a concept of inert matter and its properties, and try to fit the biological sciences into this framework of explanation. But this procedure (though it has been found to work pretty well) is not a self-evident one, and before about 1700 the normal scientific attitude was the opposite one: the scientist started with ideas of growth and maturation, as observed in plants and animals, and tried to accommodate the facts of physics and chemistry into *this* framework of explanation – accounting for the facts of chemistry, for example, by such concepts as germination and maturation, as is done in alchemy. This change in scientific outlook, from a universe basically biological to one basically mechanical, explains a good deal of the difference in the 'feel' of the universe for a renaissance man and a modern man.

So, in using in *The Winter's Tale* constant images of germination and maturation, for example in the imagery of the seasons, Shakespeare is presenting the universe in terms of the science of his day. Simultaneously, as we have seen, he reminds us of man's techniques for domesticating nature. I suggest, therefore, that through its imagery the play constantly reminds us of man's control over nature by means of his 'arts', and by means of the scientific understanding of nature on which these arts are based. This is a much more 'modern' attitude than is usually attributed to Shakespeare, who is often thought of nowadays as a near-medieval figure, with practically nothing in common with, say, his contemporary Bacon. I think there is more Baconism in late Shakespeare than is normally

[1] See especially Stephen Toulmin, *Foresight and Understanding* (London 1961), 62-81.

recognized. The same theme, for example, is found in *The Tempest*: Prospero is the magician-scientist (the two were commonly equated) who controls nature through his arts and his knowledge. It is important that Prospero's magic is not presented as being damnable. In Marlowe's *Dr Faustus*, from the early 1590's, the practice of magic arts is presented as being wholly damnable. In Chapman's *Bussy D'Ambois*, from the early 1600's, the presentation of the magician-friar is deeply ambiguous, leaving it open to the audience to see his arts as damnable or holy. But in *The Tempest*, from the early 1610's, the magician-scientist has become a wholly beneficent figure.

Another theme of the play is the continuity of human history, the way life goes on generation after generation despite all conflicts and disturbances. This is suggested by the seasonal imagery itself, for the seasons are cyclical. It is also suggested by the images given more than once in the play of the generations of man stretching backwards and forwards in time. It has often been pointed out that the play contrasts the young with the old, the children with the fathers, and shows how the conflicts of one generation are healed by the mediation of the next. But there are also many phrases that make us look backwards or forwards along the perspective of many generations. In the first scene of the play, Camillo says of the young Mamillius that he

> makes old hearts fresh; they that went on crutches
> ere he was born desire yet their life to see him a man.
> (I. I. 36-8.)

The man who went on crutches before Mamillius was even born obviously belongs two or three generations back, and he wishes to live yet another generation beyond the present one, until Mamillius is a man. The sentence evokes very economically the sense of many generations stretching back and forward in time, with the present as a nodal point in the sequence. Another example comes in the scene where Perdita's recognition is described; it is said that Leontes

> thanks the old shepherd, which stands by like a weather-
> bitten conduit of many kings' reigns. (v. 2. 54-5.)

The shepherd here becomes a type of the continuity of rural

life, with its toughness ('weather-bitten'), its life-giving qualities, and its channelling of tradition (both suggested by
conduit, which presumably carries water). This life continues
whatever goes on at court: 'of many kings' reigns' not only
evokes the perspective of history, but also suggests a fabric of
local life which is tough and enduring through the vicissitudes
of political history: kings may come and go, but the conduit
and the old shepherd remain. It is also worth noticing how
old the shepherd is; after the revelation of Florizel's identity
he says

> O sir,
> You have undone a man of fourscore-three
> That thought to fill his grave in quiet, yea,
> To die upon the bed my father died,
> To lie close by his honest bones.   (IV. 4. 444-8.)

The story does not require him to be so old; but he is made to
belong to yet an earlier generation than Leontes (whose place
he takes as Perdita's father), and the sequence is stretched back
still further by the reference to dying on the same bed as his
father.

This sense of the human generations stretching back and
forward seems to imply an acceptance of the processes of history,
an acceptance of the work of time. And it is interesting to see
what Time himself says in the play. He is introduced as a
chorus at the beginning of Act IV, and there is perhaps a
tendency for the reader to skip through this quickly – to treat
it as just a theatrical dodge to bridge a gap in the play. But
Shakespeare is not casual in the way he puts words into peoples'
mouths, least of all with a symbolical figure like Time:

> I, that please some, try all, both joy and terror
> Of good and bad, that makes and unfolds error,
> Now take upon me, in the name of Time,
> To use my wings. Impute it not a crime
> To me or my swift passage that I slide
> O'er sixteen years, and leave the growth untried
> Of that wide gap, since it is in my pow'r
> To o'erthrow law, and in one self-born hour
> To plant and o'erwhelm custom. Let me pass
> The same I am, ere ancient'st order was
> Or what is now receiv'd. I witness to

The times that brought them in; so shall I do
To th' freshest things now reigning, and make stale
The glistering of this present, as my tale
Now seems to it. Your patience this allowing,
I turn my glass, and give my scene such growing
As you had slept between.   (IV. I. 1-15.)

This makes the processes of history into a kind of organic
growth, to be viewed with the same kind of detachment as other
processes conforming to this scientific paradigm. The life of
human society is compared to vegetation ('leave the *growth*
untried', 'To *plant* and o'erwhelm custom', 'give my scene such
growing'); and this implies an acceptance of historical change
as natural and inevitable. Time can plant and o'erwhelm
custom: and *custom*, we must remember, is a key word for the
whole contemporary social set-up (one of the major social and
economic changes of the seventeenth century was the replace-
ment of custom by contract, for example in the matter of
rents and land tenure); but custom here is seen as something
mutable, not as an absolute. The collocation of *plant* and
o'erwhelm suggests that a social order grows to maturity and
decays, like a plant, but at some stage may be violently destroyed (*o'erwhelm* rather suggests a flood) and another 'planted'
in its place. There was an ancient order, there is a present-day
order ('what is now receiv'd'), and this in turn will one day be
replaced by another: the present (the things that now *reign*)
will one day seem as 'stale' as my old tale now seems to the
present-day audience. Social change, then, is accepted: the
passing of the 'order' and 'custom' of the present day is something *natural*, part of the growth-processes of Time. This is in
strong contrast to the attitudes expressed in, for example,
King Lear, where attitudes in conflict with traditional custom
are depicted by Lear and his friends as *unnatural*.

What Shakespeare has done, I think, is to put the tragic
conflicts and disorders of his age into a wider historical perspective. In the great tragedies, the breakdown of order and the
agonies arising from a change of custom and of world-view fill
the picture. But in this play he has stepped further back, and
these conflicts have become merely part of the picture, disturbances in the continuum of human history. The kind of
attitude implicit is seen at the end of Act III: Antigonus is

killed by the bear, the ship sinks with all hands, but the scene ends with the old shepherd saying

> 'Tis a lucky day, boy; and we'll do good deeds on 't.
>   (III. 3. 142.)

This is not just callousness: we have already seen the old shepherd take up Perdita for pity. It is rather acceptance: the acceptance of human life as a continuing process in which there is death and tragedy, but where nevertheless it is always a lucky day for someone.

I suggest then that the play is about the process of social change in seventeenth-century England: the division between court and country, the mastery of nature by the arts of man, the toughness of traditional rural life in the face of political change, the hope for a regenerated England through a reunion of court with cottage, the acceptance of the processes of history. The weaknesses of the play are a result of what it leaves out. The society actually depicted in the play is, as Time himself says, an earlier one than that of Shakespeare's day. It is a simpler society, with nothing in it apart from courtiers and peasants. The actual agents of change in Shakespeare's England – the engrossing merchants, the enclosing landlords, the smart lawyers, the rising yeomen – have no place in it. The Old Shepherd, indeed, could be taken as a type of the New Men of Shakespeare's day, for he is

> a man, they say, that from very nothing, and beyond the imagination of his neighbours, is grown into an un-speakable estate.   (IV. 1. 43-45.)

But this is a result of Perdita's 'faery gold', not of his own business acumen. As a result, the 'country' that is opposed to the court in the play is a different thing from the 'country' that was opposed to the court in contemporary political dialogue. The only character in the play who stands outside the simple opposition of court and peasantry is Autolycus. It has often been remarked that Autolycus is one of the great sources of vitality in the play. This vitality, like that of Falstaff, seems to arise from the fact that he is *déclassé*: he has contracted out of the social order and is therefore able to view it critically and amorally; and his energies are unhampered by the accepted code of the effete and artificial society from which he is an outcast. He is, he tells us, an ex-courtier, brought to his present condition by gaming and whoring (IV. 3.); but at the end of the play he is about to be restored to a position at court, through the intervention of the Old Shepherd and his son; even for this one unconforming element there is to be no place in the regenerate society.

It is this simplification of society, I think, that explains the Arcadian atmosphere of the play. The critics who have called the play escapist, or who have emphasized the fairy-tale elements in it, have surely not been entirely unjustified. In particular, the peasant society of the fourth act is seen in a kind of golden haze. Wilson Knight has commented on the 'realism' of this act; and certainly it is in strong contrast with the artificial Euphuistic pastoral of say Lyly or Greene. But this 'realism' is largely a matter of homely detail and of natural-sounding speech. There is a more important sense in which it is not realistic at all: it is seen nostalgically as a kind of Golden Age, a Garden of the Hesperides, an idealized pastoral picture of the kind that has been painted by townsmen in all ages; the harshness and narrowness of rural life are entirely omitted, and the whole thing presented in a somewhat rosy light. Moreover, because of the simplification of the society depicted, and the omission of the actual social forces which were making for change in Shakespeare's day, the reunion of Court and Cottage becomes something merely wished for, an act of faith. Hence the supernatural operates in the play as a substitute for plausible natural causes. It takes one miracle to cure Leontes of his tyranny, and another miracle to bring regeneration to his kingdom; and Shakespeare had to use miracles to bring these things about because, in the social framework that the play presents, he had left himself no other way of doing it.

SOME CURRENT USES
OF "SHAKESPEARIAN"

Alick West

In a note on the back cover of the Penguin edition of *Malone Dies* by Samuel Beckett occur these words:

> the power of Beckett's writing lies in the free play of an unanchored imagination and in a mating of words and ideas which is at times Shakespearian in its suggestiveness.

The same comparison was made in the account by a young American producer, Charles Marowitz, which was published in *The Observer*, of his experience as assistant to Peter Brook in the recent Stratford production of *King Lear*:

> In discussing rehearsals our frame of reference was always Beckettian. The world of this Lear, like Beckett's, is in a constant state of decomposition. The set pieces consist of geometrical sheets of metal that are ginger with rust and corrosion. . . . Apart from the rust . . . there is nothing but space – giant white flats opening on to a blank cyclorama.
>
> It is not so much Shakespeare in the style of Beckett as it is Beckett in the style of Shakespeare, for Brook believes that the cue for Beckett's bleakness was given by the merciless *King Lear*.[1]

There is a similarity of theme in a volume of essays, translated into French under the title *Shakespeare Notre Contemporain*, by the Polish critic Jan Kott. I will briefly summarize the underlying conception in his interpretation.

There are two ways, Mr. Kott says, of regarding history. One may believe that history has sense and direction, that it

---

[1] In line with this was the review of the production by Milton Shulman in the *Evening Standard*: "It is also a comment on man's futility and despair as poignant and contemporary as anything written by Samuel Beckett".

accomplishes its objective tasks, that it is reasonable and rational or can at least be grasped by reason. What is then felt in history as tragic is the price which humanity must pay for progress. He who endeavours to resist history, either by retarding or accelerating its pitiless movement, becomes a tragic figure: being at odds with history, he is crushed. This was the conception of history, and of the tragedy of history, held by Hegel. It was shared by Marx; and therefore he liked to quote from *Hamlet*

> Well said, old mole! Canst work i' th' earth so fast?
> A worthy pioneer! (II. I. 162-3.)

For the pioneer will make the way up into the light.

One may also believe that history has no sense and no direction; it does not move from the spot; or it repeats without respite its terrible cycle. It is an elemental force, like the hail, the storm and the cyclone, like birth and death. It is a mechanism, like the moving platform at the fun-fairs, on which you can only maintain your balance if you move, neither too fast nor too slow, in the opposite direction; but inevitably you lose your balance, to the amusement of the spectators. There is no tragedy in history, only the grotesque.

There is an eternal conflict, says Mr. Kott, between these two views of history, between the tragic and the grotesque conception of life, between the philosophy of the priest and of the clown. Nor is there only conflict in the vision of life; there is a similar conflict, similarly eternal, in the act of living. This is the conflict between the political and the moral. For politics is a mechanism to which morality is irrelevant. Speaking of *Richard II*, Mr. Kott says:

> There are not good kings and bad kings; the kings are only kings. Or, in different words, and using contemporary terminology: there exist only the situation of king and the system. A situation which does not permit of freedom of choice. At the end of the tragedy, the king says these great words which Hamlet might have spoken:
> They love not poison that do poison need . . .
> Between the order of action and the order of values there exists a contradiction. This contradiction is the human condition.

The conflict between the two views of history, between the tragic and the grotesque conceptions of life, is also the conflict in life between hope that the contradiction of action and values can be resolved and the absence of this hope.

This eternal conflict 'becomes particularly brutal' in periods of social disintegration. For then, Mr Kott argues, the belief in meaning – in God, in moral good and evil, in the meaning in history – is lost; and consequently the tragic sense is lost also. Hence the similarity between Shakespeare and Beckett: in both the grotesque dominates. Equally in *King Lear* and *Endgame* the contemporary world has broken up – 'the world of the Renaissance and our own'. Although the closing essay, where Mr. Kott draws a most stimulating comparison between Prospero and Leonardo da Vinci, is in a different key, the dominant mood of the book is rejection of the belief that meaning can be found in history; it is its eternal meaninglessness which makes Shakespeare and ourselves contemporary.

I think that such comparison of Shakespeare with the contemporary theatre, whether one agrees or disagrees with Mr. Kott's judgment, is valuable. It restores to Shakespearian criticism what it had tended to lose with the nineteenth-century reaction against romanticism. The later nineteenth-century discussion of the plays in terms of the characters as self-existing people in real life rather than in terms of Shakespeare's activity obscured the truth of Coleridge's criticism that there is a relation between the creative imagination manifesting itself in Shakespeare's work and society as an organism. The comparison between Beckett and Shakespeare raises once more this fundamental question, but with the difference that the dramatist is now seen as being in a society of disintegration.

This assumption of society's disintegration is, I think, a source of contradiction in Mr. Kott's philosophy.

The conflict between the two views of history, between the tragic and the grotesque, and the conflict in living between the orders of action and of values are presented in this view as eternal. Yet, at the same time, they are presented as intensified by the disintegration of society. There is thus a relation between the conflict and the condition of society within which the conflict goes on. Since change in society is recognized – the disintegration first of the world of the Renaissance and then of our own world implies an intervening integration – what grounds are there for certainty that the conflict is eternal? Or rather, since the human condition is presented not so much as conflict but rather as powerlessness in the face of conflict, as the inevitable defeat of the order of values by the order of action, what grounds are there for certainty that there can be no victory? Mr. Kott does indeed recognize change not only in society but in the issue of the conflict: the priests are being defeated. Today, as he says in a passage of great importance, the absolute is absurd.

> That is perhaps the reason why the grotesque employs so often the image of a mechanism which, having once been set going, cannot be stopped. Various sorts of hostile and impersonal mechanisms replace the God, the Nature or the History of ancient tragedy. This notion of an absurd mechanism is the last metaphysical concept still surviving in the contemporary grotesque. But this mechanism does not stand in a relation of transcendance to man, still less so to the human species. It is an ambush which man has prepared for himself, and into which he has fallen.

If, then, our response to the Shakespearian and Beckettian theatre of the grotesque is not to involve suppression of what we know, we must watch with the consciousness that metaphysics has had its day and that in the grotesque is its last refuge; with the consciousness that we ourselves have made the moving platform on which the characters fall about ridiculously; and – since the mechanism of the grotesque transcends the human species even less than it transcends the individual man – with the consciousness that our hold upon this knowledge is the more sure the more we are aware that we are both individual and species.

But Mr. Kott's interpretation of Shakespeare does, it seems to me, involve suppression of this knowledge which has come not from the disintegration of our world but through our changing it.

Since the comparison with Beckett is an integral part of this interpretation, I think it necessary first to speak of *Waiting for Godot*.

II

In the introduction of his book *The Tragic Sense in Shakespeare* Professor Lawlor stresses that pleasure is an essential part of tragic experience. He quotes Wordsworth:

> We have no sympathy but what is propagated by pleasure: I would not be misunderstood; but wherever we sympathize with pain, it will be found that the sympathy is produced and carried on by subtle combinations with pleasure. . . .
> However painful may be the objects with which the Anatomist's knowledge is connected, he feels that his knowledge is pleasure; and where he has no pleasure he has no knowledge.

The quality of the pleasure and the content and value of the knowledge are related.

The pleasure received from *Waiting for Godot* is that of recognizing what in certain moods we feel to be our situation. The recognition is more than only recognition: for our situation is given heightened and unsuspected significance by the penetration and clarity with which it is presented; and the situation is elevated, and, as it were, sanctioned, by being given public performance in a theatre.

The quality of the pleasure depends upon what it is to which heightened significance is given: inactive waiting as the necessary response in the face of reality. To quote the conclusion of the play:

> *Vladimir,*   Well? Shall we go?
> *Estragon,*   Yes, let's go.
>   *They do not move.*

It depends still more upon the necessity not to examine the intellectual implications of the technique by which the significance is heightened if the pleasure experienced is to be received and accepted as a source of knowledge and illuminating vision.

The technique creates a sense of the stage which I have never before experienced, and which was impossible in Shakespeare's day; and it changes the relationship between the actors on the stage and the audience.

The stage is not only the visible stage, but also what surrounds it in the wings. The bare, obscure visible stage is itself a nothingness, with one stunted tree; surrounding it, there is a greater, unimaginable nothingness. Within this mystery the visible stage is a faintly illuminated enclave of humanity, whose representatives, Vladimir and Estragon, seem to lose in stature against the encompassing emptiness. In the unnameable environment are their unseen adversary 'They'; and beyond, Godot. The sense of being in the presence of the incomprehensible is heightened because through the dialogue and the silences and pauses of inaction the structure of space and time becomes uncertain and baffles the mind; and the talk turns in upon itself, and thought becomes lost. The felt mystery in and beyond the wings, and the knowledge that 'They' and Godot are within it, creates and sustains a religious sense that on the visible stage the human figures are moving, or sitting without movement, in the presence of a greater metaphysical power.

Imposed already before the entry – from where? – of Pozzo and Lucky, this sense of the visible stage dominated by the invisible imposes also acceptance of the relationship, against intruding knowledge of reality outside the theatre, that Pozzo should be absolute master and Lucky absolute servant. For the tension of the visible stage surrounded by and at the capricious mercy of the incomprehensible is the opposite to freedom. So we feel it natural that the servant does not think except when his master tells him to, and that his spoken thought should be melancholy gibberish. And the darkness beyond the stage is of such a quality that one can believe that Pozzo, since he also, though master, shares the powerlessness of humanity, should be strangely blinded in it; and since the servant is the appendage at the end of the master's rope, the disappearance of Pozzo is the disappearance into the same nonentity of the master-servant relationship – or, in the language of contemporary reality, the relationship of capital and labour. Only when that has been removed from the action, can the waiting for Godot – a compromise God, who exists and does not exist – be resumed again as the absolute and endless condition of humanity.

But men have not inertly waited for Godot. They have been active and themselves created God. Then, knowing themselves to be the creators of God, they have become conscious of their humanity, and the servant has broken the master's rope. To accept the pleasure given by *Waiting for Godot* is to forget humanity's power and progress. Beckett immobilizes and denies the energy that created the very language he uses, and dramatic form and content, and the tree now stunted on the stage – the tree of life and knowledge and of Golgotha on which the representatives of humanity now think of hanging themselves and with their last involuntary ejaculation impregnating the earth to bring forth shrieking mandrakes.

Thus there is in the pleasure, it seems to me, the tone of destructive self-pity; and in the knowledge associated with the pleasure there is self-ignorance. It is true that much of our time we sit and wait, but not in metaphysical darkness where 'They' are hidden. 'They' fight us and we fight 'them'; and towards others we are ourselves 'they'.

The bright stage, on which in Shakespeare's time all action was in the open, in a ring of people, the mainspring of the action visible and intelligible in the conflicting energies of the characters, is now the gloomy scene of inaction watched by and dependent on invisible presences in the wings; and the audience is, as Vladimir says when he comes to the front of the stage and looks at us, 'that bog'.

III

If *King Lear* is interpreted according to Mr. Kott's conception of the grotesque, our pleasure is again in the recognition of our own unchangeable condition as we watch the antics of men in that wordless presence which is the absence of God.

Mr. Kott quotes Gloucester's lines as he kneels at what he imagines to be the brink of the cliff:

> O you mighty gods!
> This world I do renounce, and in your sights
> Shake patiently my great affliction off.
> If I could bear it longer, and not fall
> To quarrel with your great opposeless wills,
> My snuff and loathed part of nature should
> Burn itself out.   (IV. 6. 34-40.)

'Gloucester's suicide,' he comments, 'has sense only if the gods exist. It is a protest against undeserved suffering and against the injustice of the world. The protest is addressed, explicitly, to somebody. It makes appeal to an eschatology. Even if the gods be cruel, they must take this act of suicide into account. It will have weight in the final reckoning between gods and men. It has value only through reference to the absolute. But if the gods do not exist, nor the moral order of the world, Gloucester's suicide changes nothing and resolves nothing.' Therefore Shakespeare makes him, after his lofty address to the gods who do not exist, fall flat on his face on the bare boards of the stage, like a clown. His suicide is a flop. 'The pantomime is grotesque. But so is the whole situation. From the beginning until the end. It is a waiting for a Godot who does not come.'

To wait for Godot implies that his coming is conceivable. The waiting for a Godot who does not come is dramatically moving only if the absence of God is mourned as the absence of what the mourner believes to have once been present, only if the meaninglessness of religion is felt as the loss of what was once real, as its continuing presence in negation.

Felt through this absence of a God imagined as having once been real, the response to Gloucester's clown-like fall on the moving platform is, as Mr. Kott says, the last refuge of the metaphysical; and his interpretation, it seems to me, retains the transcendance of the metaphysical. It requires that we should feel Shakespeare's stage, like Beckett's, to represent humanity in a surrounding 'otherness', to use Mr. Steiner's word in his *The Death of Tragedy*, and that to keep our pleasure in this representation of our condition we should refrain from recognizing in the 'otherness' our unidentified selves who make our history.

Waiting for Godot is a denial of history. Unlike *King Lear*, the scene is nowhere, and so when the play finishes it might start over and over again; for there is no difference between the beginning and the end. The interpretation of *King Lear* in terms of the grotesque of Gloucester's fall must leave out of account the difference that Shakespeare's tragedy cannot start over again. The end is not the same as the beginning; and the turning point in the human action that brings the change about is when a servant draws his sword against the inhumanity of his master.

IV

The word 'Shakespearian' is also applied, as Mr. Kott says, to the work of Bertolt Brecht. One cannot accept both uses. According to whether the similarity is found with Beckett or with Brecht, the conception of Shakespeare is radically different, as is clear from the following passage in Brecht's *Kleines Organon für das Theater*:

> The theatre, as we find it, shows the structure of society (represented on the stage) not as subject to influence by society (in the auditorium). Oedipus, having sinned against principles of his society, is executed; the gods see to that, and they are not to be criticised. Shakespeare's great individuals, in their own breasts the stars of their destiny, run amok and come to ruin . . .; the catastrophe is not to be criticised. Human sacrifices galore! Barbaric entertainment! The barbarians, we know, have their art. Let us make a different one!

Except perhaps when Estragon in sudden fury kicks the prostrate Lucky, he and Vladimir do not run amok; nor would the characters in a Beckettian Shakespeare be charged with such energy.

Classical criticism in the seventeenth and eighteenth centuries also called Shakespeare a barbarian; but it judged by a different standard and assumed that civilization was already attained. Brecht applies the term with the meaning that we leave our barbarism behind in the degree that we understand why the apparently passive society in the auditorium is not exempt from responsiblity for the social catastrophe on the stage.

In a postscript to the *Kleines Organon*, Brecht relates how Einstein once told the physicist Infeld that since he was a child he had really done nothing but think about a man running after a beam of light, and what complications had resulted! And so, Brecht said, all the talk about Brechtian 'alienation effects' had come from his applying to the theatre Marx's sentence that it is not only a question of interpreting the world but of changing it.

The world, for Brecht, is not the unchangeable absence of God; and our life is not the estranged condition that we are vainly impelled to find meaning in meaninglessness. Our life must deliberately be made strange to us; it must be made strange through art in order that we shall not think that no other life is possible.

His meaning is best expressed in one of his poems:

> Observe the conduct of these people closely:
> Find it estranging even if not very strange,
> Hard to explain even if it is the custom
> Hard to explain even if it is the rule
> Observe the smallest action, seeming simple,
> With mistrust
> Enquire if a thing be necessary
> Especially if it is common
> We particularly ask you –
> When a thing continually occurs –
> Not on that account to find it natural
> In an age of bloody confusion
> Ordered disorder, planned caprice,
> And dehumanised humanity, lest all things
> Be held unalterable.

Therefore the theatre must not represent the structure of society as not capable of being changed by society. The audience must not be made passively to contemplate upon the stage a metaphysical 'otherness'; they must know that they are watching themselves, and they must criticize the catastrophe in order that, outside the theatre, they can remove its cause.

For this, says Brecht, is the age of science and of the beauty of science; and not only the science of the natural world, but the science of society. As Galilei watched the swinging of the pendulum, so we must see our own social action with the same wonder and the same sense of being on the brink of truth.

Since this is the age of the consciousness of science, and no longer of the unconsciousness of religion, we must make a different theatre from that of Shakespeare's time. But, as Brecht stressed, the old principles of the art of the theatre still hold; for its purpose remains to give pleasure. 'To demand or to approve that it should do more, is to set one's own purpose too low.' For the energy, and the understanding of the necessity, of the revolution must come not only from the intellect, but from the knowledge inherent in pleasure, from body and soul exalted, as through the work of Shakespeare, by the meaning beyond words in gesture, intonation and rhythm, in the tension of dramatic action, in the expressiveness of particular form.

There is therefore both continuity and the necessity of change. The plays that delight us from the past must be so produced, Brecht says, that we are aware of their coming from the past in order that, knowing the transience of the society in which they were written, we shall know the transience of our own, and look forward, with the hope which is inseparable from pleasure.

V

Such consciousness that we, and not only Shakespeare, are the subject of social change, is, I think, necessary.

The knowledge which in his *Shakespeare's Doctrine of Nature* Professor Danby so well communicates of how in that doctrine, as expressed in *King Lear*, are the warring ideas of medieval theology, Hobbes's materialism and Winstanley's communism is invaluable for the understanding of the play. But when through Shakespeare's art we, in Coleridge's phrase, become Shakespeare and thereby experience pleasure, the knowledge attained through that pleasure cannot be expressed only in terms of Shakespeare's doctrine of nature. For in an age of science and revolution nature has become different.

Yet although our interpretation of the play must be guided by a new concept of nature, our experience of the play is more than a matter of concepts and doctrines. For Shakespeare is himself a 'piece of nature'. One of the excellences of classical criticism is its insistence on pleasure as the aim of literature and its admiration of Shakespeare for the pleasure given by that unsubdued energy of nature, of which, as Pope said, 'he was not so much the Imitator, as the Instrument'. It manifests itself in that spiritual strength which can create beauty out of the terror of the world. The tempest rages, yet it fills us with exultation at the articulacy and power of man: a man equals it with his words; men, as Granville Barker said, act it; and it is the discovery by man of his own being – 'Off, off, you lendings!' Shakespeare's activity as an instrument of nature, rather than his doctrine of nature, creates and unites audiences in pleasure and knowledge, so that the theatre becomes, as Shaw called it, 'a cathedral' and 'a factory of thought'. For what must we feel awe, and what must be our thought?

If Brecht is right, as I believe him to be, that the production of the plays of the past should illuminate the transience of our own form of society, his philosophy holds also for the criticism and interpretation of Shakespeare. As the issue before society has changed, so has the significance of Shakespeare. We are interpreting what has been, and is, a historical force in the changing of the world and a focus of conflict. Classical criticism admired in Shakespeare the power of wild nature, but considered that the power must be checked by civilized restraint after the times of revolution and enthusiasm. With the renewal of revolution, Coleridge admired in him the power, not of an undifferentiated nature, but of the unity of '*alter et idem*, myself and my neighbour,' which he held to be opposed to the actual power in contemporary society, when the workers in the factories were 'mechanized into engines for the production of new rich men', thus violating 'the sacred principle recognized by all laws, human and divine, . . . that a person can never become a thing.' With the beginning of the change from bourgeois to socialist revolution, Marx found in Shakespeare the fury of man against the inhumanity of the commodity. Fear of the new content of revolution with the advance of socialism from utopianism to science, and fear of Shakespearian energy as being a source of its inspiration, is, I think, a great cause of the decline in Shakespearian criticism during the nineteenth century and of the consideration of Shakespeare's work as a statement about life rather than as itself the energy of life; just as the impossibility today of separating the interpretation of Shakespeare from the consciousness of revolutionary change has liberated it from the limitations of the nineteenth century – Professor Wilson Knight, in a prefatory note to a new edition of *The Wheel of Fire*, states that the problem posed by modern physics of discovering 'a new principle *which can unite permanence and change*' has rendered untenable the category of 'character' previously employed in the interpretation of Shakespeare.

Therefore, although I have found his book of the greatest help, I cannot but disagree when Professor Danby says that Cordelia's goodness, embodying the ideals of 'natural theology', 'requires not only perfection in the individual, but perfection in the community also'; and that since this ideal community will be non-existent, 'Cordelia expresses the utopian intention of Shakespeare's art'. I do not think that one can rightly speak of Shakespeare's art as having a utopian intention, any more than a believer in the truth of 'natural theology' can speak of a utopian Christianity; for Shakespeare's art is wholly a real occurrence and a real power. Cordelia's goodness is part of the content of the tragedy. The creative energy that makes the tragedy of which it is part, and the pleasure, knowledge and hope experienced through participation in that energy, has had real effect. It has been part of the achievement of the consciousness, not only that we prepare our own ambushes of disintegration, but that, knowing now that we make the form of our society, we can with knowledge attempt our liberation. The vision of goodness has not yet been realized; but there is real change when the pursuit of the vision is guided not by utopian but by scientific thought.

If it is wrong to speak of a utopian intention in Shakespeare's art, it is also wrong, I think, to regard *King Lear* as the allegory, in Professor Danby's words, of 'the Good Man in the Bad Society'. The good and the bad are not polarized thus, but rather in what Coleridge described as the tension between latent and actual power in the organic unity of man and society. The opposing of the good man to the bad society makes, I believe, the same kind of false antagonism as that between the order of action and the order of values in Mr. Kott's interpretation. Both orders are of our own making; the good man and the bad society are one. The conflict between what is good and what is bad, between latent and actual power, is real. The words which Shaw wrote sixty years ago are still true: 'The world will not bear thinking of to those who know what it is.' But think we must, with the knowledge that, being individual and species, we have made the world what it is and can therefore change it.

If Shakespeare is to be a living presence, criticism should not lend his name to work which celebrates nothingness nor use terms which obscure the knowledge of our responsibility and power, but terms through which it is increased with not less than the whole energy of Shakespeare's work. The turning point of the action of *King Lear* is that a peasant stands up for

tortured humanity; through the tragedy itself, and through
the pleasure, knowledge and hope it brings into life, we know
the freedom to be won as the domination of man by man is
defeated; and, in Edgar's words to Gloucester, we know the
condition of that freedom:

> What, in ill thoughts again? Men must endure
> Their going hence, even as their coming hither:
> Ripeness is all. Come on.   (v. 3. 9-11.)

INDEX